VIRTUOSO

The Story of John Ogdon

VIRTUOSO
The Story of John Ogdon

by

Brenda Lucas Ogdon

and

Michael Kerr

Hamish Hamilton   London

First published in Great Britain 1981
by Hamish Hamilton Ltd
Garden House 57–59 Long Acre London WC2E 9JZ

British Library Cataloguing in Publication Data

Ogdon, Brenda Lucas
  Virtuoso.
  1. Ogdon, John
  2. Pianists – Great Britain – Biography
  I. Title
  786.1'092'4   ML417.03

ISBN 0–241–10375–4

Photoset, printed and bound
in Great Britain by
REDWOOD BURN LTD
Trowbridge & Esher

CONTENTS

ILLUSTRATIONS

(between pages 182 and 183)

ACKNOWLEDGMENTS

The authors would like to thank the many people who helped them in the preparation of this book – particularly Brian Masters, not only for ransacking his memory, but for allowing us to quote from his diaries. Alistair Londonderry, Richard Croucher, Gerard and Carolyn Schurmann, Peter Andry, Simon and Sheelin Eccles, and Michael Johnson also willingly permitted us to take up their time.

Our gratitude too to Susan Kerr for tolerating without complaint the many hours spent on this manuscript, as well as for all her constructive criticisms.

And lastly, and most importantly – from both of us, a heartfelt "Thank you, John".

Brenda Lucas Ogdon
Michael Kerr

FOREWORD

It is something of a shock to see one's own life from the outside, as it were; to discover that one's formless day to day existence has been arranged into chapters, ordered into paragraphs, and generally given shape. And yet, even as I was reading this biography with the same expectant curiosity that I would give to a book about a stranger, I was also realising with astonishment that the extraordinary fellow in the centre of the action is, unmistakeably, me, and that here indeed *is* my own experience – of necessity distilled, but still, my own experience. It has been a pleasure for me to relive so many happy times within these pages, and it is equally my pleasure now to be able to share those times with the reader.

But, as is generally known I think, I have had my share of less happy times as well; and some people, including many of my friends, will find that the description of my breakdown makes very painful reading. I ask them to persevere and read on, because it is only by comparison with that pain that my improved condition has any real significance.

I know that Michael and Brenda gave long and careful thought as to how much they should reveal, and I am pleased that they have chosen to be as open as they have been. There is no point in writing about a breakdown or about recovery if the original shock and suffering are played down: there is no merit in glossing over expressions of mental illness which are everyday occurences in hospitals throughout the world. In short, I believe that it is in frankness, not concealment, that my integrity, and even my duty, lie.

Here then, included in this book, are some of the harsh facts behind the words 'severe mental illness' and 'serious nervous breakdown' which the press has been using about me so often lately. Not that I am complaining about the press! – I was thrilled by the sympathetic and wide-spread media interest that came my way both before and after my return to the London concert stage in February 1981; and I was, and am, deeply moved by the warmth, encouragement, and enthusiasm that have been given me by the music-loving public.

In health as well as sickness, I also owe a thousand emotional debts to my friends and colleagues. And I must say a most special thank you to my wife, Brenda, for many reasons which there is no need for me to list here. This book speaks not only of, but for me.

Perhaps, in some ways, I am lucky. Perhaps, in 1981, I am getting a chance few people ever get: the chance for a new beginning.

JOHN OGDON

Part One

The Early Years

1

It was a hot summer afternoon in 1955, and I had been so engrossed in practising a Mozart piano sonata that I hadn't noticed how time was passing. If I didn't hurry, I would be late for the day's last assignment, which was to accompany a fellow student at Manchester's Royal Northern College of Music during his violin lesson. I hurried to the stairs which led to the Main Hall.

A cascade of notes drowned out my footsteps; I slowed down, then stopped to listen. Someone in the Hall was performing the Liszt B minor piano Sonata with a tempestuous and passionate conviction that I had never heard matched in the College before – not even, for that matter, in a concert hall. For a moment I thought someone might be playing a recording – by Horowitz perhaps. But no, the sound was unmistakeably real.

I started down the stairs again, and tiptoed into the Hall. Several other people, most of them students, had got there before me; they were standing like statues, their reflections frozen in the polished parquet floor, staring towards the raised platform on which a young man was playing a black Steinway grand. He was crouched close over the keyboard, as if he meant to tear it apart and devour it; he was huge, dwarfing the piano stool on which he was sitting. Beneath the mop of dark curly hair, sweat glistened on the softly-contoured face, now strengthened by his total concentration. Oblivious of everyone there he was pouring his soul into the music.

The notes cascaded around us in a torrent, racing dangerously fast – the man's ferocity was almost beyond belief. I forced my eyes away from the piano, back to his audience: a few more people had crept into the hall, but no one else had moved. Every person there was listening in what I can only

3

describe as a stunned silence.

... I had kept the violinist waiting long enough: I crept away self-consciously, though nobody noticed me. But at the door, I turned back for a last look at the massive figure at the piano: and I felt a shiver running through me, an almost tangible charge from the electricity he was creating.

I walked faster as the music faded behind me. Fascinated and even awed though I was, I had to admit that something in me was resisting this phenomenal talent. It wasn't jealousy – I had an arrogantly youthful faith in my own abilities. But both by temperament and by training, I felt more at home with Bach, Mozart and early Beethoven than with the nineteenth century Romantic repertoire – on top of which the young man's approach was for my taste too undisciplined ... in some disconcerting way, too self-revealing.

What sort of man must he be to play that way, I wondered? Volatile, passionate – a dominating personality, surely. And what was his name? Of one thing I was certain even then – I and the music loving public would be hearing a great deal of it one day.

By the time we were introduced a few days later in the student canteen, I had found out that his name was John Ogdon. And once again I was taken aback by the man – on this occasion by the gentleness of his personality, which seemed so at odds with both the passion of his playing and the power of his eighteen-year-old physique. Equally unexpected was his inarticulate shyness: behind the thick lenses of his glasses, his eyes seemed slightly puzzled, though his smile, which he used rather too often as a substitute for words, was strangely sweet. I also remember that he sported an uneven growth of stubble and a very dirty shirt, neither one designed to appeal to someone of my fastidious upbringing. Our meeting was polite, but nothing more than that: I neither liked him nor disliked him.

It may seem surprising that John and I, who were both studying the piano at the College, should not have come across each other until the latter part of the school year. But as students, our lives were fragmented: we were coached individually on the piano rather than in groups, while our approach to training and to practise was invariably self-centred. At least,

4

it was for those of us who were determined to make our mark as concert artists.

And many of us were unquestioningly determined to make that mark. It never occurred to us that in living memory only a handful of British artists had made international names for themselves: in fact, it didn't cross our minds that few musicians from anywhere achieve far-reaching recognition. We knew, of course, that music is an international language: but we didn't realise that consequently the same small handful of brilliant artists dominate the concert stage from New York to Buenos Aires, from Edinburgh to Leningrad.

But even if we had appreciated the obstacles facing us, we would have ignored them, so certain were we of our potential to succeed... Perhaps in a way such blind ambition is sad: the overwhelming majority of would-be maestri, from my and every other generation, have ended up at best teaching full time. And yet, however many the casualties, this same innate confidence and drive is an essential ingredient in the make-up of every performer; because without it, however talented he may be, he has no hope at all of succeeding.

And I for one certainly had that confidence – in spades. I was utterly and totally obsessed by music; it was no less than my life.

Every morning I left my parents' house in Hyde at seven thirty to catch the trolley bus for the 8 mile ride into Manchester. In summer, when the sun was up, I did not mind the early start: but I remember with less affection the bleak winter mornings, the long waits at the bus stop while the air's sooty undertow scratched at my throat and halos of misty breath framed the heads of my neighbours in the queue. And then the scramble to get a seat when the bus turned up at last – the bright "ping" of the conductor's ticket machine and the blunt northern accents – "Where to, luv?" ... "Ta, Ducks" ... The slow progress through blackened suburbs, the roof tops slowly becoming sharper in the tentative, drizzly light...

But however tired or depressed I was, however damp or dreary the day, my heart would leap at the sight of the College. With its brown-bricked façade it looked more like a reformatory or a Dickensian orphanage than a temple·of learning, but for me, it was the centre of the universe. I would rush inside, praying I wasn't too late, that the professors' unlocked teach-

5

ing rooms hadn't already been filled by other, even keener students. These early mornings were the magic time for me – the time when I had the opportunity to practise on the teachers' own pianos, marvellous and responsive instruments compared to those that were officially available to us. And there in the teaching room I would stay, in proud and jealous possession, until the official academic day began and I was turfed out into the corridor to fend for myself.

After that, finding any kind of piano to work on was a struggle, such was the demand, unless I went home again to practise. But there was rarely time for that, there was so much to do at the College – private lessons, other students to accompany and a hundred and one budding talents both from at home and abroad to hear and assess.

It was an exclusive life that we students led. The outside world scarcely existed for us, and people for whom music was not the breath of life we considered boring, to be tolerated but not taken seriously. The Royal College was our oyster, and for the most part we felt safe, fulfilled and happy in its shell.

I heard John Ogdon for the second time in a so-called Open Practice.

Open Practices were concerts given by the more talented students, and as they were open to the general public, we always prepared for them with an excitement tempered with fright. They gave us our first whiff of that intoxicating communication with an audience; and we could not have put our hearts into them more completely if we had been playing at the Royal Festival Hall.

I was impressed by the authority of John's physical presence when he walked on stage – it is an authority that cannot be taught, and one that instills an audience with confident anticipation from the very first moment. But to my disappointment, his programme was exclusively Romantic, and again I was disturbed by a driven quality in his playing. At the same time, I was left with no doubt that, of us all at the College, he was easily the most naturally gifted. And alongside all the *Sturm und Drang*, the extraordinary *tempi* and the staggering runs, I began to hear a tender and lyrical voice that was unexpectedly moving.

How strange, I thought again, that someone who could communicate so vividly with an audience should be so reserved off the stage. Oh well ... it was no concern of mine: after all, John and I weren't friends.

And then, one late afternoon, as I was walking down Oxford Road to catch my trolley bus home, I heard steps clattering along the pavement behind me: I turned to see John racing towards me. No, it *can't* be me he's after. I thought – unless perhaps I've dropped something ...

"Brenda ..."

I stopped. He tried to catch his breath without success: he went on panting heavily in the slanted evening sunlight. "Brenda" he began again in his rather drawling northern accent, "I was just wondering if you would go to the cinema with me."

"When? Not now!"

"Any time. There are some good films on this week. Any time."

I looked back into his earnest, good-natured stare. His hair was a mess and very long for those days, his clothes were untidy and his waistline was large. The picture did not appeal to me: "Thank you, but no, John," I said – adding for good measure "I already have a boyfriend."

His nod and his smile were crestfallen, but he made no protest as I walked off and left him.

In retrospect, I don't know why I aroused as much masculine interest as I did in those days: I was innocent and not a little prim, and though I had large dark eyes and a more than passable figure, I had almost no time and less money to spend on making the physical best of myself. Besides, I looked on most of my would-be Romeos as an irritating distraction from music-making – though perhaps my very lack of interest was a magnet of some kind.

Not that I lied to John about a boyfriend, or not exactly. For one thing, I was still getting over a passion for a member of the College faculty. He, I'd been sure, had returned my feelings. but he was married with three children, and an open liaison with a student would have led to his immediate dismissal. Besides, my convent-educated scruples had ruled an affair out of the question. But though I had realised our love had been doomed to die without flowering, that knowledge had not made the love any less real to me, or easier to bear.

7

But by now the worst was over, and I was finding some consolation in a University student called Patrick who lived, like me, in Hyde. My feelings for him, of course, were much less exalted – and the fact that he did not understand music or my close, exclusive world raised an inevitable barrier between us. But he was tall, handsome and athletic, sharing with me a love of tennis and other sports, and he was usually a warm and welcome companion on my evening trips home on the bus. Patrick was in love with me, which was nice, but without being demanding, which was nicer. I didn't want complications.

I had forgotten all about John Ogdon and his offer by the time I arrived at the College next day. I found an empty practice room and went to work.

Things were going well, I was wrapt in the music – when I heard the door handle turning, breaking my concentration. A second later, John walked into the room.

Oh no, I thought, irritated. I stopped practising and asked him what he wanted.

"Nothing particularly. Just to have a talk".

And to my amazement, talk John did. He talked fluently, excitedly, even magically – he talked about music, musicians, interpretation, approaches to performing. Idea followed idea so fast I couldn't keep up – I was dazzled, stunned, and, I must confess, intellectually out of my depth. I could hardly believe what was happening – that I, Brenda Lucas, was now the one at a loss for words.

Suddenly I found myself getting up from my piano stool to make way for John: he didn't actually ask me to move over, he simply took possession. He had been carrying the score of a Mahler symphony, and he wanted to explain something, he said, about the composer's approach. Whereupon, squinting through the lenses of his glasses, he played through an entire movement by sight – nine or ten staves interpreted on one inadequate piano. Technically, intellectually and imaginatively it was a breathtaking accomplishment – one I'll never forget any more than that Liszt Sonata in the Main Hall.

Afterwards John went on talking and occasionally making a point at the piano as though nothing out of the ordinary had happened. He didn't seem to mind that I was contributing little or nothing to the dialogue; he was obviously enjoying himself. And I was enjoying myself too – suddenly it didn't matter that he was so overweight and untidy . . .

Two days later, John interrupted my practice session again: a couple of afternoons after that, he was back once more. The next week, the pattern was repeated – and the next.

He was by no means always as articulate as he had been on that first occasion; quite often he would be diffident and shy. At other times, he would hardly talk at all; he would stand frowning slightly, seemingly staring at something within himself. On these latter occasions, his physical presence became a tangible intrusion, seeming to swell till it filled the room; I found I could neither concentrate nor practise. "What do you want?" I'd snap.

"Oh, sorry, Brenda" he'd say, apparently contrite. "Am I disturbing you?"

Only when it came to expounding anything about music was he never at a loss for words. He was almost impossible to resist as he communicated his joy in Liszt, or as he talked about a composer he considered shockingly neglected, Ferruccio Busoni. "When I make a success as a pianist" he told me. "I'm going to play him as often as I can." His death in 1924, he insisted, had been a serious loss to music – he was not only a great composer, he had been an editor, a writer, a philosopher, and the greatest pianist since Liszt. He was an intellectual giant, there was no one alive today to compare with him. John was determined to see him restored to his rightful reputation.

The trouble was, I was becoming far more concerned over the neglect of my practising than I was about the neglect of Busoni. John was starting to be a nuisance.

"You're much too ignorant about modern music" he told me one day. "You should come along to one of our New Music recitals."

"I don't want to."

"You should, if you're ever going to be a really rounded musician . . ."

"John! I'm not interested in modern music! Now please leave me alone to practise!"

"And I'm not interested in your technical perfection! There's more to music than that – its overall shape, not the details . . ."

"That's all right for you!" I jumped up, furious. "You can

9

play anything you like without even thinking, you don't have to try! But I do – so get out of here!"

He gave me a sudden thunderous look from under his brows, his head held low in his shoulders. Then he turned and left, slamming the door.

I stared after him. For that brief moment, he had looked so threatening that I had been genuinely scared. It took me a heart-pounding minute or so to regather my wits and start practising.

Only a day or two later, John was back, our contretemps apparently forgotten: and the regular pattern of his visits began all over again. By now, though, I had no compunction about asking him, politely, to go – except that too often he paid no attention. Remembering the effect of my shouting, I was wary of repeating the experience; but on the one or two occasions I was driven to it, he went with no sign of resentment.

Perhaps it was in the hope that John would leave me alone during practice sessions that I began to include him more often in my casual social life at the College: though perhaps such a development was inevitable. He would sometimes join me and a few other students for a coffee and a Danish pastry in a local café – that is, when we could afford them – or stretch out with us in the park when the weather was fine at lunch time.

As the weeks passed and I began to know John better, I realised that he loved having people around him; his eyes would light up with pleasure at the very suggestion of a party. And though my mother had placed pubs out of bounds for me, I was told that if he ever spied a bar piano, however honkey tonk or out of tune, he would be more than likely to rush over to it and launch into a technically stunning version of, say, "Rhapsody in Blue" or some of the evergreen Gershwin songs – much to the amazement of the patrons. After a drink or two, John even became convivial.

I discovered, too, that he was an ardent fan of the cinema, taking special pleasure in slapstick: nothing would have kept him away from a Chaplin revival. And he was surprisingly well read, with a catholic taste ranging from the Brontës to literally any ghost story he could lay his hands on. As for science fiction – when he wasn't actually reading it, he was ready to talk about it by the hour.

But of course his over-riding passion was music; if possible he was more obsessed than the rest of us. Even so, he was far less conventional than I in the way that he went about studying. Not for him those early morning sessions on good pianos – often he didn't turn up at the college until the late afternoon! But then, in some areas he already knew more than his teachers, and his phenomenal natural technique had developed in such a way that he felt uneasy with formalised disciplines.

But for all his talent, for all his brilliance and bouts of articulateness, John was completely incapable of conventional small talk: the little things of life that make up the bulk of other people's conversation simply didn't interest him. In addition, he was absent minded, and he could be so withdrawn into himself that it sometimes seemed a miracle that he could find his way around Manchester: indeed, he had been known on more than one occasion to completely forget where he was going.

One thing that was guaranteed to snap him out of even the deepest reverie, however, was the sight of a pretty girl. And rather to my surprise, I found that in their turn, most women responded to John. Several of my own girl-friends were adopting an attitude towards him that was deferential, even awed, yet at the same time maternally protective. I pictured the fantasies they must be having – dreams of pampering their man-child, of feeding him and dressing him up before sending him on to the concert platform to astound the musical world. And now that I was getting to understand John a bit more I was convinced of another thing too – no one would be happier to live out such a fantasy than he . . .

Oh well, I thought, I leave them all to it. If ever a way of life were foreign to me, that would be it. It was against my nature, and against everything in my upbringing.

2

Thrift, hard work and clean living – those were the values I had been raised to prize above all others.

I grew up in Hyde, a suburb south east of Manchester, in a cold, four-bedroomed Victorian house. My father, who worked for the National Assistance Board, was an easy-going sports-loving man who would make a joke about everything. Even about serious or sad things. It was his way of keeping the world at bay, and he taught me and my younger sister Janet to do the same.

He used to play cricket for the local club, and some of my happiest childhood memories are of spending sun-warmed summer afternoons watching the interminable game. I never really understood it; but seeing my father fielding in his white flannels, or striding out to bat in cap and pads, I felt that the world was a safe place to be, and knew with a glowing certainty that I loved him.

But the real head of the family, and the dominating influence on my development, was my mother. A teacher, and later headmistress, at a local infants' school, she was the epitome of Northern common sense unembroidered with flights of fantasy. She was not unkind, but charity to her mind was far from synonymous with money – and though money was a topic that dominated our lives, Janet and I saw very little of it. It was something to be earned, not given – and by the time we reached our teens, we were expected to pay for our clothes out of our own meagre and hard-won savings.

My mother was not a person in whom I or anyone else could confide – to her, uncomplaining self-reliance was all. Personal crises, family tragedies were ignored – she simply pretended to herself, as well as to others, that they weren't happening. In time, such an attitude was bound to show painful cracks – but that was still many years in the future.

Ours was not a musical household. But when I was seven, an upright piano was delivered to the house: and from the moment I realised I could play "Bewitched, Bothered and Bewildered" with no trouble, by ear, I knew that everything the instrument represented was to be of vital importance in my life. And I have no complaints about the way my parents reacted: they were not only tolerant of my long hours at the keyboard, they actively encouraged me to practise.

Two years later, I was sent to the Harrytown High School (For the Daughters of Gentlemen, as the sign outside proudly proclaimed). It was convent school, and by comparison with its enforced standards of behaviour, my mother's seemed almost on the wrong side of permissive. Girls only spoke when spoken to: at other times, in corridors as well as classrooms, silence was the strict and holy rule. Religion cloaked the days as the habits cloaked the nuns, dark and somehow threatening: our lives were surrounded by the whisperings of sanctimonious skirts. The alternative to the nuns' way of austerity was Sin, and therefore Damnation. Some of the braver girls, including my sister Janet, rebelled, at least in secret: but not I. I was determined not to go to Hell if I could help it: even Purgatory seemed a very bad idea. Outwardly, and even, where possible, inwardly, I became resolutely blameless.

But my purity did not make me happy. Only music made me happy – and I was lucky to have a nun called Sister Mary Angela as my teacher. This good and talented lady taught me all she knew, and she taught me well: at fourteen, in my so-called Grade Eight exam, I scored the highest marks of any student in the country.

It was time to move on. I went for private lessons to the Russian pianist and teacher, Iso Elinson. Short and energetic, he played a vast repertoire from memory, and, so it seemed to me, when he wasn't performing or giving lessons, he spent every moment in practising. I was more than ready to follow his example, and found him an inspiring instructor.

By this time, my parents had given me a room in the house to use as my own studio. For all her traditional attitudes, my mother did not believe that a woman's place was exclusively in the home: and so, respecting and understanding my dedication rather better than its subject, she let me limit my domestic

13

chores to washing up for the family and making my bed. I didn't learn to cook, nor did I want to learn.

When I was sixteen, a day came that I had anticipated for months, indeed for years: I became a full time student at the Royal College of Music. As I stood waiting for the trolley bus on a nippy autumn morning, I was more elated than apprehensive: at last I was entering a world of real music and real musicians, a world in which each day would being new progress, new revelations.

The reality proved less glamorous. To a girl brought up in a convent school, the college curriculum seemed ludicrously free. If students didn't want to work, they didn't – at least, not very hard: if they preferred lounging in a coffee shop or (like John) staying in bed all the morning, nobody seemed to mind. Several of the professors were old and uninspired: too many of the lectures had a depressing air of 'déjà entendu'.

After a life of imposed discipline, I was forced to understand that it was my own responsibility and no-one else's to make the best use of my time. Single-mindedly, I set about turning myself into a star pupil: I practised harder than ever, I accompanied other musicians, and played in chamber groups whenever I could. Gradually I began to enjoy myself, and after my first year, my efforts were rewarded with a scholarship.

But though I learned how to cope with, and exploit, the College's curriculum, I did not find it as easy to adjust to some of the other students. The less talented, and certainly the lazier than myself, I regarded with a mild contempt – if I regarded them at all. More difficult to come to terms with were some of the brighter students, men and women whose attitudes and way of life were totally alien to me. I had been trained to believe that visible order and neatness were essential to achievement; these people, disturbingly, proved otherwise.

Some of the most unsettling of my contemporaries belonged to a group called New Music, Manchester, who played, as their name implied, largely modern compositions including works by their own members. In addition, they performed for enterprising music clubs, some as far away as London.

But successful though they were, at least in student terms, not even their most devoted admirers could ever have called them "neat". They were unkempt and very shaggy, wild-haired and wilder-eyed: and for me, their music was no better. I found it disordered and discordant: I would never have believed, then, that so much of it would prove to have a lasting quality. Nor would I have predicted with any confidence the future success of Harrison Birtwistle or Elgar Howarth; though the group's uncrowned leader, Alexander – "Sandy" – Goehr, was already outstandingly brilliant. There was also a wiry young man with eyes of a frightening intensity called Peter Maxwell Davies: defensively I described him to myself as yet another mad genius.

And of course, there was John Ogdon – as scruffy and unconventional as the best of them, and, like most of the others, a composer as well as a performer. It was with these passionate and argumentative young men that he seemed to be most at ease: he was more relaxed and very much more articulate than in any other company.

With the other members of New Music, at least, I didn't have to come to terms; they were as indifferent to me as I was remote from them. But with John, things were different: John was seeking me out. I would not, like my mother, pretend that what I did not understand did not exist. If John and I were to remain friends, I would have to try to become more tolerant; I would have to make more effort to understand him.

It wasn't easy.

3

My reaction on being invited to John's home for the first time was one of simple shock.

The Ogdons lived on the other side of Manchester from Hyde, in a suburb called Besses o' the Barn, which hardly lived up to its romantic name. The house, a small modern semi-detached, was anonymous enough from the outside – but inside, I entered a world different from any I'd experienced before. The place was very untidy, with sheets of music and books lying open on the furniture, over the carpet, and on ledges and shelves everywhere. And it was noisy too – John's father, Howard, would happily practise on his trombone while in another room John or his elder brother Karl, or even an older sister would play the piano by the hour. And on the rare occasions when no one was actually working at the keyboard, Howard would fill the silence with gramophone records – usually Wagner, played fortissimo, which can be very fortissimo indeed!

Though, in time, I was to become devoted to John's parents, I could never describe his father as anything less than eccentric. He was a small, short-haired man with bright blue eyes, and he was as slim as John was bulky; by profession an English teacher, he spent most of the time shut away in his study, working on jealously guarded manuscripts. He was extremely fussy about his meals and usually he would insist on different foods from the rest of the family, which he would eat at different times. Like John, he found it difficult to sustain a casual conversation; but unlike John, he was anti-social, being reluctant to leave the safety of his home. For Howard, night was the time for living; day, whenever possible, he preferred to spend in sleep. And yet for all his oddities, he was enormously clever, and kind.

Obviously marriage to such a man was far from easy for John's mother, but she behaved as if the Ogdon way of life was the most natural in the world; her ability to cope filled me with a rather puzzled awe from the moment I first met her. She was taller than Howard, always simply dressed, with her grey hair drawn back into a bun; her face was strikingly beautiful, with a calmness to it, a serenity, that conveyed reserves of inner strength. When I knew her, she seemed to spend all her time in the kitchen, preparing separate meals for her difficult husband and her indulged youngest son; if she had any life of her own, I for one was never aware of it. And yet, inseparable from this self-sacrificing drudgery, there was a core of fearsome stubbor-ness, as I was to learn to my cost some years later.

For Dorothy, the phenomenally talented child she had borne provided a consolation for the hardships of her life. And her life was and had been, hard, particularly in John's earliest years, when Howard had suffered a nervous breakdown.

He had been diagnosed as schizophrenic; he had been con-fined in hospital, unable to work, for a couple of years. And even though he had recovered, the experience had left deep scars – and amongst the manuscripts he had worked on so hard in his study was a long and exhaustive account of his sufferings, both in his tortured mind and in reality.

During his illness, money – always scarce in the Ogdon household – had threatened to run out altogether. It had been up to Dorothy to run the family financially as well as in every other way; lodgers had been taken in, and somehow she had managed. But however severe the straits, she had determined that John should not suffer.

The youngest of five children by six years, John Andrew Howard Ogdon Jnr. had been born on 27th January 1937; late both to walk and talk, he had grown into a delicate child, suf-fering from ear trouble and short sightedness. But his extra-ordinary musical talents had shown themselves very early. By the age of five, he could already play the piano better than many a gifted adult; while at nine, he had started to compose – simple pieces, but astoundingly sophisticated for one so young.

It says a great deal for John's parents that they did not allow him to be exploited financially and artistically as a child prodigy. But it is far harder to understand why, when he was

17

ten, they permitted his official musical training to stop. John himself is vague about the reasons: he says that though he had already had lessons at the Manchester College of Music for two years, Howard and Dorothy had "agreed with the Principal that I would benefit from a wider education." Today, I wonder if they had sensed something over-obsessional in John's approach to music – but perhaps I am reading his future into his past.

Whatever the reasons, he was sent to Manchester Grammar School to study for his General Certificate of Education: and maybe, as a result, his outlook and interests *were* broadened. Very occasionally he was allowed to play for his old piano teacher, Nellie Houseley; but the fact remains that in the crucial development years between ten and sixteen, John was virtually self-taught as a pianist. And however gifted a child may be – even if gifted to the point of genius – training is essential, above all to stop the development of bad technical habits.

John himself has written "the most difficult thing is to keep the logic, the thought of the music, without letting the notes get in the way." Not that the notes themselves, in the most literal sense, have ever given him any trouble – for him, they were the easiest part. But to put his point more prosaically – technique is a matter of physically knowing how best to control and shape the sound: it is a matter of bodily discipline, of posture, wrist position, elbow control. John had to learn, or try to learn, these vital aids to performing for himself.

Of course, my criticisms of John's education may seem hard to justify when even then, as now, he could play some of the most difficult virtuoso pieces ever written with breathtaking ease – pieces on which even the most outstanding of his colleagues would spend several months of effort. But John does admit that a teacher in these years would have helped him in his approach to the classics. All his adult life, he has found the precision and exactness of Mozart and Bach harder to master than the technical bravura of Tchaikovsky or Rachmaninov: and even today, he will sometimes say "I must work more on Mozart, I really must try harder."

Teachers or no, Dorothy Ogdon never doubted for a moment that her son was destined, eventually, to become a great pianist: and she believed, and deeply so, that it was her

18

reward, as well as her duty, to nurture and protect him. Between her and John there was a tacit pact that in return for his hours of practice and study, she would cater to his every whim. This she did throughout his days at Grammar School, and she continued to indulge him just as much on his return to full-time study at the College of Music.

John never made a bed, never lifted his discarded clothes from the floor – not because he was deliberately exploiting Dorothy, but because it never occurred to him to do so. Such domestic details didn't matter to him – if, in protest, she had left his bed unmade one day, he probably wouldn't have noticed. He *would* have noticed, however, if she had skimped or economised on his food. She fed him enormous, gargantuan meals: I remember the high teas at his home, when, in summer, mounds of ham would disappear from his plate – and, when winter came, how he would devour whole steak and kidney pies, slice after slice of thick-cut bread and all the many variations of northern stodge which helped insulate us against the cold of the stone, unheated houses.

As I had hoped, my occasional visits to John's house were helping me to understand him a little better; but after all, that did not mean that he was proving much easier to deal with.

At my own home, when the telephone rang, it was almost always John at the other end of the line – his persistence soon became a family joke. Sometimes he would be quite talkative, more often the opposite. "Why are you calling?" I'd ask him – and then one of his silences would follow. These interminable pauses would drive me mad – "What do you *want?*" I'd demand. His most usual answer was a request to come to the house – not to see me so much as to use the baby grand given to me so generously by my aunt Marion.

I remember my mother's repressed disapproval when she discovered the extent of his appetite – and her shock when he would disappear into her larder and casually help himself to anything that caught his fancy. Indeed, at first I had been worried about what my parents would make of him, and was hardly surprised that they thought him an "odd fish". And yet John was so unpretentious, so much, in his own way, himself, that they came to accept him without question – even becoming fond of him.

My own fondness, too, was imperceptibly deepening. Though it never crossed my mind that our friendship could be anything but platonic, he could catch me off my guard with a refreshing charm, and when we were alone together, we got along for the most part with no trouble. It was in general company that things were often complicated.

In spite of all my efforts, John's social finesse was not improving. If I took him along with me to the house of a friend for tea, he was perfectly capable of sitting the entire time without saying a word. Sometimes he would not even try to look interested in the conversation, but would sit with a heavy and serious scowl that disturbed me and dampened others. Or he would get up from the table and, turning his back, would silently study the bookshelves.

On the other hand, his attempts at sociability often met with no more success. In the most unintellectual of gatherings, he would turn to his neighbour with a bald "What do you think about Chopin?" – or "Which do you prefer, Charlotte or Emily Brontë?" The result, of course, was usually that the conversation stopped dead, with his companion floundering for words.

I found myself, unconsciously, becoming more aggressive with him. "Change your shirt" I would tell him, "you've worn it three days now!" Or "John, you've dropped egg all over your lapel – wipe it off" – or "I won't be seen out with you until you shave!" And always – almost always – he would obey with docility. He even seemed to enjoy my carping – though it hardly needs an expert to point out that in my way, in spite of all my convictions, I was after all beginning to look after him.

I remember once getting a phone call from a mutual friend of ours, Frieda, whose home boasted a grand piano and who regularly invited the two of us for meals and musical evenings. On this occasion she was close to hysterical – John had been invited to tea along with other friends, and he had not shown up.

This, it seemed to me, should not have been upsetting or surprising to anyone who knew John as well as Frieda did – after all, as I pointed out, he had always been vague about keeping engagements, however often he'd been reminded.

"But Brenda, he stayed here at the house last weekend . . ."

"So?"

"Well..." The tight voice was silent a moment. "He was very ... very *amorous* ... I mean he ... *we* spent most of the time – you know – *kissing!*" Another pause: then she blurted out "He even tried to undress me!"

For those days, this was strong stuff indeed – and evidently it had been enough to persuade Frieda, who was a fervent fan of John's, that she and the budding maestro were virtually engaged. "And now after all that" she wailed "he hasn't turned up to tea!" She was deeply, bitterly hurt, and her mother was beside herself with righteous indignation.

Only minutes after my conversation with Frieda, John himself called me. He didn't deny his weekend behaviour, he simply begged me to rescue him from Frieda's attentions, which he was finding rather more overpowering than he'd bargained for.

"All the same, John" I said reprovingly, "you shouldn't have stood her up for tea."

"Tea?" he repeated innocently. "Oh! Tea! I forgot all about it – really I did!"

I was sure that for once his acknowledged social vagueness had been put to calculated use, though I didn't say so.

It took time, several phone calls, and more patience than I usually credit myself with to smooth that situation over; but eventually I managed to calm both mother and daughter. John was not accepted back into the household immediately, however, though after some months he and Frieda once again became good, if physically distant, friends.

At the time, I found the incident funny: certainly I felt no jealousy. But looking back, it stands for me now as the beginning of a role that John has imposed on me ever since – and one which, to be fair, I have always accepted. I became important to him not only because he found me attractive, not only because of our shared love for music, but because he trusted me to save him from scrapes of his own creation, from which he would not – could not – take the consequences.

But alongside John's gaucheness, his vacillation and uncertainty, there was always his profound belief in his talent. Just how profound, I discovered one quiet evening after supper in my parents' house.

John told me, sitting alone with me in my studio, that he believed he was one of the great musicians of all time, in the line of Beethoven, Brahms and Busoni. He said it quietly, simply, and with total conviction.

I was stunned. I fell back on my father's habit of cloaking embarrassment with a joke, making some bantering reply. But I knew that John had meant what he'd said – and what's more, that in a way I believed him.

The great world outside the College still had to judge him, however. It would have its first chance soon, in May 1956, when he entered the Queen Elisabeth Competition for pianists in Brussels.

4

I too had decided to take part in the Queen Elisabeth Competition. I had made the decision independently from John, and it was another student who first told me that he was considering entering.

"Considering" turned out to be the right word. "Yes" he said, when I broached the subject, "I would like to go to Brussels."

"Well – have you done anything about it?"

"Not yet. You see . . . I'm not quite sure how . . ."

And so once more I found myself taking charge – checking that he filled in and posted the right forms, making his travel arrangements, and so on. Just about the only thing I didn't arrange for him was his accommodation – he'd been given somebody's address by a fellow student, he said, and I could leave that up to him.

I was very excited at the prospect of Brussels; the competition is one of the most prestigious in the world – and though I had no illusions that I would win, I hoped I wouldn't disgrace myself. Also I would hear and meet the finest young pianistic talents from all over the world – and last, but not entirely least, Brussels was "Abroad."

The previous summer, "Abroad" had acquired a special magic for me. I had gone to Salzburg to study at the Mozarteum – all expenses paid, of course, from my own savings. I had studied the Beethoven Fourth Piano Concerto with Heinz Scholz, playing on his wonderful Bösendorfer piano; I had basked in perfect weather, thrilled to the towering scenery and the eighteenth-century elegance of the town, and gorged myself on cream cakes and coffee. I had even lived in a castle and had met other young musicians from America and Germany with whom I had been to many Festival concerts as well as playing chamber music far into the night. In short, the weeks I had spent in Salzburg were amongst the happiest in my life – and the return to England had sent me crashing into depression. All at once, Manchester struck me as unbearably grim – and after the charm and warmth of the Austrians, the blunt take-it-or-leave it manner of our northern people had been almost more than I could bear.

So amongst its other attractions, Brussels offered the chance of escape: and perhaps it would bring me one more taste of the musical cameraderie I had so much enjoyed in Salzburg. I set to work on my practising with a will.

But as time passed, my anticipation began to dwindle, my nerves to increase. The works I would have to play were difficult – I spent hour after painstaking hour working on the obligatory Handel suite, on the Brahms Handel Variations, and compositions by Chopin and by Liszt. This competition, it was dawning on me with increasing vividness, really was serious stuff.

John, on the other hand – who was offering an even more daunting repertoire than I was – seemed not a whit concerned. He continued to pursue his wider musical studies under Claude Biggs, Iso Elinson and Gordon Green – men who, to someone of John's ability, were even then advisers rather than teachers: and his New Music meetings continued as before. Not that he didn't prepare for Brussels – of course he did: but only as one more aspect of his musical activities.

And so the weeks passed by quickly – and suddenly the day of our departure was upon us. For both of us, the serious work was now over; all that remained was to play – and to be judged.

John was quiet on the plane trip, which was not unusual – I was even quieter, which *was* unusual, but then my heart was in my mouth. I had to make a conscious effort to seem relaxed when, at the airport, I was met by my host for the duration of the competition, one Monsieur Janssens.

No one was there to meet John. Monsieur Janssens offered him a lift to the address where he said he would be staying, but something about John's manner worried him. "Are you quite certain" he asked in his accented English "that you are expected there?"

"Oh yes," John replied – then added "at least, I think I

24

am."

"You *think*?"

"Well yes – I do *think* it's been arranged." But quite how it had been arranged, and whether his lodgings had been confirmed, he was obviously not at all certain.

Monsieur Janssens and I waited outside in the car while John rang the doorbell to the building: we watched him with baited breath as he stood there . . .

After what seemed an interminable wait, the door opened: without a backward glance, John disappeared inside. He had not come out again a few minutes later.

Monsieur Janssens and I looked at each other, and both of us broke into laughter. As we drove to his pleasant home in a fashionable section of Brussels, we agreed with each other that it was unbelievable than anyone could be quite so casually vague.

The Janssens had eight children, one of whom, a daughter, was very soon going to be married; so the large house was buzzing with preparations. Under the circumstances, the young English stranger in their midst might have been considered a nuisance at best: but in the event they were exceptionally kind to me, inviting me to share their always delicious meals and making me feel like one of the family.

But still I could not relax – it was all so new, so strange. The briefings, the sheets of paper, the long lists of instructions – and the other competitors to look at and wonder about. So many intense young men and girls in strangely cut clothes, chattering in languages I couldn't understand – there were close on seventy competitors, most of them, I was sure, far more brilliant than I. And unlike Salzburg, no one here was interested in me, no one reached out to me: there was little friendliness or mixing, least of all with the Russian party, which was "protected" by bulky and sinister-looking guards.

But after only two or three days in the Belgian capital, names began to extract themselves from the general anonymity – we picked them up almost unconsciously, they seemed almost to reverberate in the air around us. Gradually, too, a pointing hand, a flurry of whispers, helped add faces to those names – Peter Frankl, a bulky and scholarly looking Hungarian: his fellow countryman Tamas Vasary, a pale young man with

25

strikingly beautiful blue eyes: a volatile, eccentric and brilliant Pole called Andre Czaikowsky. There was a girl too, from France, called Cécile Ousset – and a slim, dark American John Browning.And then, glimpsed occasionally between his ever-present guards, there was a small beak-nosed youth with a mop of black hair and button-bright eyes – a Russian by the name of Vladimir Ashkenazy.

In the middle of this strange new world, I thanked God for John. He too was affected by the atmosphere, but positively so – I sensed an excitement in him, a new determination. But still he remained the same old John from Manchester – as disorganised as ever, and as comfortingly familiar.

Quite what his arrangement was with his hostess, I never discovered – if there was one, it very soon went by the board. He decided that as I was staying with the Janssens then he must be welcome as well – above all at meal times. Madame Janssens was at first surprised by his presence, later mildly indignant, finally – as happens so often in John's case – affectionately resigned.

One day, when he was with us at the lunch table, I opened a letter from Patrick, who was still my number one "steady" back home in Hyde, and who wrote to me regularly during my three weeks in Brussels. As I read, I became vaguely conscious that John was scowling down at his plate: I felt a mild irritation but nothing more, after all, I was used to his moods.

After lunch, when he had gone, Madame Janssens said "That John, he's jealous."

"Jealous? What of?" My hosts and my excellent accommodation I wondered?

"Of the man who wrote you that letter."

"Patrick?" I stared at her. "No – no, I'm sure not."

Her smile was small. "John's in love with you, Brenda. Can't you see it?" She repeated "He's in love with you."

Vehemently, I denied it. But she would not be convinced, so instead I made a joke about it. And then I forgot all about it – after all, there were weightier things on my mind . . .

The morning came at last when I was due to play in the preliminary round for the judges. My mood was in no way helped by the fact that John's services had been called on elsewhere, and so he was not around to lend me moral support.

I made my way to the wings of the stage to await my turn; There was one person to go before me: the American, John Browning. He was black-haired, black eyed, and handsome – and to my eyes, he also seemed wordly and suave. What was more, he looked as cool as a cucumber, while I was undergoing a savage attack of nerves.

John noticed my condition, and in a deep persuasive voice, he did his best to reassure me. But I was in no state to listen; and anyway, soon he was called on to the stage, where he proceeded to play Chopin's C Sharp Minor Scherzo with an apparently effortless perfection. It really wasn't fair, I told myself – talent, sophistication,and a matinee idol's profile into the bargain. Some people were born lucky!

Then it was my turn to face the judges.

I got through my Handel and Chopin, but I played them well below my normal standard. Usually, once I'm at the keyboard, my performing nerves desert me: but not on this occasion. It was an ordeal I will never forget.

John Browning had waited backstage to hear me. "You see?" he said smiling, "I said you'd be fine." He was sure, he told me, that I'd be passed into the second round. I didn't believe him, but I was grateful to him all the same.

And then a reaction set in – I was barely able to get back to the Janssens before my over-taut nerves finally snapped. Nauseous and weeping, I collapsed into bed, and a doctor had to be called.

Mine, of course, was a severe case of over-reaction. But I wonder if the public who flock to these competitions have any idea of the enormous strain experienced by the young men and women taking part? Are they aware of the sleepless nights, the hard knot in the stomach, the almost unbearable suspense? So much work has gone into the preparation of the repertoire: so much is at stake – a whole future . . .

Amongst some musicians, there is a conviction that competitions are not only an ordeal for the participants, but that they are misleading and unjust to boot. After all, these critics point out, music is an art, not a horse race – there is no winner provably first past the post. And every performance is a mixture of technique, personality, musicality – how, in the circumstances, can the judges lay claim to an objective opinion?

On the other hand, no one is forced to go into a competition. But for an ambitious musician, a major award is the quickest and most effective route to a concert career – not only because of the publicity and prize money involved, but because important orchestral engagements are guaranteed to the winners. Anyway, most competitons are as honest as is possible – and usually the really outstanding talents are easily recognisable, and do make it through to the finals. Even those who aren't placed are guaranteed some useful exposure before a discerning international audience.

But back in Brussels in 1957, I was more concerned with my own frayed nerves than with the pros and cons of artistic competition. In my darkened room, my certainty of failure was confirmed: I was no longer in the running. I was so upset I missed hearing John play in his preliminary round: but I soon learned he had caused a sensation.

Nobody that year offered a more daunting or challenging repertoire – it included Beethoven's Hammerklavier Sonata, Brahms' Paganini Variations, Liszt's "Dante" as well as his B minor Sonata, Alkan's Etude for the left hand, and Balakirev's Islamey. After hearing him, the critics acclaimed him as a phenomenal talent, and there was a sudden sharp buzz of excitement along the competitor's grapevine.

But John, too, was failed by the jury.

Nowadays, he claims that this failure did not upset him – that the experience given him by Brussels was what had mattered most to him all along. But I remember things differently. Somehow, I was able to get out of bed and join him in listening to other, more successful competitors; he would sit next to me hunched and lowering deep in his chair, obviously making comparisons with his own effort, often unfavourably.

And yet, there could be no doubt that the standard of these other pianists was dauntingly high – in fact, in terms of talent, this must have been one of the most outstanding competitions that has ever been held. Vasary, Frankl and Czaikowsky all played as brilliantly as the whispers had foretold, and John Browning again impressed us with his fluent professionalism. Today, I can still remember a stunning account of Liszt's "La Campanella" given by Cécile Ousset.

And above all, for me at least, there was a haunting and

magical performance of Chopin's Etude in C major, Op 10 No. 1 by the Russian Vladimir Ashkenazy. As a personality he remained shadowy to us, cut off by his ever present escorts: but as a pianist, there was no doubt that here was one of the great talents of our time. We were convinced we would be hearing him again – little guessing the dramatic role he was destined to play in John's future . . .

In short, the pianists we were hearing were not only gifted: they were superbly trained and thoroughly prepared – far more so than the small contingent from Britain. John was left with no alternative but to face up to the fact that he had not deserved to win. His preparation of the repertoire had been too confident and slapdash, and his technique was still too unpolished.

For John and me, Brussels was an eye-opening experience. We benefitted enormously just from listening – but the more ravishing the playing, the more painful that learning process was. For the first time, we realised that the world of music, at least in its higher reaches, was a tough, merciless and infinitely demanding place. For both of us, the time for dreams was now over.

We did not stay in Brussels for the end of the Competition – apart from anything else, the semi-invalid I still was proved too much of a burden on top of preparations for the wedding, and three weeks after my arrival, Madame Janssens kindly but firmly insisted I catch a plane back to Manchester.

Chastened and shaken, John and I returned to the College. In a way, on this occasion, it was good to be home again – but naturally we both grabbed at any scrap of information about the competition's progress that came our way, phoning each other at once to pass on the news.

When the final results came through, we weren't surprised to hear that Vladimir Ashkenazy had won first prize, with Browning second, Czaikowsky third, and Ousset fourth . . . How remote it seemed already, that bright and dangerous world out there – yet how provincial did the College appear to me now! Oh well, I reminded myself, my time as a student was fast running out, and there was still plenty of studying to do.

Just as we had settled back into the familiar academic routine, John was asked by the College to perform the Brahms

First Piano Concerto in D minor with the student orchestra at the end of term concert – a concert open to the general public. The conductor was to be none other than the local musical hero, the man who had turned the Hallé into one of the finest orchestras in the country – Sir John Barbirolli.

This would be John's first performance under the baton of a world-famous conductor. The invitation galvanised him into a bout of unprecedented industry – never before had I known him to work so hard on a single composition. Inevitably, I saw less of him than usual: but he did tell me how Sir John – a flamboyant and romantic figure in his flowing black cloak – was unstinting in the time and care he devoted to orchestral rehearsals. He went through the concerto alone with John as well, and was full of suggestions and useful encouragement.

The night of the performance in July, the concert hall was packed with the concert-going public of Manchester, as well as by every student in the College who could squeeze in. I remember that my throat was dry, and my heart beat harder as the orchestra tuned up and the audience lights slowly went down . . .

Only a few minutes into the performance, I knew that something special was happening: there was a silence in the audience, an almost tangible tension communicating itself between player and listener. As the last movement built towards its close, I could feel – and share – the contained excitement that was straining for release: and with the last chord it exploded into a thundering, whistling ovation. John, with that mysterious presence he always conjures up on stage, was pushed forward by a proud and applauding conductor – he was called back time and time again. For the nineteen-year-old pianist, the performance had been a triumph – the first big public success of his career.

Afterwards, I overheard the enthusiastic comments from members of the audience as they pushed along the aisles: while backstage, in the wings, the orchestra players were still lingering, discussing the performance in terms little short of awe. John was surrounded by a crowd of friends, all eager to congratulate him: Sir John was amongst them, unqualified in his praise, and referring to John, as he always did afterwards, as "my boy". John stood there, perspiring, nodding, and smiling a bemused sweet smile, not quite believing what was happening.

I waited a moment, catching an occasional glimpse of him through the throng. With playing like that, I thought defiantly, he could after all have matched the best of them at Brussels – I was convinced of it. Dammit, I was proud to know John Ogdon. Very proud!

5

My mother raised her voice amid the general applause: "John has won everything!"

It was true. At the end of his time at the Royal College of Music as a full time student, John collected every possible award and gained all his diplomas with distinction. I had expected as much, but I was thrilled for him all the same.

My own success could not match John's, but I was very pleased with that too. He came over to congratulate me after the official ceremonies were over: we shook hands and promised that we'd keep in touch. And somehow, under all the excitement, neither of us could hide a genuine regret.

By and large, our student days had been very happy – and (the experience of Brussels apart) they had allowed us to drift on a music-filled, magical cloud. But now reality claimed me, and I fell to earth with a bone-jarring bump.

My mother wasted no time in making it clear that though I was welcome to stay on in the house, I was expected – not unreasonably, of course – to start making my living at once. And so I began a gruelling routine that was to last for over three years.

I took part time teaching jobs at schools around Hyde, and I gave private lessons to neighbourhood children. At the same time, I continued to go into the College for lessons with Iso Elinson, while on my few free days, I would practise for five or six hours. I was also engaged, with increasing regularity, to play all over the North West of England – dates had originally been booked for me through the College, but, as I became known to the Music Clubs, there was a gratifying snowball effect. The pianos were often atrocious and the fees were no more than tokens: but I can still remember my excitement at being hired to play a Mozart concerto in Ashton-under-Lyne.

It might not have been the Festival Hall, but it was a start!

At home, I was still not expected to cook, and as a special concession I was given the occasional use of my father's car: but I continued to take part in almost all household chores, washing up still being my forte. These domestic duties on top of my teaching, practising, studying and public performances meant that I lived in a state of constant exhaustion, with almost no time for social life.

What little there was, I largely devoted to Patrick. John, whom inevitably I had to see less than before, would sometimes say that instead I should make more time for him: but I didn't take these complaints very seriously, and our friendship continued to jog along in a comfortable, unquestioning way. Much of our conversation when we did meet centred around the struggle to start our careers, and our worries if we would ever succeed. John's professional dates at the time were still few and far between – although he did have one big advantage: he was getting the occasional radio engagement.

Like me, he was still going back to the College for secondary piano studies, and he was doing some teaching as well: he continued to increase his already huge repertoire and read about music voraciously. All in all, he seemed quite happy, I thought – certainly happier than I was. But his mother, Dorothy, was as dedicated as ever to cushioning him from life's hardships.

A year after leaving the College, John and I managed to take a break from our home-based routines by each making a working trip abroad. I returned to my beloved Salzburg and the Mozarteum, while John, on a grant given him by the College, went to Basle in Switzerland for lessons with the great Dutch pianist, Egon Petri.

Salzburg was all I remembered and more – and the visit was capped when I was invited to play a movement of Beethoven's Fourth Piano Concerto in public under the aegis of Antal Dorati. But important though that visit was to me, John's time in Basle was to have much further-reaching consequences both to his playing and to his career.

He spent over three months as Petri's student, returning to Manchester early in 1958. The master proved to be an approachable and volatile old man with an irrepressible penchant for puns – which didn't prevent John regarding him with

33

a totally genuine awe. Not only was Petri an acknowledged giant of the keyboard – he had studied with John's idolised Ferruccio Busoni, and had even premiered the mammoth piano concerto in Britain under the baton of the composer himself.

He gave John insight into Busoni by insisting that the interpretation of his works should often be subdued, almost classical – an approach, incidentally, which Petri thought equally applicable to Liszt. He also stimulated John's interest in the near-forgotten Alkan: and in addition, works by Beethoven, Brahms and Chopin were studied in depth. And John's benefit was technically practical too: the old man tolerated no faking or hard-to-hear short cuts when it came to the notes. "Your little finger is too high" John remembers him insisting. "In fifty years, that finger is going to be very tired if you keep on playing that way!"

Years later, Petri is supposed to have claimed that he had nothing to teach John: "He knew it all already" he said. But in truth, under his perceptive guidance, John's technique improved remarkably, and the experience was vital to his development as an artist.

Immeasurable though Petri's influence was, John was to meet someone else in Basle who was to have a profound, though very different, effect on him.

One day, as John tells it, he left his lodgings to go to the local music shop, where the proprietor rented out a small upstairs room with a piano on an hourly basis. John was studying Beethoven's Third Piano Concerto, and he became so engrossed at the keyboard that he forgot about time.

He was practising what he now concedes was his own rather florid cadenza for the Concerto's first movement when he became aware of another presence in the same room: he looked round to see a tall and dark young man standing by the door.

John stopped playing at once; his hour, he realised, was up, and this was obviously a student who had also rented the room.

"Don't stop" the young man said to him in English; "I couldn't touch the piano myself after hearing playing like yours. But do you mind if I stay and listen?"

John needed no more encouragement; and after the second hour's session was finished, his admiring listener introduced himself as a fellow student of Petri's: his name, he said, was Alistair Londonderry.

And so, in a Swiss music shop, began one of the most important friendships of John's life.

Superficially, perhaps, the young men's rapport might have seemed unlikely. Alistair was everything John was not: aristocratic, strikingly handsome, articulate, and socially adept – while at the same time he was demanding, restless, and easily bored. Yet it was perhaps on these very contrasts that their friendship blossomed and thrived. Certainly John claims that he felt at ease from the very first moment. And perhaps Alistair found John's lack of pretension refreshing: while he continued to look on John's talent with a deeply committed enthusiasm.

And so, over the next weeks, these two improbable friends whiled away endless afternoons and evenings discussing all matters musical. They discovered they were both fierce champions of Liszt, including his often frowned-upon transcriptions of operas – equally, they revelled in Busoni's transcriptions, unacceptable though they were to strict purists. In a different vein, Alistair did his best to awaken in John a still dormant passion for Mozart; and he revealed an unexpected talent for jazz drumming, which John looked on with happy indulgence. He was an accomplished pianist, too, though he adamantly refused to play for John.

What John didn't know then, and did not learn till later, was that his new found friend and admirer, the Marquess of Londonderry, was also one of the wealthiest men in all Britain – one who, furthermore would be more than willing to use his influence and patronage on John's behalf when the time was ripe. But that was not yet . . .

I had returned to England from Salzburg long before John was ready to leave Basle: and my homecoming was even more depressing than it had been the first time.

Over a year had gone by since I'd left the College, my mother reminded me, and it was time I reimbursed her more realistically for the studio where I practised and gave private lessons. So now, in addition to my former teaching jobs, I took on pupils at a boys' prep school for several hours a week, as well as teaching juniors at the Royal College of Music every Saturday morning.

But in spite of the day to day drudgery at home in Hyde,

there was the studio itself, with its royal blue wall to wall carpeting and my music and books on the shelves. And there was my dear easy-going father, always a warm and reliable presence.

And there was Patrick.

Now that music was my livelihood, I sometimes needed release from it – and that, Patrick was able to give me. When I had time, I would watch him play rugger on Saturday afternoons, admiring his aggressive masculine grace: or we would swim, or play tennis, or go on long walks. We were a social twosome as well – we were invariably invited out as a couple. My mother began dropping unsubtle hints, pointing out that we'd been going steady for three or four years, and looking at me with mounting disappointment as one after another of my friends announced their engagements.

But time passed and I was twenty one ... twenty two ... and still Patrick didn't propose to me. The problem was that his family was Irish Catholic, and of particularly intransigent convictions. His parents did not want to know about me, and never once, in all the time I knew Patrick, was I invited into their home. They would have disowned him if he had asked me to marry me, and, without discussing it openly, we both knew as much.

But in all honesty, if I had married Patrick – and I might have, given the chance – it would have been more because of the middle-class conventions of the time than from any deep personal conviction. The way things were, I still had the best of both worlds: support and easy companionship, but no ties to stint my ambitions.

Though I had missed John from moment to moment while he'd been in Basle, I was surprised how happy I was when he came home to Manchester again. His eccentricities, his vagueness, his silences, were unexpectedly reassuring and familiar: at first I thought Basle had left him completely unchanged. But gradually, I began to realise that he was bringing a taste of a wider world into my overworked life.

He told me more about his new friend Alistair, who was now revealing an exciting talent for unearthing rare or out of print scores. Often, he would send them to John – I still remember John's incredulous excitement when the Liszt/Busoni "Don

Giovanni Fantasy" was delivered by the postman one day.

Later, in the autumn of 1958, Alistair was to provide John with yet another committed and lasting enthusiasm – this time for the new Lady Londonderry, the former Nicolette – "Nico" – Harrison. After first meeting her on a visit to London, John could talk of little else for some days: "She is" he assured me, goggle-eyed, "one of the most gorgeous girls I have ever seen in my life. Honestly, Brenda!"

Even knowing John's weakness for a beautiful face, his reaction seemed excessive to me – surprisingly, I felt a bit slighted, and also very curious indeed . . .

Throughout the summer and autumn of that year, John worked hard both composing and practising under Dorothy's approving eye. He also began making regular visits to London to study with the pianist, Denis Matthews.

Denis tells a revealing story about John. On their first meeting as teacher and pupil, he says, he asked John to play him something by Mozart – whereupon John launched into the "Don Giovanni Fantasy" (or, to give it its correct but less-used title, "Réminiscences de Don Juan") to which Alistair had first introduced him! In the following months and, indeed, years, Denis was to prove particularly helpful to his young student in his interpretative approach to the classics; and the two men soon developed a personal friendship, sharing, amongst other things, a delight in Marx Brothers films.

John was not yet playing regularly in public – though the few dates that did come his way were increasing in prestige and importance. Soon after his return home from Basle, my family and a group of friends crowded round the living room radio to hear him perform Beethoven's Third Piano Concerto with the BBC Northern Orchestra on the Home Service; and within only a matter of weeks, he received complimentary critical attention for his interpretation of Liszt's then rarely heard "Totentanz" with the Royal Liverpool Philharmonic.

But it was John's next appearance with the Liverpool orchestra that was to prove crucial in his early career. In those days, under its conductor John Pritchard, the orchestra was unusually enterprising: and so John was re-engaged for November 1958 to play his beloved Busoni concerto.

This is no ordinary concerto. It has five movements and lasts for well over an hour – and in the final movement, a male voice choir joins in: little wonder, then, that it is almost never performed. The piano part itself is subordinate to the overall design, but at the same time it is one of the most gruelling in the repertoire, demanding unusual virtuosity and stamina. The first movement alone has monster arpeggio following monster arpeggio yet it also contains the most subtle washes of colour: other movements call on every resource from feathery finger work to massive and thundering sonorities. It is a work that any pianist would approach with awe, and John was not an exception.

This was his chance to embark on his dreamed of Busoni crusade, and an opportunity too to show how much he'd learned about the composer from Petri – and he threw himself into his practising with a fervour unmatched since his preparations for the Brahms with Sir John Barbirolli. In fact, so passionately did he practise on this occasion that he almost ruined things for himself.

I went to his house to see him a week before the concert was due to take place and was horrified to see that his fingers were covered in bandages. "I've been working so hard" he explained. "The pads have got sore – they're a bit swollen."

"But what on earth are you doing about practising?"

"Oh" he said, almost nonchalantly "I take the bandages off for that – but when the pain gets unbearable, mother puts them on again for me."

Only the day before the performance did John remove the bandages for good.

He played the concerto without the aid of a score, in itself an astonishing feat. I must admit, though, that it is not my own favourite music – apart from anything else, it is so very long! – but naturally I went to Liverpool to hear it, taking my mother along. And whatever my reservations about the work, it was an overwhelming experience to hear an interpretation of such powerful and confident brilliance. We were stunned, and so was the rest of the audience.

If I had to put a beginning to John's British career, this Liverpool concert would be it. Both the little known concerto and the performance itself attracted widespread attention: and from this moment on, when John's name was mentioned in professional circles, the answer would not inevitably be "Who?"

But if fame had started to beckon, however shadowily, from the wings, fortune had given the performance a miss. When the applause had died down, when the crowds of well-wishers had left the dressing room, when only personal excitement and a sense of achievement were left, John was handed his fee for the performance.

It was twenty guineas. Not enough to cover expenses.

6

In those days, twenty guineas was the standard fee for those of us labelled "student pianists": I was to earn it myself from the same orchestra a few months later, in the March of 1959.

The engagement came about through my own belated audition for the BBC – then, as now, musicians without an international reputation have to be officially "approved" before they can be hired for a broadcast. Luckily for me, one of the BBC jury (which passed me) was the manager of the Liverpool Philharmonic, Gerald McDonald – and on the strength of what he heard, he hired me for three performances of the Grieg concerto.

I was over the moon with excitement. At the first opportunity I rushed to the phone: "John" I shouted when he answered "I've been hired to play the Grieg with the Liverpool!"

There was a long silence at the other end of the line.

"John?"

"Good" he said, and at once changed the subject.

Neither then nor later did he congratulate me; and any encouragement he did give me subsequently was tempered by an amused condescenscion, as if the Grieg were merely a trifle, hardly worthy of serious attention. I was astonished and hurt: I may have been blind, in Brussels, to his jealousy over a love letter, but it would need a greater moron than I not to notice his resentment where just one professional engagement was concerned.

As time passes, I have become more convinced that men – particularly when they're young – are naturally more jealous than women. Desperately though I wanted a career, I can honestly claim that I have almost never been resentful of somebody else's success (though I may have been surprised by it, but that's another matter!). Always, when I have cared most deeply, it has been for John much more than myself.

John has mellowed over the years – in those days, though, it was as if every good review, every major engagement, for another pianist was both a threat and a personal loss. But of course, he was far from alone in reacting in such a self-centred way. The most soulful and sensitive of musicians are driven by ruthless ambition and, side by side with ambition, by the very real fear of being overtaken, outshone, and forgotten . . .

But if John seemed less than generous to me on a professional level, it did not seriously mar our friendship. In fact, we were seeing more of each other than at any time since leaving the College, largely because the reason for John's earlier and purely personal jealousy had removed himself from the scene.

My mother's complaints about Patrick had been growing louder with each passing month "You're twenty three already!" she'd say, as if I was well into middle age. "Brenda, soon you're going to be left on the shelf! If Patrick's not going to marry you, at least he should let you find somebody else!"

And so, at last, my mother did succeed in raising the spectre of my becoming an unwanted and lonely old maid. "Are we going to get married?" I asked Patrick directly one day. He looked at me a moment, his expression gentle: but his answer was equally direct. "No" he said.

So that was it. Exit Patrick to study in Birmingham.

And enter John more strongly than ever to fill the void that had been left behind.

Between my teaching and general studying, I had been practising for the Grieg until I could have played it in my sleep. All the same, I was nervous as the time for the performances approached. It is hard to convey what it feels like to walk out on to the boards of a brightly lit stage, to see the huge black piano waiting silently, and to know that whatever is going to happen at the keyboard, in front of hundreds of people, is one's responsibility and nobody else's. John Pritchard – who had also conducted John's Busoni concerto – was sensitive to the way I was feeling, and he was wonderfully reassuring – a quality for which not all conductors of his standing are famous.

41

Considerate too was the orchestra's assistant conductor: he was a strikingly handsome, dark skinned young man, and, though I admit I did not sense an aura of success about him, I have nonetheless never forgotten him. Today he is one of the most celebrated conductors in the world: his name is Zubin Mehta.

The first two performances, at Glossop and Ellesmere Port, went well. The third, in Liverpool itself, was of course, the most important – and John swallowed whatever lingering vestiges of professional resentment he might still have been feeling, and arrived to lend me unqualified support.

To my astonishment, Patrick turned up as well, with an armful of deep crimson roses – some of which, romantically if impractically, he'd hoped I would wear as a corsage.

I was very pleased with my performance, and the audience's reception was warm. Afterwards, excited as I was by the congratulations of friends and strangers who had come backstage to my dressing room, I was still able to notice, with amusement, the formal indifference with which John and Patrick were acting towards one another.

But Patrick's unheralded appearance disturbed me. I had thought our story well over: now I was reminded how close we'd been to each other – and how attractive he still was to me. Part of me was tempted to turn back the clock, even though we could have no realistic hope of a future . . .

The superb reviews next morning helped restore me to my sense of proportion. My music and ambitions, I realized again, were things Patrick could not understand, and in which there was no place for him. I resolved not to lose any more sleep over him than I ever had over John – which, of course, was no sleep at all.

By this time, John and I had both become regular visitors to Liverpool – not only for the occasional concert, our own included, but because we were studying with Gordon Green, a hale and hearty man we admired as a teacher and loved as a friend. His wife, Dorothy, owned a small restaurant called "The 23 Club", which had become a centre for the city's musicians and intellectuals; and sitting there, while animated discussions ebbed and flowed all around us, it was easy to imagine we were in a sort of Café Flore or Deux Magots of the English North. We both loved the place – not least because Dorothy

42

could be so uncommercially generous!

One day soon after the Grieg, John was opposite me at a Club table when he said "Brenda, I think I want to grow a beard."

"A beard?" I studied his round face a moment – everything in it, I suddenly thought, was rounded, from the frames of his glasses to his nose. "Yes" I said, "you know, I think it might be a good idea. Only keep it . . . sort of long."

"Bushy?"

"No, not bushy – long! To give your face more length."

"How long – to here?" He raised his hand, palm flattened, somewhere across his chest.

"No silly – higher . . ." I leaned over the table, and raised his hand to throat level. "About there. But John, please not bushy!"

He began growing a goatee the next day – since then, he has never shaved it off, and it has become inseparable from his public image.

For both of us, the most important thing that happened in Liverpool that year was the second major piano competition of our lives. Though it was being held for the first time that May, it attracted over sixty young men and women from countries all over the world, while the jury was a distinguished one, headed by the pianist Solomon and of course, the Liverpool Philharmonic's conductor, John Pritchard. There were to be three rounds – and the twelve finalists would all play with the Orchestra in concerts spread out over several nights. Interest from the national press as well as the local music-loving public promised to be very high.

All the same, the atmosphere, to me at least, was not nearly as pressured as Brussels had been: for one thing, the repertoire – which included Liszt and Schumann pieces, Ravel's "Ondine" and a specially written Toccata by Peter Racine Fricker – was one I personally found less demanding. And of course, on this occasion there were no planes to catch, no problems with the language, and I was familiar with the concert hall, and even with members of the orchestra.

For John, though, these same factors, if anything, only made the strain worse. He was beginning to make a name for himself, which he did not want to jeopardise – and a defeat on his home ground would not pass unnoticed, as it might in some foreign town. And the fact that the repertoire was not so demanding was no consolation to him – he felt that he would be left with less opportunity to shine.

So by the time May arrived and the competition began, John was more tense than I. The first round was closed to the public, I remember; and the jury, to ensure scrupulous fairness in so far as fairness was possible, sat behind screens, unaware of the contestant's identity. To my relief, I played very well, and so did John: and both of us were passed into the second round.

This round too – which was open to the public – went without any mishaps: and to our immense excitement, John and I found ourselves amongst the dozen finalists. The lessons of Brussels, we told ourselves, had been well and truly learned.

Except that they hadn't. Not by me, at least.

The Beethoven Fourth Piano Concerto which I played in the finals went beautifully, and, I learned later, had been commended by Solomon himself. But in a moment of misplaced bravado, I had also elected to play the Rachmaninov Paganini Variations, which I had not yet mastered completely. I did not disgrace myself in front of the packed out house, but even before the performance had finished, I knew I had no hope of getting a prize.

The Rachmaninov Paganini Variations were also played by a Spanish pianist, Joachim Achucarro, who was a favourite for the first place. Unusually blond for a Spaniard, he was always unfailingly courteous: I liked him and wished him well – though after he'd been playing for only a minute or two, I realised that he needed no wishes of mine. His was a brilliant performance, no less exciting because of its meticulous accuracy.

Of the other finalists, only two gave performances that seriously threatened Achucarro: Aldo Mancinelli – and John Ogdon. John had chosen the Liszt No 1 Concerto in E Flat: there was a wonderfully tender quality to much of the playing – but above all, this was a no-risks-avoided performance that was triumphantly brought off. When it was over, the audience was shocked into silence for a moment before letting loose in an ovation; I and John's other friends shouted ourselves hoarse in his support.

And then, at last, the time came when we were all summoned backstage while the jury considered its verdict.

The suspense was knife-edge – it was by no means certain who was going to win. The minutes ticked by like hours; John tried to appear relaxed, but sweat was beading his forehead and shining on his flushed cheeks.

In fact, though it seemed much longer, only ten minutes passed before the finalists were summoned on to the stage to hear the final decision, which was announced by the conductor John Pritchard. Aldo Mancinelli came third: John Ogdon second: and "by the narrowest margin" Joachim Achucarro was proclaimed winner of the first prize.

Later, we were told that there had been some disparity in the jurors' opinions. Evidently Solomon and another jury member, Cyril Smith, had considered that John's technique, for all its breathtaking facility, still wasn't quite polished enough – and it was their opinion which had finally carried the day. Be that as it may, I was glad that if John had to be beaten by anyone, it was by a man as nice as Achucarro.

And in the event, the second prize proved very far from a disaster for John. He was given rave reviews in the national press – the *Guardian* talked fulsomely of "his outstanding and creative sensibility" and "total musical command". From this point on, John's British career was assured.

But I remember the Liverpool competition not only for the practical success it brought John's way: I remember it too for a much more intimate reason. While we had been backstage in the dressing room waiting tensely for the jury to make up its mind, John had eased me towards him and had kissed me for the very first time.

It had been a surprising and rather unsettling experience – with so old a friend it had even seemed mildly incestuous. When we were called back on to the platform, I could still feel his lips against mine – until in the excitement of hearing the results, their imprint faded, and vanished.

7

The seal was set on John's success when he was signed up by Ibbs and Tillett.

Ibbs and Tillett at that time was the most powerful musical agency in Britain – not only where important dates were concerned, but in its virtual monopoly of smaller music clubs all over the country; in other words, it controlled, almost single-handedly, the vital "bread and butter" dates by which a young artist survives. The agency's address, 124 Wigmore Street, was known to every aspiring musician in England – inside was a rambling shabby warren of offices, almost Dickensian in atmosphere with dust covered files piled high on the shelves. But disorganised though the place may have seemed at first glance, it – and its staff of young men – was run by Mrs. Emmie Tillett with an autocratic, school-marmish efficiency: she believed, too, in keeping the artists she represented under as tight a control as she could. This latter aim she achieved by the simple expedient of keeping their fees very low – a wealthy musician, as she herself would explain, was liable to develop an irritating mind of his own.

Emmie Tillet was tall and imposing, with short gray hair: she could, when she wanted, be the epitome of charm, but there was also an aura of power around her that could make grown men tremble – and did. Her business was her life; and like many dedicated people, she was prepared to be ruthless in support of those in whom she believed. She soon came to believe in John as a musician as well as liking him as a person: so, though she might not make him rich, he was aware – as was every one else – that she would prove an invaluable ally in getting his career off the ground.

John, of course, had another very important ally: the Marquess of Londonderry. And it was Alistair who decided, in

1959, that the time was ripe to launch John's talent on London. He booked the Wigmore Hall for the 29th September, and undertook to finance and promote the debut recital himself.

So, by the summer of that year, things had really started to buzz for John – though in terms of day to day drudgery, he was working nowhere near as hard as I was. Still, we were managing to see a great deal of each other – in fact, by now we were almost inseparable. Tired and overworked as I was, he was always ready with much needed sympathy and support: sometimes I found myself wondering how I would manage without him . . .

One of our favourite haunts in those days was the Midland Hotel in Manchester, which we thought very grand and sophisticated. Equally glamorous to our stodge-raised northern palates were the spaghetti suppers that were served in the snack bar, and we indulged in them fairly often. One night, after a particularly good Bolognese, I offered to give John a lift home in the car, which my father had lent me for the evening.

John climbed into the front seat beside me – and before I knew what was happening, he'd pounced.

I resisted him with convent-school firmness – he leaned away at once and looked at me, the car park lights reflected in his glasses. "Will you marry me?" he said.

I stared back at him in astonishment.

"Please . . ."

I found my voice with difficulty: "No."

"Brenda . . ."

He sounded hurt and rather wistful: I was sorry that I'd been so blunt, and I put one hand on his arm. "Dear John, thank you . . ." I fell back on the obvious cliché: "But really, we're good friends and that's all."

"I'm in love with you, Brenda!"

"Well, I'm not in love with you. I'm sorry!"

He leaned back in his seat with a sigh. "Think about it" he said.

We drove off in an eloquent silence.

After dropping him off, I raced home. I left the car outside in the street and hurried into the house.

My mother and my father's sister, Aunt Agnes, were in the kitchen. "Mother" I blurted out, "John Ogdon has asked me to marry him!"

"Oh Brenda!" Aunt Agnes was thrilled, and my mother also seemed pleased.

"But I don't know!" I told them plaintively. "I don't know if I want to get married, particularly to John of all people!" Again, a cliché served me best – "I've got to have time to think!"

During the following two weeks, my mother played devil's advocate – trying, I suppose, to help me know my own mind. On the one hand she would prey on old fears: "All your friends are married now – you're the last one left. You may not get another chance!" But then, when I seemed to waver in John's favour, she would say "Do you really think you ought, Brenda? He's overweight, he's not athletic like you are – and he's short-sighted and has always had ear trouble . . ."

"But he's a great pianist" I'd protest – adding "And he's in love with me!"

"But are you in love with him?"

"No – not that way!" For an instant, that seemed to clinch matters – but then I remembered my doomed passion for the faculty teacher, and another ill-fated but consuming romance I'd suffered through when I was sixteen. "But I only ever fall in love with the wrong kind of men!"

The one person who seemed unperturbed and completely relaxed when I saw him was John. I began to suspect, resentfully, that he wouldn't very much mind a refusal – his home life was comfortable, he was pampered by his mother, and our friendship would almost certainly survive . . . Perhaps he only thought he *ought* to get married, and I happened to be the most convenient choice.

I looked away from him as we finished yet another spaghetti dinner in the Midland's snack bar. I must tell him "no" and get it over I thought: I'm not going to become a substitute mother for anyone, least of all because I am handy. And my own mother is right – he has hundreds of alien habits like staying up all night and then lying in bed all the morning. He's hopeless about almost everything – everything except music that is. Now that's something different. Musically, I've been incredibly lucky to know him – he's broadened my horizons, taught me so much, often truly inspired me . . . How strange that a man so enormously talented should be so lacking in insufferable ego. I mean ... even apart from the musical side, think how kind he's been these last months, how concerned because I'm working so hard. Without him, I don't think I could have survived ...

I caught myself short, and suddenly tears were pricking my eyelids. "John" I told him gently "It's yes."

He looked puzzled. "Yes what?"

"Yes dammit!" I snapped. "Yes, I'll marry you!"

So in July 1959, John Ogdon and I became officially engaged, and he presented me with a large and beautiful Victorian ring, composed of a ruby, sapphire and pearl with three little diamonds on either side.

Life didn't change dramatically, as I had half expected it would. Deeply fond of John though I was, I was no closer to falling in love with him: and apart from being more overtly affectionate, John's behaviour towards me changed hardly at all. Often I thought music and the upcoming London recital were on his mind far more than I was – and almost certainly I was right, because years later I was shown a letter John wrote early that August to Alistair. After discussing a variety of subjects including his Wigmore programme, a Godovsky transcription and his lessons with Denis, he squashed a tiny note into one corner: it read "P.S. Have just got engaged."

But to be fair, another subject brought up on that letter was the state of John's nerves, which was bad – he was tense because Emmie Tillett had asked him, at only a day or two's notice, to stand in for an indisposed pianist at a Promenade Concert in London's Royal Albert Hall. The concerto was to be the Liszt E flat, which he had performed in the Liverpool Competition.

I couldn't get to London to hear him, but by all accounts he played magnificently. For John, it was an awesome experience; he remembers standing on the stage taking his bows, looking out into the vast dark cavern of the Hall with its circular tiers of red-curtained boxes on which gold glinted dimly, and hearing those great waves of applause surging and crashing around him. It is for moments like these that performing artists can drive themselves so very hard – having given all of themselves in performance, they get such an elatingly warm reward back.

It had been an auspicious London debut, and one which

gave him useful confidence for the Wigmore recital to come.

Back in Manchester, all was not going so well.

I should have forseen trouble, of course. Dorothy was not unpleasant to me at first, but she made her reservations quite plain. "You do realise, Brenda" she would say, "that the wife John needs must be very devoted."

"I *will* do my best, you know" I would counter her haughtily.

Darling eccentric Howard Ogdòn was kinder during his irregular sorties from his study. "Watch out for John when he gets angry" he told me – "particularly with broken inanimate objects which he's always too clumsy to mend. I warn you, he has a terrible temper – it'll frighten you when you see it."

I didn't tell him I had already had a glimpse of it once, when I'd shouted at John to get out of the College studio in which I'd been practising. The memory made me uneasy – deliberately, I put it out of my mind.

As the weeks passed, Dorothy's onslaught grew ever more direct, her disapproval ever more plain. John had always been looked after, she reminded me – he would expect the same treatment after our marriage. He needed a "little woman", devoted solely to his pleasures and needs – not an ambitious career girl who was looking out above all for herself. I was all wrong for her son, she conveyed – utterly and totally wrong.

There were one or two open rows between us, but mostly, in face of her stubborn resolve, I managed to fight back the tears and the protests. What made things harder for me was that in my heart I thought she might be right.

I turned to John for support – and to my chagrin found virtually none. "Of course I expect to be looked after", he told me, as if that was the most natural thing in the world; "any man expects to mean more to his wife than a professional career of her own."

With difficulty, I bit my tongue; now was not the right time for a showdown. John was very soon leaving for London, where he would be the guest of Alistair and Nico at their house in South Eaton Place. With only days still to go before the recital debut at the Wigmore, he was taut and white-faced with nerves: so I decided our relationship could wait until after the concert was over.

50

The programme John had chosen was by any standards a mammoth one:

3 Fugues from the Art of the Fugue	Bach
Sonata in E major Op 109	Beethoven
Variations on a theme of Paganini (both books)	Brahms
Interval	
5 Preludes	John Ogdon
Sonatina Seconda	Busoni
Islamey	Balakirev
La Campanella	Liszt/Busoni
Mephisto Valse	Liszt

A programme like that is in itself a challenge, even a boast, laying claim to unusual artistic and pianistic powers before a note has been played – and unless it is superbly pulled off, it can break a reputation far more easily than it can make one.

I had travelled to London by train for the concert, and by the time people started to assemble in the little hall, I was feeling scared stiff for John. Never had I seen a more worldly and wealthy audience – never had I seen so many beautiful women, such glossy hair and sparkling jewels – never had I been surrounded by so many confident, well-dressed men. These people were used to the best: they would certainly be no easy pushover.

And then John came on to the stage – his shambling figure and the dark mop of curls producing, as always, a little ripple of surprise. He sat down, hunched his shoulders over the keyboard – and started to play . . .

He has rarely performed better in his life. There is little that I can or want to add except that the concert was a sensational success. The audience, for all its glitter, responded like teenagers at a rock concert – they were amazed, they were stunned, they were delighted. At the end, the applause swelled to deafening proportions; John was called back for encore after encore. How he found the energy after so gruelling a programme, I don't know: I myself was limp and exhausted just from the excitement of listening to it all.

Afterwards, John's dressing room was pandemonium – but eventually, with Alistair's help, it was cleared, and John and I were rushed off to South Eaton Place for a buffet supper party thrown in his honour.

I had met Alistair earlier in the day, and had been as impressed by his charm as I'd been led to expect. But John had not prepared me for his London home. The ceilings were lofty, the mouldings magnificent, the chandeliers glistened like rainbows: art treasures were spread through the rooms as naturally as ashtrays were scattered at home. A butler and maid were in evidence, and I heard references to a cook ... I hadn't known that people still lived so well, I had thought this way of life only survived in front of canvas sets in the theatre or elaborately false mock-ups in films.

And the people – so elegant to my eyes, so dauntingly sophisticated! Alistair's sisters, Lady Jane and Lady Annabel Vane-Tempest-Stewart – and of course, Nico, Lady Londonderry herself, every bit as blonde and as beautiful as John had described her to me. At supper, I found myself next to Sacheverell Sitwell, someone I'd read about but had never imagined I'd meet: he turned out to be human after all, and full of enthusiasm for John's talent.

For an unsophisticated girl like myself, all this was heady stuff indeed. What was more extraordinary was that no one made me feel dowdy in my off the peg sweater and skirt, which would have required no effort at all.

As for John – I saw with amazement that he seemed to be in his element: smiling, nodding, and taking to the surrounding luxury as though he'd been born to it. Here, in this company, his gaucherie seemed almost an asset, his eccentricity a positive strength. The bejewelled and titled ladies presented no threat to him: on the contrary, he revelled in them – the more so the prettier they were – with a simple and natural pleasure. In the face of such competition, I was completely forgotten.

Too soon, it was time for me to leave; I had to catch the overnight sleeper to Manchester. John kissed me on the cheek and would have let me go to the station alone: it was Alistair who gallantly prompted him "John, I think you should see your fiancée on to the train."

I lay on the bed in the sleeping-car wide awake, listening to the clatter of the wheels on the track. It had been a very special evening – one I knew I would never forget all my life long. And it had prompted me to two vital decisions.

The first was that I would become, to the best of my ability, like those women at the party – the women John had so blatantly admired. I would study to make myself as elegant and glamorous as they were – and I would lose my northern accent if it killed me, and learn to speak just as they did.

And my second decision was that I would refuse to enter this privileged world as an appendage to John's apron strings. His mother was right, I was ambitious; I wanted to succeed on my own. I would, I decided, break off our engagement.

8

The next morning, I bought the late editions of all the national papers and tore them open to the review pages. However great an audience success, whatever one's personal enthusiasm for a performance, the critics are an unpredictable quantity; one must always be prepared (though one never is) for nasty shocks.

As it turned out, I had no need to worry. One paper described John as "the reincarnation of Busoni" and he was generally proclaimed as the most outstanding talent to emerge in England for many years. I am not overstating the case when I say that John's was one of the most successful London recital debuts in living memory.

When he came home, he was, of course, thrilled and happy; yet in a way he appeared untouched by the praise, by the lionising that had come his way. He seemed to accept it all as an unquestioned right, just as he accepted his mother's domestic ministrations. This belief in his talent was not arrogance, I was beginning to realise, nor an unwarranted conceit: it was almost as if his musical abilities existed on their own, separate from, though contained within, himself – and it was his duty, as a man, simply to give them expression.

It was dawning on me at last how his confidence could be reconciled with humility. "Dear Alistair" he wrote after his home-coming to Manchester, "I am very glad that I did not so to speak 'let you down' at the Wigmore: I felt so nervous . . ."

I waited until the euphoria in both our families had abated a little before announcing my decision to break off the engagement. On hearing the news, Aunt Agnes was noisily aghast, my mother prim-lipped but resigned: while Dorothy Ogdon, predictably, was serenely, approvingly, content. As for John, though later he claimed he was deeply distressed, he appeared at the time to be unperturbed.

Although he accepted back my beautiful engagement ring, he continued to act as though nothing between us had changed. Whenever I wasn't working and when he was not off on a tour – and in spite of my attempts to be distant or formal – he still contrived to be with me.

He wasn't in Manchester nearly as often as before, though – not with Emmie Tillett as his agent. That autumn he began his serious rounds of the bread and butter circuit, playing all over Great Britain. In many ways, Mrs. Tillett looked after him well, handling all his travel itineraries and hotel bookings – but she remained true to her dictum of keeping the fees to the absolute minimum. Incredibly, John continued to earn a mere twenty guineas a performance – so in spite of the concerts he was giving, he still remained a poor man.

I would miss him while he was away, but at the same time I dreaded his return: I knew that no sooner would he be home than I would hear his slow northern drawl on the phone, or see his bearded figure come through my door. I couldn't get rid of him without being cruel, without shattering the friendship I valued. Was he as unaware of our broken engagement as he seemed? I was seriously beginning to doubt it: I was beginning to believe that his vagueness in social and personal matters might after all serve as the most useful of covers for a determination as strong as his mother's.

This situation, I told myself ever more frequently and with a continually mounting frustration, was little different from a sort of unconsummated marriage in the demands it was making on me. And I could not have made it more plain that I wanted a career of my own: if we were married, John could not in fairness prevent me pursuing it. And if he didn't like it that way, he would have himself to blame and nobody else . . .

So in the end, John proved the stronger of the two. I was conquered not by romantic love, but by his dogged and unwavering persistence.

One day early in 1960, in the middle of a conversation in my blue carpeted studio, I realised I could bear it no longer. "All right, John," I interrupted him. "You can give me back the ring whenever you want."

A slow smile spread over his face, and I could swear it was

the smile of a victor. "Oh good," he said, and came over to give me a kiss.

The next day I got the ring back, and we decided to get married that summer.

A hectic few months followed; I was teaching and studying, as well as playing more concerts in the North West, while John was away on tour increasingly often. In April, he gave a second recital at the Wigmore Hall, the expenses this time being carried in toto by Ibbs and Tillett. Again I went to London to hear his programme, which included Beethoven's Op. 111 Sonata, Ravel's "Gaspard de la Nuit", and Liszt's Fantasie (or "Dante") Sonata. The next morning, the critics confirmed their earlier opinion – a major new talent had burst upon the scene.

Later that summer, John gave what was to prove another important recital: he offered a long and difficult programme at the Contemporary British Music Festival at Cheltenham. His dedication to modern music – particularly British modern music – earned him much grateful praise: while among the works that he played were his own Variations and Fugue Op. 4. It was at this point of his career that the critics first began writing about him as an example of a composer/performer in the rare tradition of Rachmaninov and Prokofiev.

Early in July – the month we were to be married – John went on his first foreign venture as a performer. Again through the influence of Lord Londonderry, he was invited to play in Italy at the Spoleto Festival, which was – and is – run by the composer Gian Carlo Menotti. On his return after a gratifyingly successful reception, he told me that another participant had been John Browning, the American pianist who had tried to sooth my pre-performance nerves in Brussels. I was happy to hear his career was beginning to soar in the States.

There was one recital that John gave at about this same time which – though it attracted only limited attention – proved memorable to everyone who heard it. Given at Park Lane House in London, and composed entirely of contemporary music, it included premières of works by Ronald Stevenson and Dennis Todd – and, counting the interval, it lasted for almost three hours. Afterwards, the bemused audience stag-

56

gered exhausted into the night, and only a sweat-stained John was left full of vigour and eager for more.

I myself gave a solo recital for the same society, playing, more conventionally, Beethoven's 32 Variations in C minor and Mozart's D major Sonata K576. I remember it particularly because it was held on 17th July – only six days before we were married. As always, I had prepared for it meticulously – but looking back now, how I found the time I cannot imagine.

At home, all around me was hustle and bustle – guest lists, catering arrangements, fittings – all the usual preparations for a wedding. On top of all this John and I had been looking for a place to set up house together – and we'd been lucky: we'd found a delightful maisonette in Didsbury Park, on the west side of Manchester, at a rent we were able to afford. We had to furnish and carpet it ourselves – but our friends rallied round with useful presents and my parents gave us two armchairs.

We also arranged an exchange of possessions with Howard – and the manner in which the deal was effected was typical of the man. John was summoned to his father's study, and a bit of paper covered with script type was put in front of him. It read:

This article witnesseth the unconditional exchange of one antique Welsh dresser owned in the first instance by John Andrew Howard Ogdon the elder and one upright Squire and Longson pianoforte with metronome owned in the first instance by John Andrew Howard Ogdon the younger
whereby
the aforementioned pianoforte with metronome becomes the unconditional property of John Andrew Howard Ogdon the elder, and the aforementioned Welsh dresser becomes the unconditional property of John Andrew Howard Ogdon the younger.

Solemnly, in front of family witnesses, father and son added their signatures to the document, and the dresser was officially John's.

Dear Howard! I treasure both the dresser and that touchingly ludicrous document to this day.

Meanwhile, as the wedding approached, my relationship with Dorothy had, predictably, again been growing in tension. In part, the trouble was caused because John had been

engaged to play with the Hallé Orchestra in Buxton, Derbyshire, four days after our marriage, which put paid to the
honeymoon I very much wanted – but there was no point in
postponing the wedding because John and I had crowded schedules well on into the autumn. So I suggested he should cancel
Buxton.

Dorothy was outraged. All her life had been devoted to promoting her son's interests: "Under no circumstances" she told
me "will John cancel anything!"

"But it's only one concert" I countered, "surely the organisers will be sympathetic! I mean, we're only going to be married
once – a few days alone together somewhere romantic isn't that
much to ask!" I begged, I pleaded, at last I shouted my angry
defiance – to no avail. Dorothy was adamant, and John kept a
meaningful silence.

I had no choice but – tearfully – to give in.

And so at last the day of our wedding arrived – a beautiful,
warm sunny day. I was by now very excited just by the idea of
being a bride, and I felt very important and glamorous in my
cream brocade dress and with my bouquet of red roses. There
was a slight hitch to the proceedings when John turned up
without a carnation in his buttonhole, and a cousin had to be
sent post-haste to scour the district for a florist. But after that,
all went in traditional story book style – we were married in a
simple ceremony in the Church of the Holy Trinity in Gee
Cross, and followed it with a reception for thirty four guests at
the West Towers Country Club near Marple in Cheshire.

Our best man was the composer, Peter Maxwell Davies, late
of New Music, Manchester. He and John had remained good
friends since their college days; while his dark and piercing
eyes no longer scared me as they had in the past. He made a
fluent and exquisitely-phrased speech at the reception, extol-
ling John and his talent: our down-to-earth relatives, I remember, expecting the usual platitudes and innuendos, were very
much taken aback.

John made a surprisingly confident answering speech – and
after more toasts, many hugs, and the occasional tear, Mr. and
Mrs. Ogdon stepped into their hired limousine and were
driven away to Derbyshire.

"Brenda and I had a nice time in Buxton" John wrote to Alistair later (forgetting to mention the wedding). That was a barefaced lie.

We had an absolutely awful time. Buxton is an attractive health spa, but it is hardly a young bride's dream of exotic romance: in any case, it rained solidly all the time, penning us indoors. Our one form of public relaxation was a putting game on a miniature golf course; for company, we had only the genteel, the aged and the infirm, sitting around the cavernous hotel lobby like lonely hunchbacked crows. I was in no mood to bear the martyr's crown with resignation, and John responded to my complaints and tears with a furious silence.

I sulked because I wanted John to comfort me, to make me feel more important to him than his concert: I wanted him to thank me for sacrificing our honeymoon so nobly. But he was having none of that: and I came as close to leaving him in the first four days of our marriage as I have at any time since.

We never formally called a truce. We didn't have to. When the time came to leave Buxton, we were so relieved that we forgot we were meant to be quarrelling.

We went straight to our new home in Didsbury Park. And very soon – in only a matter of weeks – a remarkable thing happened. I fell in love with my husband.

9

John – spoiled, eccentric and untidy John – proved after all to be affectionate, passionate, understanding – and fun. My flawed genius became, in my eyes, a compulsively huggable great teddy bear of a man. I was deliriously happy, and no one could have been more surprised or grateful than I was myself. And John was equally enchanted by our new life together.

The maisonette we were renting was part of a much larger house, but it had been sealed off as a separate unit. It was small but remarkably pretty, with an attic studio, two bedrooms, and an open plan kitchen and dining room. It also had a living room which was completely taken up by John's Bechstein baby grand; if we wanted to use the room for anything other than practising, we had to squeeze round the piano and sit cramped uncomfortably in corners.

I found running the place far easier than I had anticipated. Out of necessity, I learned simple cooking fast, relying, I admit, a little too heavily on tins of curry and on steaks. To someone of my upbringing, washing up and cleaning were no problem – and John, the male chauvinist who had once claimed my role was to look after him, proved after all eager to pitch in and help me. Alas, a less domesticated person would be hard to imagine. Those fingers which had mastered the keyboard could not be relied on to wash the stoutest of mugs without breaking it: and somehow, he just couldn't manage to clean up the bathroom after he'd used it, or to pick his discarded clothes from the floor. "I'm sorry, Brenda" he'd say meekly, when I remonstrated. "I'll try to remember next time." But he never did remember – and he never has remembered to this day.

Our landlord, a saturnine and highly strung television producer, lived in the same house – and in return for my doing some babysitting, his wife let me use her washing machine. This was a convenient arrangement but sometimes a difficult one, because soon after we moved in, our relationship with them began to deteriorate.

The trouble, not surprisingly, was the piano. We were allowed to practise between 8 am and 6.30 pm every day – a generous allowance, on the face of it. But for the two of us, who had previously been able to study at almost any hour of the evening, the adjustment proved difficult to make: though selfish preference itself was the least part of the inconvenience we faced. We were, after all, working professionals – and though we did not have to keep normal business hours, our lives were regulated by them none the less. The day was the time when shopping had to be done, and – in my case – students taught on a part-time basis at the Royal College; it was also the time when our agents had to be consulted, itineraries agreed, programmes argued over, and all the other time-consuming adjuncts to a soloist's career dealt with. It is hard to convey the frustration when, after a long day spent entirely in shops, travelling and on the phone, we found ourselves forced to sit looking at the piano, so beguiling and yet sentenced to silence.

Things were worse at the very beginning, when we only had the one piano – John's – to work on between us, and we were forced to draw up a shift pattern. Later, when my own boudoir grand was delivered from Hyde, I was able to move it up into the attic, so at least we could both practise at once.

It can't have been easy for our neighbouring landlord, I realise that: but rightly or wrongly, both John and I felt ears were pressed against the walls in case we overstepped our schedule by so much as a second or two. We found ourselves getting distracted and self-conscious, rather as I feel if I'm writing a letter which someone starts reading over my shoulder... Once, in deliberate defiance, I admit, I started playing a dreamy Chopin Nocturne just after the six thirty deadline: moments later the landlord was pounding on our door, and only my father's presence prevented an unpleasant scene.

But these tensions did have one positive aspect – they brought John and me ever closer together, lovingly united against the harasser at our door.

Ibbs and Tillett were continuing to provide John with a steady stream of concerts, which took him away from home for an average of three days a week. I too was getting engagements, though less frequently – but I was quite happy preparing for them as well as adding new compositions to my repertoire. And I was also working with John on a very exciting new project: our first two-piano recital, which was to be one of the "fringe" events of the 1960 Edinburgh Festival.

It was a thrill to go to that austere and beautiful city, crowded with culture seekers from all over the world – to know that everywhere operas and symphony concerts were being presented, as well as recitals by world famous artists, plays by leading companies, revues by students, street shows by buskers, and to feel a contributing part of it all. We played an adventurous programme, including works by Chopin and Schumann, both of whose centenaries the Festival was celebrating. The recital was very well received – and we resolved that the Ogdon/Lucas duo (I still play under my maiden name) would become a permanent feature of our careers and our lives. So much for the "little woman" Dorothy had wanted for John, I thought triumphantly: she might have pleased him by seeing to his board and making his bed, but she could never have managed his concert platform as well!

There was another first for John that year – his first record. In December 1960, HMV, knowing that he was a specialist in Busoni, asked him for some of the composer's shorter pieces: he obliged with the Sonatine Number 6 (Chamber Fantasy on Bizet's "Carmen"), Turandots Frauengemach – Intermezzo (No. 4 of "Elegies"), and nine variations on a Chopin Prelude. The second side of the record was made up of two virtuoso Liszt pieces – the Dante Sonata and the popular Mephisto Waltz (No. 1). For me, it was fascinating to be in on the recording sessions – the complicated equipment, the faders, the dimmers, the jargon, the retakes, the discussions about balance and splicing... The producer was a man with a faint Australian twang, named Peter Andry, whom I liked very much from the start. In time he was to become a key figure in EMI Records, and also a true friend to John and myself in the darkest of our nightmare years. But those years were far in the future, undreamed of, as yet inconceivable...

62

The December that John cut the record is memorable to both of us for another reason – I discovered I was going to have a baby. The pregnancy was unplanned – and my initial reaction was one of dismay. What would happen to my precious career, for which I'd worked and yearned all my life?

But my darling John was thrilled, as proud as a paunchy Punch – and only days after my condition had been confirmed, all my own reservations collapsed beneath a wave of overwhelming contentment. I became a model mother-to-be, greedily reading books on baby care, going to ante-natal classes regularly, and exercising as conscientiously as I worked at the piano.

And so the months passed happily; I continued practising hard, I looked after the house and proudly managed to make ends meet – and slowly, inexorably, I grew larger. John, when he was at home, treated me as though I were made of the most fragile china – an attitude which, though touching, alarmed me if I thought of those broken mugs!

In July, when I was seven months pregnant, John took me with him on his second visit to the Spoleto Festival. We were lodged in an unattractive and run-down house, with cheap furniture and primitive plumbing: but the glorious town, perched so picturesquely on its mountain slope, more than made up for the discomfort.

The Festival was – and is – an informal one, and daily lunchtime concerts, which were held in a little theatre on the main square, were often shared between three or even four artists. John, whose repertoire for the visit included Beethoven's 109 Sonata and Ravel's "Gaspard de la Nuit", was well remembered from his visit the previous year, and he was clearly an audience favourite. Indeed, he was lionised at Spoleto, and he revelled in it.

I remember one very hot night going to a party held in a large villa above the town: the company was cosmopolitan, and I was all set to enjoy myself. We strolled out into the garden, where lanterns nestled amongst the leaves and the cloudless sky glittered with stars. I was pleased for John when a stunning-looking Italian woman came up to him and started singing his praises. I didn't mind when they were joined by

63

another beauty, and then by a third. It wasn't so much fun when the fourth and fifth arrived – and it was downright humiliating when I was slowly elbowed away from his side, and he was completely enclosed by an adoring bevy of feminine bodies.

I stood on the outer edges, alone and ignored, glowering at the glossy hair and the sleek bare backs. I felt unattractive and uncomfortably pregnant – and knew I'd been totally forgotten.

Suddenly, I'd had enough. Unnoticed, I shoved my way back through the garden and out of the house, and started to run down the steep mountainside towards the distant lights of the town.

The shadows were long and very black, and I didn't see the young peasant until it was too late. He caught hold of my arm, saying something in Italian: I couldn't understand the words, but his meaning was clear. I pulled away, but he held me tighter; I struggled with him, but he was strong and I knew there was violence in him. Driven by terror, I somehow managed to break free and began to scramble back up the hill: I could hear his harsh breathing as he came after me.

Headlights shone through the darkness. I waved my arms and yelled – I thought the car would pass us when there was a screech of brakes and a man in uniform jumped out. The peasant turned and raced away into the night, and my saviour, an army officer, eased me gently into the passenger seat. Sobbing and shaking convulsively, I was driven back to the party.

John had to be sent for – he had not yet noticed that I had left. When he saw the state I was in, he went pale, frightened for the baby as well as for me: he took me back to our lodgings at once.

He tried to comfort me, but I couldn't forget how unattractive, how unwanted, I'd felt. But gradually his concerned and contrite attentions, combined with the feast of marvellous music and the soothing, balmy evenings in the old church square combined to restore my equilibrium: and after a difficult day or two, romance revived and blossomed again.

John returned to England and another heavy schedule of concerts. I stayed at home in Didsbury Park, cossetting myself and preparing for the great event. On the 1st October, after an eighteen hour delivery in Manchester Royal Infirmary, I gave birth to a girl.

John wasn't with me at the time (for some reason, none of the family turned up until afterwards) – he was away on a concert engagement, and he didn't know that he was a father until an uncle and aunt of mine met him at the railway station with the news. He rushed to see me and the baby, beside himself with excitement.

We named our daughter Annabel – and even allowing for a mother's pride. she was adorable. The entire family, on both sides, succumbed totally to her charms, with Dorothy – by now reconciled to our marriage – insisting she was unmistakably an Ogdon. As for John, he was the picture of a devoted young father.

I had to give up all thoughts of concerts or teaching, at least for a while – but I didn't mind in the least. Little Annabel had the sweetest of natures, and never gave John and me any trouble – the sleepless nights endured by most couples were completely unknown to us.

Which was just as well, because in addition to his professional engagements, John was preparing for another competition, which was due to take place in the January of 1961 – the Franz Liszt Competition. This was not a regular fixture – it was tied up with the promotion of a movie about the composer called *Song Without End*: but the film company's involvement did guarantee the maximum publicity. Also the competition itself was conducted to the highest standards: the jury was headed by Louis Kentner, and in addition to John, those taking part included such talented young men as David Wilde, Benjamin Kaplan and Hamish Milne. To our delight, the two heats were held in the beautiful old Londonderry House: now it no longer exists, but in those days it still belonged to Alistair – who did not, of course, have any say in the judging.

I had come to know the Londonderrys a little better since our marriage, and I thought of them as an enchanted fairy-tale couple – wealthy, aristocratic, and beautiful. Not, I hasten to add, that they were perfect – they were far more interesting than that. Alistair could be easily bored; he liked to have talent around him, and he expected his friends to entertain him. He was unpredictable, too, with almost no sense of time – he could not be relied upon to turn up for every engagement even when he was the host. As for Nico – if she was present as well, that was considered a positive bonus.

She was present on the afternoon before the finals; and never in my life had I seen anyone look so exquisite. Her long golden-blonde hair was perfection, her black silk dress redolent of high Paris chic. John, who to no one's surprise had sailed through the competition's first round, was open-mouthed in admiration.

Well, I thought, I've worked hard at my accent and it's getting much better (except when I lose my temper and all those northern vowels keep crowding back): but on this evidence I've still got a long way to go in the glamour stakes. And from that day on – not fully consciously at first, but deliberately all the same – I did everything in my power to imitate Nico, copying her hair colour and, so far as my limited budget would allow, her style of dress. Just because I wanted to be a famous pianist, there was no reason why I shouldn't look stunning as well!

That night, in the finals, John gave an inspired performance of the Liszt B Minor Sonata – the same sonata which he'd been playing the first time I had heard him, before I'd known who he was. He had come a very long way since then – all the old excitement was there, but now there was masterly control, a heart-warming edge of restraint. I was able to sit back and listen with no nerves to mar my enjoyment because I was convinced he was going to win. And win he did – by the unanimous decision of the jury.

To John's already burgeoning British career, the result was no less than electrifying. There had been television coverage for the finals, and an enthusiastic reception from the next day's national press: these factors combined with the recent release of the praised Liszt/Busoni recording resulted in a torrent of offers – more than he could possibly cope with. Our life, we very soon realised, would never again be the same – even though Emmie Tillett insisted his fee should be raised to no more than thirty five guineas . . .

We decided the time had come to think about moving south to London. It was the centre of British musical life, added to which Ibbs and Tillett were there and it was a more convenient centre for travel. In any case, a move was now due: Annabel was growing fast, and we badly needed more space.

At the same time, John made another important decision. He may have conquered the British concert scene, but purely national recognition, in the music world, constitutes a living but not a career. John was very sure of his talent, and he was quietly but desperately determined to join that small and elite band of soloists who are known all over the world. There had to be some way of achieving this – and the best way that John could think of was to enter one of the most important, gruelling and hotly contested piano competitions the world has ever known. It was to be held the following May, and already there were rumours that the brilliant young Russian who had won first prize at Brussels, Vladimir Ashkenazy, was going to take part.

It was a formidable challenge, and one that John could not resist: and so he became a competitor in the 1962 International Tchaikovsky Competition in Moscow.

10

So eager was John to expand his professional horizons that the previous year he had fully intended to enter another major international competition, which had been held in Texas. He had told me of his plans very soon after Annabel's birth: but she was still so helpless and little, and I was so very much in love with John, that I could not bear the thought of him flying off and leaving us alone. I cried bitterly, begging him not to go: generously, lovingly, with no word of reproach, he stayed at home in Didsbury instead.

This time, things were different. Even before the Liszt Competition, John had been able to pay a local girl to give me some part time help in the house: and now, inundated with engagements as he was, he could afford a nanny as well, and I was able to return to part-time teaching and my regular practising sessions. But much more important – by the time the Moscow Competition took place, John would be 25 – and if he wanted to make an international name for himself through winning a major prize, he couldn't afford to wait very much longer. And as this Competition was held only once in every four years, I wasn't going to stand in his way.

Opposition did come, however – it came from Emmie Tillett, who proclaimed it a "hare-brained" scheme. How could John possibly expect to beat Ashkenazy on his own home ground, when the Russian, at the same age as John, was already something of a legend in musical circles? What good would it do John when he lost? And where was the money coming from, pray – out of his own pocket? John was living in a fool's paradise – he must forget the whole idea!

And besides, Emmie pointed out triumphantly, he had already been engaged for concerts in Wales that May. She felt very strongly about the sanctity of engagements under all circumstances – I remember a few years later, when Jacqueline du Pre and her husband Daniel Barenboim stayed in Israel during the Six Days War, risking their lives by giving concerts close to the front lines, that Emmie was besides herself with fury. "Jackie's meant to be at the Norwich Festival" she fumed, as though the poor girl were on holiday. "She really is *very* naughty!"

John protested that the Welsh concerts did not have to be cancelled, they could be postponed instead. Emmie would not listen – she would not, she insisted, permit such behaviour. Shades of Dorothy, I thought grimly.

But John was even more stubborn. Come hell, high water, or even Emmie Tillett, he was determined to make it to Moscow.

Meanwhile, the offers for engagements in Britain were still pouring in – and he accepted every one he could manage. He needed each penny they were bringing in – not only to pay for Annabel's nanny, but because, as Mrs. Tillett had pointed out, he could expect no outside support towards the cost of the trip to Russia.

And John played not only his own concerts; whenever it was physically possible, he would stand in for indisposed soloists the length and breadth of the country. Ever since he had substituted for the sick pianist at the Albert Hall over two years ago, Mrs Tillett had only to ask him … and ask him she did, again and again. He was away from home almost all the time now: and already he had earned the nickname that has stuck throughout his career – Slogger Ogger.

Sometimes I was worried that he was doing too much – that he would accept a date for an unfamiliar concerto, for example, at too short notice to give it the necessary preparation. But he was brimful of confidence and enthusiasm, his energy never flagged – and I had to admit that musically he was at the peak of his form.

In January 1962, he cut the first of his orchestral discs, again for HMV – it was Rachmaninov's Second Piano Concerto, with our friend John Pritchard conducting the New Philharmonia Orchestra. John received, I remember, what then seemed a princely sum to us – a once and for all flat fee of £200, minus commission. Babes in the financial wood that we were, we knew nothing in those days of royalties – though to be fair, no one could have predicted with any certainty that the record would become a best seller and remain one over more than a decade. Anyway, what we lost in potential income we gained in hard-won experience.

After the recording had been completed, and whenever his concert engagements permitted, John threw himself heart and soul into preparing for the Competition. He began taking lessons in London with the Hungarian teacher, Ilona Kabos – and even the death of Howard, his father, whom he had loved and now missed very deeply, did not undermine his inflexible purpose.

I too was practising very hard with some help from Ilona, as my own Wigmore recital debut was due on 3rd April. Part of my time was taken up also with an unforeseen problem caused by the comparative new affluence of our lives – trouble with the servants, or, more specifically, with the nannies.

There was more than one of them in those early months of 1962. I must take much of the blame. I wasn't used to servants, I wasn't sure how to treat them – particularly when they were usually so much older than I, and so much more experienced with young children. But then the nannies proved to be no more adaptable than I. Most of them had worked in far larger establishments, and – regulated parental visits apart – the children had been entrusted into their virtually exclusive and all-knowing care. Now suddenly they found themselves living in a matchbox in which two pianos competed with each other in a deafening cacophony of sound: no rigid schedules were kept, the master worked at night and came home at all hours, if at all – in short, we did not live like the proper predictable people a good nanny expects to employ her. Worst of all, they accused me of acting towards them as though they wanted to steal little Annabel away.

They were probably right in the latter point. I wanted their help with Annabel, but not at the price of abdicating my responsibility for her. And so the rows flared, notices were handed in, and dismissals made. John kept out of it all, and I didn't ask for his help: if a nanny had refused to accept her notice, or had demanded six months wages before getting out of the house, John would have smilingly agreed rather than risk a head-on confrontation.

April came, and with it my Wigmore recital, which included

works by Mozart, Beethoven, Ravel, Rawsthorne, Liszt and Bartok. To my relief, it was successful, and John was openly, expansively, proud of me.

And suddenly May was upon us, and it was time for John to fly off to Moscow. I didn't go with him; even if I'd been granted a visa, which was unlikely, I didn't want to leave Annabel for up to a month, besides which John's return ticket cost £85, which was a lot of money for us in those days. But I saw him off with my love and my heartfelt good wishes.

In Moscow, John was met by an interpreter, and whisked off to the Hotel Ukraine, which was a short taxi ride from the centre of the city. *If* John could get a taxi, that's to say – the drivers are not bound to accept a fare unless they feel like it, which all too often they don't.

He learned that there were fifty five other pianists entered for the competition, and that lots were to be drawn for the order of playing. In the first round, twenty four young hopefuls were to be selected to go on to the second heat, from which only twelve would be passed to the finals. The required pieces for these earlier rounds included a Bach prelude and fugue, a Beethoven sonata, a major romantic work, a Tchaikovsky sonata, and some Shostakovitch preludes and fugues. As his additional personal choice, John offered some shorter pieces by Busoni and also Ravel, Balakirev's Islamey, La Campanella and Mephisto Valse by Liszt, Scriabin's Fifth Sonata, and several other equally demanding works.

The surviving twelve competitors would be required to play the Tchaikovsky First Piano Concerto in B-Flat Minor with orchestra, as well as another concerto of their own choice – the finals were to be spread over several nights, of course. For his own choice of concerto, John again opted for the Liszt No. 1 in E flat. All the heats were to be conducted in public, and the jury was to be headed by the fine Russian pianist, Emil Gilels.

To most people involved in the competition, John was an unknown quantity. But from the moment he stepped from obscurity, as it were, and on to the lighted stage, he made an indelible impression on his audience. There was the usual gasp of surprise, on this occasion a little louder than he was accustomed to hear: this big and bulky man with the dark curly hair and prominent beard was so unlike the conventional idea of an

71

Englishman.

The first piece he played, Bach's Prelude and Fugue in C sharp minor, marked him immediately as someone to watch. His performance of Liszt's La Campanella brought him the first of his rousing ovations, and it is still remembered as a highlight of the whole competition. By the end of the recital, the Russians had taken this modest and brilliant young musician to their hearts, and John was passed triumphantly into the second round.

But his next recital did not start well. One of the compulsory works was Tchaikovsky's long "Bolshoi" Sonata, which is rarely heard outside Russia – deservedly so, I think! He played it too fast for the Russians' taste, and his audience was clearly disappointed.

Sensing the finals slipping from his grasp, John seemed to call on his every inner resource; and his performances of Ravel's Ondine and Scarbo were ranked with his Campanella as one of the most memorable experiences of the competition. Again he was passed by the judges – this time into the finals.

But victory was very far from certain: in fact, at this stage popular rumour placed him about eighth in the jury's estimation. And, as everyone had expected, Ashkenazy was playing brilliantly: his rendering of Liszt's Feux Follets equalled anything John had yet done.

But wherever John might be placed eventually, he could have no doubt that he had set Moscow, literally, by its ear. In the press and face to face, critics and performing musicians wrangled furiously over his merits. No one denied the perfection of his trills and octaves, the ease with which all technical difficulties were overcome – no one faulted his command of tone and colour. Everyone seemed to agree that not since Busoni himself had a foreigner shown such masterful technique. The arguments occurred because some people thought of him as an outstanding virtuoso, but little more than that.

His defenders claimed that on the contrary, his pianistic brilliance was such that it blinded people to the fact that his was a thoughtful and totally individual voice. They talked of his integrity, his creative force and – a description that was to be applied often and prophetically in the coming years – his demonic quality. His interpretations, they insisted, were not meant to be examined through a magnifying glass, detail by

detail, phrase by phrase – his was a broader conception, sometimes sacrificing the "letter" for the "spirit" in the interests of
the whole. It was a challenge also to audiences to change their
habitual listening habits, to be able to stand back and see the
broader pattern.

These Moscow defenders had listened well to John's
playing. The approach they were describing was identical to
the one he had explained to me himself, all those years ago in a
Royal College studio, when he had needled me about sterile
note-perfect correctness . . .

While controversy reigned, John quietly tried to make the
most of Moscow. He did not listen to many of his rivals in the
competition, being determined to keep a clear and unin-
fluenced head, but he made friends amongst some of the other
competitors, notably the British pianist Arthur Thompson and
the cellist Leslie Parnas. The Russians and other Iron Curtain
competitors, predictably, were kept apart from the others, as
they had been at Brussels, and contact was fleeting at best.
Ashkenazy remained a remote and mysterious figure: rumour
had it – rightly or wrongly – that the authorities had kept him
in six months' seclusion while he polished his competition
repertoire.

John gradually got used to the long delays in restaurants,
and the sudden inexplicable changes in the menu: the paper-
thin hotel walls he found harder to accept, and finally, after
being kept awake all night by his neighbour's snoring, he
shocked the desk staff by stubbornly insisting on his democra-
tic right to change his room. He was a little oppressed by the
dim May light of the city, by the greyness of the clothes, by the
sheer bulldozer bulk of so many of the women – and it was difficult to adjust to shopping centres where any neon signs or coloured posters showed only pictures of Lenin or strident party
slogans. But he liked the city with its simple houses – many of
them, unexpectedly, yellow – its wide streets and vast squares,
the many trees. And among the repetitive institution-like rows
of apartment houses, or behind the huge and ostentatious
pointed towers known to Muscovites as "Stalin Gothic", one
could still find a cobbled street with painted nineteenth
century houses, and colourful little gold domed churches.

John told me all about this during the competition itself,
shortly before the finals. No, I didn't fly to join him after he'd

73

spent three weeks in Moscow: I took a train to see him in London. I can think of few other musicians who would conceive of jetting back on Aeroflot at this vital point in the proceedings to keep an engagement at the Festival Hall: but that's exactly what John did. What's more, he used his return ticket for the journey, and had to find the money for the flight back. But after all, he explained, it was the Tchaikovsky concerto he was performing in London, and with the London Philharmonic Orchestra – what better dress rehearsal for the finals could there be? Both on the platform in performance and backstage afterwards he was in terrific form, though just before he left post-haste for the airport and the return trip to the Soviet Union, he told me he didn't think he had a chance of pulling off first prize.

But it was in the final round that John was to come truly into his own. After his performance of the Liszt E flat concerto, the audience gave him a four minute ovation. Mr. Khruschev was there, joining in the applause, making no attempt to conceal his enthusiasm: his wife is supposed to have demanded of him "Why does John Ogdon wear a beard? Who does he think he is – Tchaikovsky himself?" John certainly didn't think that – but to many who were present, he then proceeded to conjure up the composer's spirit in a performance memorable for its bravura, colour, and musical control. The Russians are perhaps the most spontaneous and warm audience in the world, but on this occasion, after the Tchaikovsky concerto had thundered to its climax, they excelled even themselves: they shouted and cheered, they threw flowers and crowded onto the platform, they chanted "Ogdon must win! Ogdon for first prize!" John stood there, bowing and bemused – his surprise and obvious humility inspiring his supporters to even greater acclaim.

There were two evenings of finals still to go. On both of them, just as the conductor prepared to launch the orchestra into one of the concertos, a man's voice shouted out in Russian "First prize to Ogdon!" and again the audience would respond with a rapturous demonstration. Some people were worried that these shows of support would harm John's chances of taking a prize – it was feared that the jury might resent them. In any case, though John had risen like a meteor from

74

international anonymity, Vladimir Ashkenazy remained a most formidable opponent: he was the local boy, already a world name, and playing like the great artist he indisputably is.

The time arrived at last for the jury to reach what was obviously going to be a very difficult decision. One hour passed ... two ... still the clock ticked on, and no decision was announced. The competitors waited backstage, some of them supported by friends, all of them on tenterhooks. The audience waited too, in an electric silence...

And I waited as well, at home in Didsbury Park. There was nothing on the radio news bulletins – no mention of the competition at all. No news was bad news, I told myself, pacing up and down. John had lost, of course he had lost, probably he hadn't even been placed. It was ridiculous to keep hoping otherwise...

Just before 10 pm the phone startled me. I grabbed the receiver.

"Mrs. Ogdon?"

"Yes?" I didn't recognise the voice.

"This is the *Daily Mail*. I suppose you know that your husband has won first prize with Vladimir Ashkenazy..."

I don't remember what questions the man asked me. I was in a daze: I couldn't believe what I'd been told.

As soon as the reporter hung up, I phoned my family, my hands shaking: "John's won!" I shouted "John's won, he's won!" Uncles and aunts, a few close friends, all people dear to John and me, came to our little home armed with bottles of champagne. Delirious with excitement, we drank, constantly toasting John, into the early hours of the morning.

Very late, the phone rang again: it was Moscow calling. The line was very faint, but I did hear John saying clearly "Darling, I did it for you."

I couldn't keep back the tears: I sobbed my heart out in elation.

It had taken three hours for the jury to come to its decision, which had been announced by an emotional Gilels. This was not a division of one prize, he had stressed, but the award of

75

two equal first prizes. To most of the people present, it was a just and right decision; once again, the audience cheered itself hoarse.

Afterwards, a huge party was thrown for the prizewinners and the judges in the Kremlin. John and Ashkenazy were very much together, in part, of course, for press reasons, but also because the guards were not in evidence for once, and both of them were able to satisfy a natural curiosity. Unexpectedly, the gaunt young face of the Russian would light up with a wide and warm smile, and through an interpreter, the two first prizewinners laid the basis for a mutual liking to add to their musical respect. And what a striking contrast they made, these two men still in their mid-twenties only – the bear-like Englishman and the slight, quick-moving Russian.

Khruschev was at the party as well. When John was presented to him, he threw wide his arms. "How glad I am to see you" he said, with a great guffaw. "You have enchanted all Moscow. I love you!" Then he put one hand on a startled John's shoulder. "I would like to pull your beard" he confided, "but I'm afraid that if I do, it may create an international incident!"

John was besieged by the press – by batteries of microphones, by cameras and flashlights and reporters shouting questions – from the moment he landed at Heathrow airport (this time, the flight had been courtesy of the Russians). For days afterwards – virtual prisoners in our little home – we continued to be inundated with requests for television and newspaper interviews, for celebrity appearances of all kinds, for photographs as a family and at the piano . . .

As for John's career – the effects of his Moscow win were even more dramatic than he dared hope. Requests for engagements poured in from countries all over the world: an imminent tour of the Soviet Union was confirmed: and for the United States, John was signed up by the most legendary of all impresarios, Sol Hurok. On the home front, one of the more startling, if minor, changes was in the attitude of our landlord. Nothing was too much trouble, and the 6:30 curfew sank without trace. Perhaps he held parties beyond our wall, where his friends could listen free to the conqueror of Moscow – who knows. . . ?

We couldn't help but feel ourselves to be the most blessed

couple in the world. We were proud and doting parents, completely involved in each other, and very deeply in love. There was no way, we were certain, that life could be better.

Part Two

The Years of Triumph

11

Immediately after Moscow, John was launched into an exciting but exhausting whirlwind of a schedule – life became a constant round of hotel rooms, taxis, trains and flights, of recitals and of performances with orchestra in the world's most famous concert halls – of recordings, of radio and television engagements, of interviews, parties, receptions. Whenever possible, I travelled with him – if I had stayed at home, we would hardly have seen each other at all. We seemed suspended on a wave of continually mounting success, which carried us onwards, exhilarating, dizzying, moving faster and faster, until one day the wave crashed suddenly, almost killing us both.

But in that summer of 1962, the adventure was only just beginning – and in the middle of all the hullabaloo, we had to move to our new house in Isleworth, Middlesex, not far from London Airport. With so much attention being directed John's way, it was not the ideal time in which to be packing up our belongings and arranging for the transportation of our pianos and furniture – but still, those chores had to be done. And one day I strapped Annabel into her baby seat in our Mini Minor, wedged John – who has never learned to drive – into the back seat among bulging cases – and off we all set for London, looking less like a conqueror and his retinue than it is possible to imagine.

We were sorry to leave Didsbury because we had been so happy there – but we were even more thrilled by the prospect of London, the hub of the British music world and a city that we both love. To add to our excitement, the house – which was semi-detached with three bedrooms – was the first property we had ever owned: we had been able to afford it because Ibbs and Tillett had given John an advance against future earnings. Alas, in the three years we were to live there officially, we were hardly to see it at all: all that time we were travelling so constantly that it felt like just one more hotel – and what is more, a less luxurious hotel than the ones we were fast getting used to.

We had barely moved to London before John was back in the Soviet Union on a three week tour. He played all the major towns there, but he had little time for sightseeing. "Life", he wrote to me, "is all travelling, sleeping, eating, playing and rehearsing": it was a tough routine, but one that was to become second nature to him before many more months were out.

He performed in some spas on the Black Sea, and was suprised by their sunny holiday atmosphere. "The concert tonight", he wrote from Yalta, "will be in the open air against a background of cypresses and mountains. It is a hotch-potch programme – first half Brahms Paganini, Gaspard, Campanella; second half Tchaikovsky Concerto." With typical understatement he added "It certainly is unusual!"

He returned home to find that his offered engagements would have kept three pianists busy for the whole of 1963: but though he was Britain's most acclaimed young musician, Emmie Tillett raised his concert fee by £15 only, to a meagre £75! Fortunately, foreign countries were, without any exceptions, considerably more generous with their fees, and in the coming months concerts in Scandinavia, Holland, and Italy were crammed into his schedule.

In August, for the second year running, John and I gave a two piano concert at the Edinburgh Festival: but now, of course, we were about as far away from the "fringe" as it was possible to get. John was sought after, pointed out and stared at, and people queued for hours outside the Freemasons' Hall. The programme opened with John playing Beethoven's final Sonata, No. 111, which must be one of the most demanding pieces ever written: and as at least one critic was to observe, few other artists would have dared tackle its awesome difficulties without a finger-loosening prelude of some kind. We then played Debussy's En blanc et noir together, and for a finale, Steven Whittaker and James Blades joined us on a battery of drums and cymbals, plus triangle, xylophone, and tam tam, for Bartok's exhilarating Sonata for Two Pianos and Percussion – more irreverently known as "Bartok for Bangers and Clangers".

The capacity audience, which included Shostakovich and

Rostropovich, gave us a rousing reception; and our success was capped when Lord Harewood, then the Director of the Festival, immediately re-engaged us for a repeat performance of the Bartok the following year.

But music was not the only thing on my mind at the time. More than ever determined to look at my best, I had swept on to the stage wearing a slinky off the shoulder dress in shimmering gold lurex – still a new material then. It was more suitable for Broadway than Bartok – but it got almost as much attention and comment as my performance itself received!

John, of course, was still his own unaffected self, apparently unfazed by his new found celebrity. He was as unskilled in social graces as he had ever been – as uninterested in clothes and as untidy. I remember someone remarking that he looked like a rumpled walrus – and somebody else saying yes, but with his hunched shoulders, shambling gait and his beard, he was the living embodiment of an Edward Lear limerick drawing. His somewhat puzzled expression and his ever ready smile continued to prompt protective impulses amongst most people who knew him, and many an unwary hostess would patronise him at parties. How many of them were aware, I wonder, of the inner force that drove him on so relentlessly, of the single-mindedness of his ambition . . .

Other important dates followed Edinburgh, both at home and abroad. John's several appearances at the Royal Festival Hall included two solo recitals; he played the mammoth Busoni concerto there as well, and was thrilled by the controversy the occasion aroused. In London, too, the Ogdon/Lucas duo made its Wigmore Hall debut to excellent reviews.

EMI meanwhile, had signed him to an exclusive recording contract, and the first disc he cut for them was a selection of favourite pieces entitled "From Bach to Liszt." And only a couple of months later he recorded Tchaikovsky's No. 1 Concerto in B flat minor with Sir John Barbirolli.

It was Sir John, of course, who had conducted John's student Brahms at the College, and now he treated "my boy" with a more proprietory pride than ever. But on this occasion there was a hitch in the proceedings: EMI had wanted the Tchaikovsky Third Piano Concerto on the B side of the record, but at only a day's notice, Sir John announced that he had been too busy to learn the piece. So the César Franck Symphonic Variations for Piano and Orchestra were substituted instead – subject, of course, to John's agreement. Always eager to please and professionally incapable of saying "no" to anyone, John gave his assent: and then rushed to the piano to start learning the work from scratch, and overnight! Fortunately for their peace of mind, no one at EMI found out until later that the Franck had never been in John's repertoire: though with the years he was to become famous – perhaps I should say notorious – for such hair-raising feats.

He took another, similar risk a few months later in the 1963 Edinburgh Festival, when he agreed to play all three Bartok Concertos without telling the organisers that he had never studied them before. To perform three major works for the first time ever within the space of two weeks is no mean accomplishment – particularly in front of some of the most sophisticated musical audiences in the world.

The Concerto No. 1, with Istvan Kertesz and the LSO, went beautifully, with hardly a clinker to be heard: the Second Concerto, with Lorin Maazel and the BBC Symphony Orchestra, was carried off with such panache that it seemed John must have been playing it for years. So far, so good – two concertos down and only one to go. But it was this last one that worried me most.

The orchestra was the renowned Concertgebouw, and the conductor, George Szell. Szell, one of the world's great musicians, had been a pianist himself in his youth, and he invariably demanded at least one private work-through with his soloist before the rehearsal with orchestra; and in these sessions he could be unsparingly, brutally frank. He refused to tolerate second best: he could wither the stoutest of hearts with his pale, cold-eyed stare: he was, in short, an implacable perfectionist.

Though the rehearsals went very well, John was still scared before the concert. My condition was even worse. I think it is more nerve-wracking to hear someone one loves in performance than it is to play in public oneself; there is no way to help, there is nothing to do except send out waves of support. Waiting for John to make his entrance on stage with the conductor, I was so painfully tense that the chance to applaud when they finally appeared gave me an active physical relief. John sat at the piano, Szell raised his baton – and they were off...

The performance was developing splendidly, as well as I had dared hope it would – gradually I leaned back in my seat, beginning to relax. And then, in the fugue, I was sitting bolt upright, frozen stiff in sheer terror. John had lost his way, he had had a bad memory lapse and was floundering – for the life of me, I could not see how he was going to save himself. Slowly, continuing to conduct, Szell turned his head to stare at him ... John stopped playing altogether, and looked up. Szell kept his eyes steady on John, visibly willing him back on the rails – and with a small grimace, he led him unmistakably into the piano's next positive re-entry. To my infinite relief, John picked up the cue – and from that moment on, the ensemble continued like clockwork. But several minutes were to pass before the blood stopped pounding through my ears.

After the applause had died away, I rushed backstage, wondering if Szell had devoured John whole and then spewed him out, as he was reputedly capable of doing to those who had displeased him. But I found my husband beaming and completely intact: Szell had praised his performance in the most generous of terms, and had shrugged off the memory lapse as trivial, the sort of thing that can happen to anyone. The ogre had shown himself to be a human after all, and John has never forgotten his encouragement.

And still, the pace did not let up. In September 1963, soon after the Festival, John went to the Soviet Union for a second tour, this one lasting five weeks. Immediately after his final performance there, he caught a flight to West Germany, where he joined up with the London Philharmonic Orchestra. I went along for what was virtually a succession of one night stands in most major cities of the country. Almost every day we were woken up very early: we would climb into our bus, whereupon, more often than not, we would fall into exhausted sleep. On arriving at the next town and the next hotel, John and the orchestra would go to the concert hall for rehearsals – and almost before they knew what was happening, it was time to get ready for the evening's performance. And so it went on, day after day after day.

For us, the saving grace was the conductor, John Pritchard – the man who had guided us both through our debuts with the Liverpool Philharmonic as well as sitting on the jury of the Liverpool Competition. Elegant, multi-lingual and occasionally outrageous, he is also a gourmet par excellence; he seems to know the best restaurant – as opposed to the most famous – in every town and village in Europe, and the meals we regularly shared with him helped make the schedule more bearable.

After the tour, we flew back to London. It was wonderful to be home again, above all to be with our adorable Annabel, who was by now just two years old. Of course, I was lucky to have trained and reliable nannies to look after her while we were gone – but unfortunately, now that I was away more often than I had been in the past, the good ladies proved more reluctant than ever to allow me any say in my daughter's routine. Miss Wilton, elderly and severe, came and very soon went: so did Miss Stevenson . . .

But this particular visit was too short to cause another nursery crisis – in almost no time at all, we were jetting off yet again, to Italy. While we were in Milan, we had the opportunity to hear one of John's pianistic idols, the great Arturo Benedetti Michelangeli, in a concert in La Scala. He played the Grieg Concerto and the same César Franck Variations which John had learned so hurriedly for the EMI recording; and he bowled the two of us over with his masterful control. As a person, like so many who are phenomenally talented, he is highly strung and often eccentric: I could say the same of John, of course, though his compulsions show themselves in an opposite way. Whereas John will accept every engagement he can possibly fulfil, Michelangeli agrees to only rare public performances – and then cancels many of those. Allegedly he has been known to keep an audience waiting for forty minutes because the coffee served him was not to his taste, and he would not budge until the right blend was found. But on this occasion, the concert ran to schedule, and John and I felt privileged to have heard him.

After Italy, John went to Spain. But I bowed out of that trip and flew back home again to Annabel. For the time being, I had had more than my fill of the pressured international music circuit.

Of course, not every tour is as exhausting as the West German one had been in October; but by any normal standards, the life of a successful soloist is a strange one. It is a life of hotel bedrooms, of existing out of suitcases, of constant changes of cities and languages – so much so that for John it has been a common experience to wake up in the morning and to find that for some minutes at least, he cannot remember which country or even continent he is in.

On most tours, rehearsals with orchestra take place in the mornings. Before a recital, too, John prefers to arrange early practice sessions in the concert hall, during which he has to "learn" the acoustics as well as trying out the piano. And trying out the piano can be a depressing experience – far more so than many people outside our profession realise. Singers have their own voices, violinists, cellists and other soloists bring their well-tried instruments with them – but the pianist is always faced with an unknown piano, and every piano is different from the last. The tone is different, the power of projection is different, the physical action of the keyboard is different. Even the products of the same manufacturer vary enormously – the European Steinways, for example, tend to be more sonorous but more difficult to control than their American counterparts. And so with each engagement, the performer has to adapt his technique, to some degree, to the piano he has been given.

In a few major cities, the great piano-making firms provide soloists with a selection of quality instruments reserved exclusively for important recitals and orchestral engagements. In New York and London, Steinway's basements are often full of performers dithering over the handful of pianos available: "Is the tone a bit dry for the Schumann, do you think?" – "It hasn't got the power I need for the Brahms" – "It's much too mushy for Mozart." And occasionally, a plaintive "This piano *can't* have been booked already for the evening I need it! Please, you've got to let me have it or my concert will be a *disaster!*"

But for the most part, the soloist has to accept whatever instrument he is given. And then, after he has tested it, back to the hotel; and in John's case, usually an afternoon's rest to help gather his mental and physical resources. He likes to relax by reading – occasionally classics, but more often science fiction,

87

thrillers and detective stories. Nero Wolfe, the corpulent orchid-growing armchair detective created by Rex Stout, is a particular favourite of his: he enjoys Agatha Christie too. He is a fervent admirer of William Golding and, in a different vein, John finds anything by P. G. Wodehouse and everything about Winnie the Pooh most rewarding escapes.

Sometimes, in small provincial towns or ugly industrial cities, on rainy days and in dreary rooms, the afternoons can seem endless – all the same, the time to get ready for the concert always comes a little too soon. There are very few performers who do not suffer pre-concert nerves – and John is no exception. He shows his tension by pacing up and down, usually chain-smoking the while, an expression of almost painful concentration on his face.

Then to the Hall; and at last the performance itself. In Germany, Holland and Scandinavia, the audiences will be knowledgeable and silent, and usually warm in their applause, though never matching the enthusiasm of Russia's: in Spain, they will be restless: in Italy, often noisy and talkative, though vociferous in calling for encores: in France, polite but cool. In England, as in America, they are appreciative and invariably respectful.

After the performance, the dressing room will usually be crowded with well-wishers, eager to shake the soloist's hand and perhaps get their programmes autographed. Later, there might be a dinner with friends, or a larger reception may be given. And, always, there are the people . . .

For a soloist travelling unaccompanied, life on the road can be lonely indeed, but at the same time there are agents and their staff to be seen – concert organisers, orchestra managers, society presidents, friends of friends, unknown admirers . . . So many hands to shake, so many faces that smile and say pleasant things. People just wanting to talk to John soon became a feature of his existence – except that there is always that nagging worry that one or more of these people are expecting him to recognise them. That man – is he being over-familiar, or have we met him before in another hall, or city, or country? Is he connected with music – might offending him, however inadvertently, be bad for John's career? . . The social line when away on tour can be a difficult one to tread – and one that does not get any easier.

Very rarely, in a capital city, someone might leave a party in the early hours to buy the first editions of the papers: but usually John goes to bed and waits until next morning to read what the critics have to say. Always, as he opens the paper, he experiences a familiar mixture of anticipation and dread – a mixture known to every performing artist, whatever his field may be. Then, depressed or reassured, he will close his suitcases again, catch a taxi to the railway station or the airport, and make his way to the next city, the next country, the next bout of boredom, nerves, excitement: to the next day, which will be almost identical to so many past and others yet to come – and which John would not change for anything in the world.

But if John's professional life soon became a vertiginous blur, one tour he made in the first two months of 1964 stands out vividly in our memories. No soloist can call himself really successful until he has conquered the United States of America – and it was to the United States that John was now headed.

12

The American tour was to prove as demanding as any John had yet made – there were to be thirty concerts the length and breadth of the country, and even some in Canada too. And all this during the coldest two months of the year.

His first concert was to be in the mid West of the country: but first we flew to New York, where we were to meet Sol Hurok and his staff.

New York overwhelmed us from the moment we arrived. To a European at the time, even the drive into town was a memorable experience – the maze of highways, the flyovers, the enormous direction signs: the cars festooned with lights like vast juke-boxes on wheels – and then Manhattan itself, thrusting up on the skyline, one of the most astounding man-made wonders of all time, and one that never ceases to amaze me, even now.

We had heard all the clichés about Manhattan, they have been told a thousand times: but still they could not prepare us for the experience of the place. We were ready for the hurry and bustle, the affluent crowds, the commercialism – for the skyscrapers towering above us, giving the illusion of keeling over dangerously when seen under cloud-swept skies. But the potholes and litter came as a surprise, as did the seedy hotels, the battered fire-escapes on low brown-stone houses, the beggars muttering to themselves. New York was another world to us, more foreign and far more frightening than Paris or Milan.

The Hurok offices on Fifth Avenue, too, were as far removed from Ibbs and Tillett as it was possible to imagine. They were streamlined, gleaming, functional – a real-life replica of executive suites we had seen in a hundred Hollywood films. We were warmly welcomed there, and taken at once to meet the Russian émigré who had became one of the most successful impresarios the world has ever known – Sol Hurok himself.

He turned out to be stocky, creased and ebullient: in the best tradition of living showbusiness legends, he was perched at the end of a huge cigar. He got up from behind his ice-rink of a desk and shook our hands: "John" he said gallantly in a voice that still held Russian traces, "I don't know how you play, but you sure have good taste in women!" After a few more niceties, he wished John well for the upcoming tour – expansively enough, yet in a manner that conveyed that if John knew what was good for him, he had better damn well produce the goods. Far from reassured, we were ushered from the presence.

After a couple of days in New York, still reeling from our confused impressions, we flew to the mid West, arriving under a lowering leaden sky. It was snowing the next morning when John went to rehearsal; it was still snowing for the concert, when he played Chopin's F minor concerto.

The audience received him warmly; but that was nothing to the extravagance with which we were greeted at the post-concert party. Never in our lives before had we come across so many noisy and extrovert people in one room: never had we seen such a conspicuous consumption of hard liquor. The generosity was unstinting and, someone told us proudly, "traditional mid-western": but as the evening wore on and the fat round snowflakes kept drifting past the windows, more and more people were getting drunk, their cheeks flushed and ties askew while their voices got harsher and more raucous. "C'mon, John, play us something" someone ordered, trying to push his reluctant bulk towards the living room piano: "Play, play!" others shouted, "Give us a toon!" Very reluctantly but unable to refuse, John did as he was asked. Another guest put his arm around me and began to paw me clumsily. So this, I thought, with a surge of convent-bred distaste, was America's famed vulgarity. I could not wait to leave the party, to fly away from the town.

But we could not fly away: the countryside was buried deep in snow, the airport was closed down. None the less, John was determined to keep his next engagement which was scheduled to take place in two days' time in Delaware, Ohio. So we decided to travel the several hundred miles there by Greyhound bus, changing at Columbus, Ohio, where we would stay overnight.

And so we spent hours in the enormous bus, driving on wide

91

straight snow-girt roads, passing through interchangeable towns apparently composed of neon signs and parking lots, until we reached Columbus. Here, as in Hurok's office, I felt I had entered a film set, though this time a tawdry one. The men were slow-moving and slower talking, wearing wide-brimmed hats, some of them even carrying guns: the hotel was seedily depressing, and we ate a dreadful meal surrounded by plastic plants. The mid West of America, I told John dejectedly, was a very far cry from Salzburg . . .

So it was a pleasant surprise for both of us to arrive in Delaware the next morning and to find that it was quite attractive. John was giving a recital on the university campus there, and the people to whom we were introduced were as charming and as civilized as any we had met in Europe. John played very well, and was enthusiastically received: the party thrown for him afterwards was fun without being wild. After so unpromising a start to our American experience, I could have cried with relief: and I almost did that night when, back in the hotel, John took my hand in his. "After all, Brenda" he said, looking at me with tenderness and an unexpected smile, "Austria has its faults too. I think we're going to like it over here."

A few days before John was due to give his Carnegie Hall recital, we returned to New York, to below freezing temperatures and to a round of lavish entertainment by the Hurok staff. We were taken to the Russian Tea Room next to Carnegie Hall, where we were ostentatiously seated on the right side of the restaurant, by tradition the reserve for celebrities, and served the famous vodka-based Moscow Mules. We were taken to glittering parties in apartments overlooking Central Park, or to dinners in glass walled penthouses high above Park Avenue. I remember being served my first vodka martini, clear and pale in a frosted glass; it made me feel very sophisticated. But I was not then used to alcohol, and the first sip almost blew my head off; soon I was dangerously light headed, and also at the start of a lasting aversion to that particular cocktail.

The people we were meeting in New York were very different from those in the mid West; they were witty, sophisticated, worldly, and were outwardly friendly as well. Yet I sensed a disturbing reserve. It was as if they were keeping an unstated distance from John until he had proved of what stuff he was made: as if they were not going to waste too much time on someone who might yet prove a failure.

John sensed this atmosphere too, with the result that he was as nervous as I had ever known him – perhaps more so. He was also well aware that the New York critics, particularly on the *Times*, carried a national clout that was – at least in those days – totally out of proportion: the reviews echoed across the country to the lowliest agent's rep, with the result that a New York success was a national success, and a New York failure – oblivion.

John had elected to face this challenge with one of his more mammoth programmes, made up of some tried and true war horses: both books of the Brahms Paganini Variations, the Sonatina Seconda by Busoni, Liszt's La Campanella and Mephisto Waltz, and his own Variations and Fugue Op. 4. He had played them all many times before, but that did not prevent him spending hours shut away in Steinway's 57th. Street basement, practising, reworking, polishing . . .

All the day of the concert he was restless, unable to sit still: an hour before the performance, his face was an ashen white. We got to the elegant and historic Hall to find it was sold out; we were told that the audience included many leading figures in the American music world, which, while naturally pleasing John, did not help him to relax.

In the end, and as so often on specially testing occasions, John played at his best. The audience was attentive and rewarded him with extravagant applause. A reception was thrown for him in an apartment belonging to Walter Prude, a vice-president at Hurok's: everybody there seemed excited.

This was one of the occasions when the first editions of the newspapers were brought to us in the early hours of the morning; under the eyes of the other guests, it was hard to open the pages carefully instead of tearing them apart . . . Five minutes later, we put the papers down, both of us weak with relief – there had been a few carps from the rags, and even Harold Schonberg of the all-important *New York Times* had expressed a reservation or two. But all in all, he had given John a definite "thumbs up" – "A keyboard artist who has very much to say" his review had concluded. Alan Rich, of the almost equally influential *Herald Tribune*, had not faulted the performance at all: "He is a towering, deep, original and compelling musical personality" he had written, "and his horizons should be without limit."

We tumbled into bed as the sky slowly lightened behind the dark soaring towers. We were happy: John had made it in America.

We bubbled into the Hurok offices next day, still euphoric. Walter Prude, tall and greying, ushered us into his office. "Great recital, John" he said, repeating the words he had used at the reception. "Very impressive."

Beaming modestly, John thanked him again.

"Too bad about the reviews, though."

"The reviews?" John's grin faded.

Walter sat down behind his desk and sighed. "They aren't good enough" he said bluntly. "I can't do anything with them."

We were stunned, we could not believe it. What did he want, for God's sake – Liszt himself reincarnated? But Walter obviously meant what he said.

I suspect that someone senior in the agency, maybe Hurok himself, had been personally disappointed by John's recital, and had applied the brakes to an all-out promotion campaign. Be that as it may, we were suddenly reminded that the music business is cut-throat, with almost no room at the top. Unless you have been established for many years, if they call you less than "the best", you slip before you have started.

It was an awakening reminiscent of Brussels, except that this time John's cloud of security had been not student ignorance but international acclaim. Now, as then, the world stood revealed as a hard and ruthless place.

Fortunately we had little time to brood, because we left the same day for Boston, where John was to give another recital. And from Boston, we launched on what used to be called a whistle-stop tour, except we were supposed to be travelling by plane. He played in Chicago, Philadelphia, Toronto, and all sizes of town in between: and to our relief, the few reservations of New York's reviewers were not shared by other critics after all.

But after ten days or so of constant travelling, I was already worn out. We had always known that America was big, but

94

neither of us had actively realised what that word "big" really meant. Now we were beginning to understand: "big" means that by comparison, Europe itself seems quite small. It means that it is no great shakes in America to fly the equivalent distance from London to Rome: while a hundred mile detour for dinner seems the most natural thing in the world. I am convinced that most Europeans have no conception of that country's vastness – unless they have experienced it first hand.

Things were not helped by the weather, which was the most severe in our experience. The snow and freezing temperatures meant regular closures of airports and more long and tedious trips by bus.

For John, the tour was going well: but happy though I felt for him, I was missing Annabel more with every day that was passing. We could not bring her over because the schedule was so hectic and the weather so bad, yet, though her nanny at the time was reliable, I could not keep myself from worrying. And I was feeling guilty too. I will never forget the body blow given me when the Hungarian conductor in Rochester, New York, on hearing my daughter was in England, smiled at me and said "Oh, you must be a bad mother."

I knew that however hard I tried to wear a confident and positive face, I was becoming dreary company for John: and so, after four weeks on the road, I told him I would not be going with him to California for the final leg of the tour.

He was very understanding, and agreed I should fly home on the first plane I could get. I made a reservation on a flight for the following day, which meant I would be leaving before John's first appearance in Detroit.

I was not prepared for what was to happen next. Talking on the phone to someone concerned with the arrangements, John mentioned that I would not be needing a seat in the concert hall after all. In next to no time, a woman in a glossy mink coat had arrived at the hotel demanding to see me.

She was on the Ladies' Committee, she explained. I had been expected to accompany John to the after-concert reception, and plans would be upset by my absence. So would I please change my plans and stay on in Detroit.

I could not believe she was serious. "But I've got my ticket" I told her. "And they're expecting me in England – I've sent off

95

a cable already."

"Forget about that" she said tersely. "It's no problem to telephone London."

"I'm sorry, but I really can't see what difference it makes if I'm at your reception or not."

She became openly aggressive. "I told you, you are expected! We have planned this reception for a long time!"

But I was adamant in my refusal. She was utterly charmless as she rose to leave, "Mrs Ogdon, the Ladies Committee will be considerably distressed. I think you should know that your attitude won't do your husband any good."

I could hardly bring myself to be civil as I saw her out of the room. But it was to prove a valuable insight into concert life in America. Nowhere else in the world does a musician find so heavy a stress laid on the social activities peripheral to a concert. More than once, John has been told by an agency's area representative that he is expected at a post-recital reception with the words "You've got to go to this one. It's a good series that they run here, and if Mrs. So and So likes you, most likely she'll re-engage you."

As John loves parties, and would never dream of turning one down, this in no way worries him. But it is true that such intensive hospitality is a feature not only of small music societies; every ambitious soloist who plays in America soon learns the names of certain powerful ladies to whom it would be professionally wise to pay court.

Such a situation hardly exists in Europe. I think perhaps the reason is that Europeans generally go to concerts only if they feel like it, and for no other reason; but in America, the striving for "upward mobility" is the most intense in my experience, and to support a musical occasion in the town or the community is definitely an "in" thing to do. And of course, it is even more "in" to be on the guest list for the private reception held for the soloist afterwards. In the States, a part of every audience goes as much to be seen as to listen.

Yet it would be too easy to criticise such attitudes. Europe may be more confident of its culture, but it is also more weary: and in most countries, the arts, to survive, have to be financed almost exclusively by the State. America relies on private patronage – and the party throwing hostesses so popular with John are often wealthy wives and widows who provide the financial backing for music societies and even entire orchestras. Their energies in promoting music are unmatched in our experience – and history has shown repeatedly that the arts will flower more freely when not subject to government committees. Certainly music is far more flourishing in the States than in any other country we know.

It was wonderful to be home, to be with my baby once again – and to catch up at last on some sleep! John wrote to me from California saying how beautiful it was, how much he was enjoying it there – except for the fact, he added gallantly, that he was missing me. Best news of all, he went on, was that Hurok wanted him to make another major tour of the country. So Prude's pessimism had proved to be unfounded: John, after all, *had* made it in the United States.

13

John's homecoming was a sad one: while we had been away, his mother Dorothy had died. She had been ill for some time, and the news had not been unexpected: all the same, one can never be prepared for something that is so final. And though John and I had been married for almost four years, the mere knowledge of her support and her devotion had been a source of continuing strength to him. Now, with both parents gone, the world was for John a far colder place.

The family member to whom he had always felt closest, his elder brother Karl, had emigrated to Australia some years before: and at this time of bereavement, it was Karl whom John truly missed. But as luck would have it, it was to Australia that we were bound next, in May – the second new continent we were to tour within only six months.

There were to be two important differences from the American arrangements. First, we were giving several two piano recitals, in addition to which I had been booked for many concerts on my own: these had been arranged through the offices of Ibbs and Tillett, who were by now representing me also. And second, I could not bear another separation from Annabel so soon, and so we took her along with us. Her nanny came as well – and wonder of wonders, at last I had found a treasure. She was a young, good-natured New Zealander, whose name was Frances Roberts; and in almost no time after hiring her, I came to think of her as a friend.

We flew the long and tiring journey first class all the way, courtesy of the Australian Broadcasting Commission. The tour itself started in Perth, which meant we would not be seeing Karl for some weeks, as he lived at the other end of Australia. But that gave us something to look forward to – and in any case, we both took to Perth at once. John said that with its beaches and its casual way of life, it reminded him of California.

Unfortunately, he was not there for long; after giving a single recital, he left for another concert out of town. I stayed behind, to play the Rachmaninov Paganini Variations, which had let me down in the Liverpool finals, but which by this time I had finally got right! Late that night, after the reception, I was driven to my motel by a young man who was extremely drunk and even more amorous – and I had to slam my bedroom door on him very hard indeed. Suddenly, feeling shaken by the experience, I realised how much I was missing John. I sat down on the bed – and for the first time ever, I asked myself if I really did want to be a soloist, travelling most of the time on my own. It was a question that was to occupy me very much throughout the tour ...

One of the most pleasant bonuses of the entire trip took place for us in Perth: we were introduced to a man John had long admired – the composer, Sir William Walton. Tall, with an aquiline nose and penetrating eyes, he is a person of many interests as well as a quietly brilliant wit: fortunately for us, we were to run into him quite often in other cities on the tour, and we shared many a meal of oyster-stuffed carpetbagger steaks. He was in Australia to conduct several concerts, and someone had persuaded him that he should cross the entire continent from Sydney to Perth by train. The journey through the monotonous, almost lunar desert landscape in stifling, insect-infested conditions, had taken more than a week; and his accounts of his sufferings on the way had us both helpless with laughter. "It was an experience" he told us, a caustic gleam in his blue eyes, "but not one that I would recommend – nor one I would repeat, whatever the price!"

From Perth we went to Adelaide, the most British of cities: the stop after that was Sydney, a spectacularly sited place with an informal and yet worldly atmosphere.

Annabel, meanwhile, stayed mostly with me when John and I had to separate for our concerts – even so, she had to be left in exclusive charge of her nanny more often than I would have liked. But in spite of the relentless pace and the partings, both of us were loving Australia – the friendliness, the unforced hospitality everywhere we went, the genuine warmth of the audiences. Even the critics, who have the reputation of being amongst the least generous in the world, were being kind to us.

As for the tour itself – it was easily the best-organised on which we had ever been. Wherever we went, we were accompanied by a representative of the ABC whose job it was to ensure that all our needs were met and that everything ran as smoothly as possible. So different from America, where we had been left to look out for ourselves . . . But of course, Australia is far away from the Western world in which it has its cultural roots, and the care lavished on visiting soloists is a deliberate inducement to them to make the long return trip half way round the world . . .

Brisbane – where we both played with orchestra – slightly dented our love affair with the country; it was brash and tough and very hot. And straight from its tropical climate, we travelled into freezing cold weather, though the island of Tasmania, with its mountains and pine forests, was the most beautiful place we were to see on this tour. And from Tasmania, we flew to Melbourne, for our final concerts in Australia. We liked it there but after the cosmopolitan aura of Sydney, it seemed staid; for John, though, this was a very special stop over, because it was in Melbourne that his brother Karl was living.

Like John, Karl was musically gifted, and he had an unusually high IQ; unlike John, he was slim, loquacious, and very excitable. At the time of our visit, he was working as a librarian, a job which neither stretched his abilities to the full nor did much for his bank balance; but all in all, the visit was the success we had hoped for, and a feeling of intimacy between the two brothers was re-established with no trouble at all. Certainly, when John flew away after our few days in the city, he was feeling far less alone than before.

I, however, said goodbye to Melbourne with a profound sense of loss – caused not by our parting from Karl, but by a purely musical blow. Two nights earlier, I had played the Bach D minor Concerto, and had been happy with the performance; the next morning, however, the notoriously hard to please critic, Felix Werder, had given me the first really bad review of my life, describing my technique as "student-like".

Perhaps I was over-tired; in any case, the effect the review had on me was shattering. I felt ashamed, confused, and publicly humiliated. But at least Werder's unkind words helped prompt me to a vital decision.

As I sat in the plane that took us away, as the solid mass of the Australian coastline below us gave way to the blue of the sea, I knew that those doubts I had first had in Perth had crystalised into a certainty. Much as I had liked Australia, my solo concerts had meant repeated and lonely separations from John, and they had diverted too much of my attention from Annabel. Now I decided that for some years, at least, my career would no longer be my major priority; from now on, my family would be first.

I reached for John's hand; he clasped it, and I sat back, closing my eyes. I felt a great load had been eased from my shoulders: I also felt desperately sad.

We still had several concerts to give in New Zealand. Wellington was not as sophisticated in those days as it is now: and I remember that in our hotel the first morning, we were woken at 6 am by a loud knock on the door, and the shout "Morning tea! If you don't take sugar, don't stir!"

We were not in Wellington for long; we left Annabel with her nanny's family outside Auckland while we travelled for three more weeks giving concerts. The audiences everywhere were warm and we were bowled over by the breathtaking beauty of the South Island, with its soaring mountains and fertile green pastures.

At last, the Antipodean tour was over. After the thousands of miles we had travelled over the previous six months, I was once again exhausted; and instead of flying back home, we took a holiday in Greece for three sunny and glorious weeks. We stayed first at the Athens Hilton – to our minds, one of the most glamorous hotels in the world – and then at the beach resort of Lagonissi, which at that time was completely unspoiled.

While on this holiday, I learned that I was pregnant again: the expensive Greek doctor, after giving me the news, asked me cheerfully "Do you want the child or shall we abort it?" John and I wanted it all right! Indeed, on this occasion, the news was not a surprise; my decision to curb my career had reinforced my desire for a second young Ogdon . . . I lay stretched out on the beach, feeling blissfully happy again; it was so pleasant to have John to myself for once, to see so much more of Annabel – to have leisure to do what we felt like. It was time, I thought, that we slowed down the pace at which we had been living.

Above all it was high time that John started taking things more easily. For over two years now he had been driving himself obsessively and non-stop; no hobbies had been allowed to distract him, and he had never found an outlet in sport... Suddenly, on this Grecian holiday I had my first faint pricks of alarm. At times, I even found myself thinking that nothing but music was totally real for him.

I regretted nothing that had happened since Moscow, but I felt nostalgic occasionally for those less pressured days in Didsbury four years before, with the troublesome landlord and the tins of curry and the very limited budget. We had been so childishly happy, so very deeply in love...

We were still happy together – but Didsbury was a different world from the one we were moving in now. It seemed a lifetime ago...

But if by rights John should have been more exhausted than I was, he was on the contrary brimful of energy and overflowing with confidence – and certainly far from ready to ease up the pace. He could not wait for the next round of concerts, the next new works to be studied and learned – and he used part of the holiday in Greece to get back to his neglected composing.

And, he told me, one sunny morning on the beach, he had had a sudden and important idea, one he would somehow find the time to pursue: he was determined that one day he would found a Festival of Twentieth Century Music.

14

By the time John founded his Festival, in 1967, his position as Britain's foremost young piano virtuoso was established beyond any question. In the '60s he toured the United States and the Soviet Union several more times, as well as the Far East, Scandinavia, Portugal, Canada, Switzerland, Israel, Australia, New Zealand, South Africa, Kenya, and Europe on both sides of the Iron Curtain – tours and countries, in fact, far too numerous to mention. For John, jet-lag seemed not to exist; he continued to accept all the engagements he could possibly fulfill, while he would still stand in for other, indisposed artists, most of them less well known than himself. He was to make over forty recordings, he continued to enlarge his repertoire and to promote modern music – and somehow, he found the time to compose.

People asked me then – ask me now – how such endeavour was humanly possible. It was possible both because of John's strengths and his weaknesses – in other words, his stupendous gifts sometimes make things too easy for him. His encyclopaedic musical knowledge, his imaginative and intellectual grasp of a composition's overall shape, can lead to a cavalier approach to the detail: while his technical facility and the speed at which he is able to learn can result in inadequate study and a preparation that is occasionally too lax. Stanley Sadie of *The Times* in London once wrote of him "Mr Ogdon's talent is huge, but sometimes he frustrates us by so carelessly squandering it." I absolutely agree, and wish with all my heart that John would conserve his gifts a little more carefully.

But all of that having been said, he remains a very great pianist. And as the sixties progressed, his lyrical touch, his delicate colouring and phrasing, came in for ever mounting critical praise: though a word that was used of him increasingly was one that his Moscow admirers had first used – "demonic."

The critics were describing a quality that has little to do with just playing loudly or brilliantly or fast: it is a driven quality that comes from the heart, and it can never, never be faked. Where gentle John hid his demon off stage I could not guess: but in performance, it sometimes seemed to take him over completely, leaving him, as he took his bows, euphoric but sweat-soaked and spent. Audiences, rightly, would be wildly excited: but in my experience, any artist thus possessed has to pay for it sooner or later.

Strangely enough for so individual a talent, John has always been deferential in the extreme towards the wishes of every conductor, be he a world famous maestro or a man with an amateur orchestra. I have often argued with John about this, because I am convinced that in matters of interpretation, the concerto's soloist should take the lead; but at the same time I have to admit that John's readiness to be agreeable does help explain his popularity with so many conductors.

John's dedication to neglected composers of the past as well as of our own time has led him to give some of the great names in musical history rather less than I think their due. But I am talking only in terms of potential, because his classical repertoire is still as great as, indeed greater than, that of many other artists.

Of the many Beethoven works that John plays, he particularly loves the Fourth Piano Concerto, while he believes the Third to be a superbly balanced composition not allowed its worth even today. Chopin is dear to his heart, and he is awed by both Brahms concerti – though to his mind, the First is the best. His affinity with Liszt, of course, has been lifelong; he finds the music's adventurous qualities as thrilling now as they must have been the very first time they were heard. Liszt's output was admittedly uneven, but he is almost always a challenge to play – and John thinks the strict control of form shown, for example, in the Symphonic Poems, tends to be much underrated.

He finds a similar control in Busoni, and he compares the composer's search for a classical 'feel' to that of Stravinsky more recently. Over the years, single-mindedly and at first almost single-handedly, John has won Busoni a host of admirers; though today, he will reluctantly concede that perhaps Busoni is emotionally too cold ever to become a real audience favourite.

To a lesser degree, John has also championed Alkan, the brilliant nineteenth century composer. His Concerto for Solo Piano is an unforgettable piece consisting of one apparently insurmountable musical obstacle on top of another and another and another ... John's recording of it for RCA Victor is one of the great pianistic achievements of his career, and he must also be one of the very few soloists in the world ever to dare play it in public, let alone bring it off so triumphantly.

There are so many other composers John loves – Bach, Schubert, Debussy, Rachmaninov, Ravel ... Scriabin, all of whose sonatas he has recorded for EMI ... But then, John's identification with music is such that whichever composer he happens to be playing is his favourite at that given moment.

Of them all, it is still Mozart whom John finds the most difficult to work up to performance standard. The finger work is so exact, it demands a kind of precision he has never found easy; and even Mozart's musical shape seems more complicated to John than, say, Beethoven's. But his love for this composer, which Alistair Londonderry had tried so hard to awaken all those years ago in Basle, has now at last come into flower.

John's interest in contemporary music has not wavered from the time I first met him. He himself says simply that he "got into the habit of it" during his adolescent involvement with the New Music group at the college. The magnetic Alexander Goehr, our best man Peter Maxwell Davies, Harrison Birtwistle, Elgar Howarth – all those close friends of his youth have made their reputations as first rate composers, and John has played and recorded their work many times. In fact, his services to British music were recognised in 1970 with a special award given him by the Composers' Guild of Great Britain.

To claim that John's dedication to contemporary music is admirable is not to convey that he performs it from a dry sense of duty – on the contrary, his pleasure is real and profound. His dedication is admirable because commercially it is unrewarding, and because the enormous energy he invests in learning a piece can end in a single performance to a very limited public.

But though some works, as even John will admit, can seem inaccessible to the point of perversity, the majority of composers still do their best to reach out to their audiences. Sir William Walton is one: so is Sir Michael Tippett: so was Benjamin Britten. I would also include Maxwell Davies.

John has played works by Tippett on many occasions, above all his beautiful but very difficult Concerto, with its first movement which the composer describes as "a jewel turning different ways." I remember two performances John gave of this work in London and Edinburgh, when he played it entirely from memory after alarmingly limited practice. He was quite rightly scared stiff when he learned on both occasions that Michael himself was coming to listen – but to John's relief, Michael professed himself completely delighted. He was pleased too with the recording John made of it for EMI, with Colin Davis and the Philharmonia Orchestra.

John also plays several of Britten's works, and among our favourite two piano pieces are the Mazurka Elegiaca and the Introduction and Rondo Alla Burlesque. Ben himself – red-faced, narrow eyed, frizzy haired – we always found utterly charming ... I remember that he had a little dachshund which he adored and which went almost everywhere with him; its name was Gilda. Once when we were at Ben's house in Aldeburgh, a colleague of ours looked at the dog's brown eyes and long, wavy red ears and remarked "Named for Rita Hayworth, I suppose?" Ben fixed him with a gimlet eye and then hissed "Rigoletto!"

Another of Ben's compositions which John and I have played is the Scottish Ballad for Two Pianos and Orchestra – once we performed it at the Aldeburgh Festival, with Ben himself conducting. It was exciting to work and rehearse with him, though in the performance itself he set an alarmingly fast tempo towards the end of the work. Whether he was deliberately stretching us, or whether he was carried away by excitement, I cannot be sure – but we had a very hard time keeping up!

In fact, working with living composers can be a dangerous occupation on occasion. In 1968, we were asked by the Henry Wood Promenade Concerts to premiere a concerto for two pianos by Alan Rawsthorne; the trouble was, though, that the concerto was not yet finished. So over the next weeks, Alan

106

would bring sections of it round to our house as he completed them, and together we would rehearse – or try to rehearse. Alan was a down to earth English gentleman who was far from averse to a drink, and he had a dry dead pan wit which had all three of us in stitches. We had so much fun together that we forgot how quickly time was passing; and in the end, Alan finished the work only a matter of days before the Prom was due to take place. John and I barely had time to learn it; John Pritchard, the conductor, had no chance to study the score in advance; and sadly, the rehearsal was not nearly long enough for the orchestra to master its complexities. The performance went as well as could be expected, but our adrenalin never stopped flowing throughout... It is a beautiful concerto, spare, with an undertone of sadness; it was, we both think, underestimated, and I hope that one day it will be revived.

John and I had begun giving public performances together in 1962, and over the years we gradually built up a solid reputation as a team. Apart, as John says, from a few Chabriers, we must have covered the entire two-piano literature, and he keeps promising to compose something for both of us himself. Alas, he has yet to do so – writing well for two pianos, he explains, is the most exacting of exercises. But he enjoys performing our duo recitals as much as I do.

One of the most unusual of the contemporary pieces we have played was called "Textures" by the American composer Henri Lazarof. We first performed it in Warsaw; Henri made the trip with us, and gave us very precise instructions about the way he wanted the music interpreted – including the use of a drumstick *inside* the piano, producing a thrilling and original sound that sent shivers the length of my spine.

John was to use a drumstick in much the same way during a solo performance of Robert Sherlaw Johnson's haunting Second Sonata at the Queen Elizabeth Hall; however, he not only had to strike the strings, he had to pluck them as well! In the third movement, he was expected to alternate between standing and sitting with the speed and endurance of an athlete; and no one who was at the recital that night will forget the sight of his portly figure throwing itself about as the sweat flew and his beard wagged with his concentrated effort. The piece must have given him some of the hardest exercise he has

107

ever had in his life – and he was rewarded with a storm of applause.

There are many other living composers John admires and whose work he plays: Ronald Stevenson, Christopher Headington, David Blake: and Malcolm Williamson, whose Third Concerto John had premiered in Sydney on our first Australian tour, and who dedicated his Sonata for Two Pianos to us. Of profound musical and personal importance to John is the American Richard Yardumian; and there is a special place in our hearts for Gerard Schurmann who, in our hard times, was to prove an invaluable friend.

And very far from least, there is George Lloyd, the Cornish composer, who in addition to seven operas and eight symphonies has written a piano concerto known as "Scapegoat". It was dedicated to John, who premiered it in Liverpool in 1964, and who refers to it in awe as "almost a masterpiece". Ruddy faced, bluff and hearty, George is a master of orchestration, and he was to give unstinting and invaluable guidance when John was composing his own piano concerto.

15

John's Piano Concerto is the most ambitious of his compositions so far. It is a forceful, even at times flamboyant work, superbly orchestrated; "he has a flair for handling big and
complicated structures" *The Times* wrote, "without losing what
the pop world would call 'the big beat'." Of course, no virtuoso
of John's temperament could ignore the romantic tradition,
and he candidly admits to echoes of Liszt in the writing – also of
Busoni and Ravel. He tried hard to keep the form clear and the
music as accessible as possible to an audience: he also attempted to simplify the musical textures to make the concerto easier
to perform (though "easy" in John's vocabulary does not mean
the same thing as in most people's). Over all, John is very
proud of this work, and he unabashedly enjoys performing it in
public.

He has played it often both in Europe and America, always
to enthusiastic reception, and he recorded it for EMI in 1970.
Its very first performance was of a particular significance to
John though, because it took place at the 1968 Cardiff Festival
of Twentieth Century Music. This was the second year of the
Festival that John had told me, on a beach at Lagonissi, he was
determined, one day, to found. Now here it was, a reality – a
dream become wonderfully true.

He had set it up with Dr. Alun Hoddinott, an enthusiastic
and straightforward Welshman who is himself an exciting
composer. Alun was also professor elect, and soon to be professor, at Cardiff University, in charge of the second largest
music department in Britain. The money for the Festival was
largely provided by enterprising local authorities, notably
Cardiff City and Glamorgan County Councils, as well as the
Welsh Arts Council.

John, of course, being John was not concerned with the

financial aspects; but during the two years that he was the Festival's Artistic Director, he gave it his time, his dedication, and conviction. It was planned to include performances by leading artists – including, of course, John himself – as well as seminars in which composers and performers would discuss their work with the public; there was also a rehearsal orchestra under John Carewe, which gave young composers the rare chance of hearing their own works being played by professionals. As for the Festival's overall aim – it was, as John himself wrote, "to present this century's music in an historical perspective," in addition to demonstrating that "at the present time music of Steinbeckian passion is being created by composers of totally opposed aesthetic orientations." He added "I think it is our duty to show these polarities of thought clearly and without prejudice".

That duty the Festival faithfully fulfilled. The music of this century ranges from Rachmaninov through Stravinsky, Britten and Boulez: Busoni, Scriabin, and Szymanovski: Messiaen, Walton and Goehr – and compositions by all of them were played at the first Festival alone. New works were specially commissioned from Alan Rawsthorne and Grace Williams: while at John's urging, compositions by Gershwin and Duke Ellington were revived. There was a place for modern jazz, too.

And, of course, amongst the many Twentieth Century composers given an airing at the Festival was John Ogdon himself. In 1967, he played his rhythmic and exuberant "Dance Suite", which was inspired by ritual dances associated with spring: and the following year – the last in which he was to give so much time to the Festival – saw the world premiere of the Ogdon concerto.

John, who has had so many works dedicated to him, has been equally generous to others. His Theme and Variations for example were composed for none other than his former rival and present good friend Vladimir Ashkenazy. Volodya, as he is known to his friends, performed it first at the Cheltenham Festival in 1966; the critics liked the work, most of them noting the Lisztian influence, but few of them remarking on the Russian ambiance John had done his best to include. One or two reviewers expressed their surprise that so mammoth a programmer as John should have written a piece lasting a mere seven minutes: but as a composer, at least, going on for too long has never been one of John's problems.

He has also written three piano sonatas, as well as five brilliant Preludes, which he sometimes uses as encores. But of all his solo piano works, I think his own favourite is one that was written for me. Just as he tried to introduce a Russian element for Ashkenazy in his "Variations", so he deliberately reflected my strengths by basing the piece's technical requirements in part on Mozart, in part on Stravinsky. John named the piece "Sonatina", and I have played it often in public.

John has also composed sonatas for solo violin and solo cello; a string quartet, a quintet for brass and within the last year or two, a sonata for solo flute. For some time, too, he has been brooding over what should prove the most daunting project he has ever attempted – a full length Symphony inspired by the work of Herman Melville.

John's growing reputation both as a writer and performer of contemporary music soon made him the obvious target for almost every would-be composer in Britain. With each morning post, it seemed, a new manuscript would be forced through the letter box; and by the mid '60s, every day of the week would bring one, two, or more calls from poverty-stricken young people eager to show John their work. On top of our already over-stretched schedules, such calls were more than a nuisance: but what made the situation even worse was that if John himself were to answer the telephone, he would always say "Yes" to his callers – he simply could never bring himself to give a flat "No". Some of these hopefuls he did see, and there was a constant flow of young strangers in and out of the house; but when he was tired or wanted to work – or felt lazy – he would inevitably call upon me to get him out of the commitment he had made. "Say I've had to leave home to stand in for someone" he would tell me: "Say I'm on tour", "Say I've got food-poisoning. Say anything!" I had to turn away so many long-haired youths and girls in baggy corduroy trousers, to inure myself to the look of hurt disappointment in eyes that had been so optimistic a moment before. As I accepted the thick and thumbed manuscripts, I could sense their resentment, even their hatred, because I was keeping my husband away

111

from them. I guessed they must think me a cold-hearted bitch; and sadly, I have learned, I was right... We went ex-directory, of course – as early as 1964; but somehow people still managed to get hold of our number.

But though John could not – and would not – see every aspiring composer, though he could not look at every new musical piece, he has never wavered in his support of neglected genius, whatever its period. Pondering this aspect, among others, of John, in an article in the *Saturday Review*, Irving Kolodin wondered whether he should be typed as a PSPE – Pianistic Scholar Par Excellence – or as belonging to an even more rarified order, CLPC – Champion of Lost Pianistic Causes: he finally decided, instead, that John's ability to identify with the music he plays, however diverse the composers, qualifies him above all as a PC – a Pianistic Chameleon. But personally, I still find myself very tempted by that category of CLPC.....

And yet, however diversified John's musical interests, it is important to stress that his taste is also discriminating, and that he will not touch any composition he does not admire, however attractive the inducement may be.

I particularly remember one occasion after he had played the Tchaikovsky Concerto in the Salle Pleyel in Paris, when we were invited to supper at Maxim's. The party consisted of about twenty people, including John Pritchard – in his element in so legendary a restaurant. Also present was a composer of enormous personal charm, who had written a piano concerto which, as he made very clear, he was hoping John would soon play in public. John, who had already glanced through the work, had not liked it; now, though, he was facing strong pressure directly, and for once he could not hide behind me. At first I feared he might crumble; but I soon realised there was no need to worry. Witnessing the determination he showed, I found myself thinking again that my husband's more usual vagueness was a most effective way of recruiting people around him to the service of an unbending will.

The very next morning, however, the matter of the composer's concerto was raised once more: it was suggested that if John were after all to change his mind, he could expect a substantial gift of some sort – say, a brand new luxury car. But still John's resolve did not waver: and where his musical convictions are concerned, his compliance will never be bought.

112

Whatever his failings and flaws, John's is a true and individual voice: and both as a performer and as a composer, he has contributed immeasurably to the musical life of our time.

16

Constant touring in the ten years following Moscow merges into a blur of huge multi-tiered opera houses and humble village halls, of thousands of faces ranged blob-like in darkened, anonymous rows. But during most of John's tours, there would be some incident that would stand out: not, ironically, the triumphs so much, as irritations and small silly incidents.

One such incident occurred the year after our first Australian tour, when, in the summer of 1965, John was asked to return to Spoleto. True, there was no signed and sealed contract, but the Festival used to be impromptu by nature; and I urged him to go and to combine the engagement with a holiday. With a little pressure on my part, John agreed.

I felt badly in need of a break at that time. On 26th April, I had given birth to a 9-pound baby boy in only two and a half hours, in a nursing home; and in what was by now predictable style, John's first brief look at his son was taken en route to the airport. Unfortunately, my post-natal care was atrocious (the place has since been closed down): I was unable to go home for three weeks, when I was still almost too weak to walk. Only on entering our house did I learn that our au pair had suddenly left after a row with my mother.

In spite of baby Richard's calm and consistently cheerful nature, it was almost more than I could manage to run the household myself. In fact, very frail as I was, I was getting close to the breaking point when I found a Swiss girl to live in. Plump, efficient and happy, she looked after me and the family better than I could have dared hope; but I could not shake off my depression, and I yearned for the hot sun of Italy.

Not a moment too soon, the time came for us to leave. John and I landed in our beloved Rome, where we hired a car and a

114

chauffeur and set off on the seventy-mile drive to Spoleto. From the start, though, the sky had been overcast – and before long it started to drizzle, and the drizzle soon turned into rain. By the time we arrived in the town in the middle of the afternoon, we were caught in a torrential downpour; the square's romantic beauty was blotted out, and water poured down the sloping streets like rivers.

The office for the Festival was not where it had been on our last visit. Telling the chauffeur to wait with our luggage, John and I braved the elements to look for it: but at siesta time the streets were almost deserted, and the very few people we did meet claimed they knew nothing about it. So we poked our noses into all the local bars and restaurants, and into the lobbies of the theatre and the concert hall: among the faces that turned to look at us was not a single one that we knew. "This is ridiculous, it's not possible!" I told John, my temper beginning to rise. "They must have booked us a hotel room – let's go and register at least!"

My hair in rat-tails and John's beard dripping like several taps, we went up to the hotel's reception desk. "No, no reservations for Ogdon, I'm sorry" – no, and no rooms to spare. No one would admit to knowing where the Festival office now was. And still there was not one person whom we knew by sight, or who appeared to recognise John: Spoleto, booked up though it was, was a ghost town on that afternoon.

Suddenly, our chauffeur charged into the lobby and started to act in the most florid of operatic styles. He was sick of this ridiculous chase, we had been here for almost three hours – he had a home, and other jobs to be doing, and if we were not ready to leave with him now, he would abandon our cases on the street and drive back to Rome on his own.

I turned from the counter to glare at John. "Well – are we staying or aren't we?"

His raincoat clung to his large body: he looked back at me solemnly through his rain-spattered glasses. "I think we might as well push off" he said.

Halfway to Rome, the clouds began to lift; fields sparkled like the ocean in the rays of the late sun. I glanced at John, he caught my eye – and both of us burst into laughter. It all seemed so ludicrous suddenly – Spoleto, the weather, even the missing au pair . . .

From that moment on, I began to feel very much better: my appetite came back and I started putting on weight. But we never heard again, that summer, from anyone involved with the Festival...

The following year, we were back in Italy once more; John had several engagements – this time, all of them confirmed! – including appearances at the Michelangeli Festival in Brescia and Bergamo.

In Brescia, we were joined by two of our closest friends, Ben and Val Worthington, who came with me to all the concerts John was giving. One of these was scheduled for a Sunday; our concert organisation had told us it was to be held in a town called Legnano, and I agreed to drive the four of us there in a car I had hired.

John had played the same concerto with the same orchestra only a day before, in another town, and consequently there was no need for an afternoon rehearsal. So only on the Sunday morning itself did Ben – a very British stockbroker – look up Legnano on the map. He frowned: "We have to drive right across Milan to get there!"

"No, it's not *that* Legnano" I said. "John gave a concert in that one not very long ago – there has to be another one, closer."

"Mmmm..." Ben studied the map again in silence. Then he said "Could it be Lignano instead of Legnano?"

"Well..." I was doubtful. "It could be, I suppose."

"In that case" he announced "we're in trouble, because it's a hundred and fifty miles from here easily – east of Venice."

"It *can't* be!"

"And is it Lignano Pianeta or Lignano Sabbiadoro we want?"

I grabbed the map away from him, and in my turn pored over it. After a few moments I said triumphantly "It's neither! Here – south east of Padua: a place called Legnaro! It's a hundred miles away at the most."

Ben came to stand beside me. "Oh yes..." A brief pause: then he added "But are you sure it isn't Legnago?" He pointed to a small town beyond Mantua. "That's a bit closer to here."

John had joined us by this time. "What about Lonigo?" he offered. "It's about the same distance away as Legnago."

Panic ensued. "Call up the concert organisation!" – no good, today was a Sunday, it was closed. No one who knew anything about the concert was reachable by phone. We did not know what to do – and what made everything worse was that not only would an audience be waiting for John, but the entire orchestra as well.

For an hour we argued – Legnago, Legnaro, or even, at a long shot, Lonigo – which was it going to be? And I have to confess that as a result of all the confusion, I have forgotten which one we eventually went to: I simply decided to act as chauffeur and leave the map-reading to Ben.

On the drive, which must have taken over two hours, everyone was in rumbustious high spirits, John laughing the most of us all. But not until we arrived at the central square and saw the posters with John's name did we know that the town we had chosen was the right one.

Three months after those 1966 Italian concerts, John set off for another tour of Austria and Germany as soloist with the London Philharmonic Orchestra with John Pritchard conducting. I, as usual, went with him.

The first stop of the tour was Vienna. Our flight landed there in the morning; there was to be a rehearsal that afternoon and the concert was due to take place the same evening.

We were still out at the airport when the worried orchestral manager, Eric Bravington, hurried up to us to tell us that John's suitcase was missing.

"Oh, no," I said. "All his clothes are inside it!"

Quietly, John added "Including my tails."

There was no chance of buying new tails in John's size before the concert. So after the rehearsal, we returned to our hotel while Eric raced round the orchestra members on the scrounge.

He returned at last with a shirt lent by one musician, a bow tie from another, cuff links from a third: John Pritchard, also a big man, contributed his dinner jacket, which fitted John adequately if not well. But there were no spare evening trousers, so John had to wear the flannels in which he had travelled, as well as his workaday shoes. And dressed in this haphazard ensemble, he walked onto the platform a short time later – and, if anyone noticed something odd about his appearance,

117

nobody remarked on it to me.

In Innsbruck, the next stop, Eric took John out shopping for a new piece of luggage and a new lot of clothes, all of which were bought off the peg. As Eric pointed out, it was lucky for John we were in Austria, because nowhere else are so many men overweight!

The tour had been as tightly scheduled as the earlier one in 1963. Soon everyone was worn out; and as John was playing the Tchaikovsky No. 1 concerto all the way on this trip, it was decided on reaching Freiburg that a rehearsal need not be called. John was for once so exhausted that he spent the afternoon in the hotel, not even bothering to try out the piano.

The Freiburg hall is a vast one, and every seat had been taken. The overture went smoothly as usual, and then the piano was rolled into its place. The coughing died away in the audience, and to a smattering of polite applause, John walked on to the platform. Reaching the piano, he stopped, bowed with his modest little smile, and turned to lift the lid off the keyboard.

It did not move. He tried again. He made a third attempt, more energetic, trying to force the lid open: still it refused to budge. Realising at the same moment as John did that the piano was locked, the audience started to titter. John stood scowling a few moments longer, staring into the wings, but no one appeared to assist him. Raising his shoulders, he strode off the stage.

The audience was kept waiting while pandemonium raged behind the scenes. Finally, somewhere deep in the basement, a dozing old man was discovered with a bunch of keys attached to his belt; he was hurried out on to the platform, and to a roar of applause, he unlocked the offending lid. John came back to an ovation – but this time he wasted no time on bows but sat down, still scowling, at the keyboard. The first chords of the concerto almost shattered the instrument with their force – and he followed them with some of the most dazzling playing he has given in his whole life. Afterwards, the audience went wild – stamping and yelling its approval. In fact, I think John had more applause at that one concert than in the whole of the tour put together.

He had another adventure with a piano less than a year

118

later, in 1967 – this time in Vancouver, one of his favourite cities. The stage in the concert hall where he was playing was raked slightly, and so to keep the piano from rolling, all its legs had to be wedged; but on this particular occasion one of the wedges had not been positioned correctly. The concerto was the Rachmaninov Third, never t e easiest of works – and John found to his horror that every ti ne he used either pedal, the entire piano would lurch drunkenly to one side. "This" one critic noted "may have been the reason why Ogdon was not as infallibly accurate as usual."

Equally alarming was a lunchtime concert he gave in Manchester in 1973, which was being broadcast "live". John was performing some Chopin studies when the piano's loud pedal fell off. Bravely, he carried on with what his radio audience must have thought was a most unusual interpretation. Meanwhile a tuner tiptoed on to the platform; and during the unusually long announcement into the following piece, he crawled under the instrument by John's feet and managed – barely – to fix the pedal back into place.

John has played so many Promenade Concerts at the Royal Albert Hall that he probably feels less nervous about performing there than anywhere else in the world. But one Prom he will never forget took place in 1967, when he had been engaged to play the Prokofiev Concerto No. 2 in G minor, under Sir Malcolm Sargent.

Sleek haired and fastidiously elegant, Sir Malcolm knew exactly what he was up to as a performer as well as a musician. Once, for example, a television producer wanted to put a camera in the middle of the orchestra to give close-ups of the conductor. Sir Malcolm, when he was approached, proved more amenable than had been expected. "But tell me" he asked the producer, "when you are actually showing me to the viewers, will the red transmission light come up on the camera?"

"Oh no, we'll cover that up" he was assured. "We wouldn't dream of distracting you!"

"On the contrary" said Sir Malcolm. "I won't let you have the camera unless I can see the light." And throughout the subsequent performance, he kept a weather eye on it: and every time the bulb would glow red, his eyebrows would arch that little more expressively, and his expression of pain or of rapture would be just that degree more intense. His musical integrity, of course, was not diminished, and the Promenaders loved him for his showmanship.

On this occasion, the rehearsal with the orchestra went smoothly and John came home to change in a relaxed and expansive mood. At that time we were living in Golders Green, and as usual I was going to drive him to the Albert Hall for the performance.

I put on a formal elegant dress, and helped John with his studs and his cuff links before giving his coat a last brush. Then we set off in heavy rain, up the hill towards Hampstead. When we were close to the top, the car sputtered, picked up again, sputtered some more – and came to a stop.

I tried frantically to restart it, but the engine would not spark. Again I tried – and again.

John, resplendent in his tails looked at me sideways. "What's wrong, Brenda?"

"The car won't go, what do you think!" His mechanical uselessness in such moments always infuriated me. I made another attempt – no luck. "Wait here" I told him.

I ran through the rain to a nearby pub and phoned a mini cab firm: "I'm sorry, Madam, all our cars are on call."

"But my husband's playing at the Albert Hall! Thousands of people are waiting for him!"

"Sorry, Madam."

A second firm proved equally busy – a third did not bother to answer. There were less than fifty minutes left before the concerto was likely to start: desperately, I dialled the Royal Albert Hall.

"This is John Ogdon's wife, we're stuck in Hampstead, you've got to send us a car and maybe change the programme order!"

The man I had spoken to said that he could not help me, but that he would pass me on to somebody else – who transferred me in turn to a third person. Not forty five minutes left now, and we had to get across London. "There must be *someone* who can pick us up!"

"I'm sorry . . ."

I slammed down the phone and hurried back to the car; I pulled open the passenger door. "Get out" I snapped. "We're going by tube."

John stared back at me, incredulous.

"Get out or you'll miss the whole concert!"

He did not argue. Together we ran across a corner of the soaked, muddy Heath and down the hill towards the tube station – pedestrians scattered in the path of John's lumbering bulk, while his cummerbund slipped up and his tails flapped in the breeze behind him. We bought our tickets to South Kensington and went down to the platform.

A train did not come for several minutes – John, puffing and panting from his effort, restlessly paced up and down. When at last the train did arrive, people stared at the wet goateed man in full evening dress, scowling as he gnawed on his nails. We changed trains at Leicester Square: we had little more than fifteen minutes to go.

At last we reached South Kensington – five minutes if we were lucky. John's breath came in noisy gasps as we raced down the long corridors under the road; then we had to brave the elements again for the last few hundred yards. A reception committee, by this time alerted to the gravity of the situation, was waiting at the Albert Hall's stage door, peering into the night. John was grabbed by anxious hands and all but carried towards the stage: in the distance, we heard the final strains of Sibelius's Seventh Symphony and the outbreak of applause. While I tried to straighten John's hair, someone dabbed at his rain-soaked jacket with a towel. Sir Malcolm came off stage, oblivious of the panic, smiled at John, and led him out, still breathless, to face the throng of young Promenaders.

Again, John played superbly. Indeed, it is my experience that an artist will often perform at his best immediately after a crisis.

In the spring of 1968, we received a letter from André Previn, inviting us to play the following year in Houston, Texas, where he was conductor of the Symphony Orchestra. He suggested an interesting programme – the American première of Tippett's Piano Concerto to be given by John: then Bach's Concerto for Two Pianos and Orchestra, and finally, Mozart's Concerto in F major for Three Pianos and Orchestra, in which Previn himself would be playing. We accepted without hesitation.

121

For me, this would be my first really important orchestral date in the States; and over the months, I practised very hard for it. The trouble was, I could not get John to study with me – in fact, he was so busy rushing from one end of the world to the other that we never sat down to rehearse together at all.

And so one Friday in March, John came home from a major Soviet tour: and the very next morning, we set off for Texas.

We had two days in Houston to recover from jet-lag before giving the first of the concerts (we were to play the programme twice) – and they were a memorable two days for both of us because of André's irresistible company. He has a spontaneous but sophisticated West Coast humour, and I at least spent much of my time trying to get back my breath between sets of near-helpless giggles. And André has other rare attributes – he looks at you as if he is genuinely interested, and, what is more, he listens in the same way.

But much as we were enjoying ourselves with André, I was a mass of nerves over the impending concerts – so far as I knew, John had hardly looked at the Bach double Concerto. As things turned out, I was right – I do not know if André suspected the truth, but John was using the orchestral rehearsal as his one chance to practise the piece. And even though we had played the Mozart in public before, he had not worked on it for a very long time – and Mozart was still not John's technical forte.

I was deeply upset – even if his prodigious talent did allow him to take such foolhardy risks, he was not being fair to himself and most certainly not fair to me. After the rehearsal was over and the orchestra had been dismissed, I insisted that John stay behind with me and practise the Mozart cadenza and all of the Bach once again.

In spite of this extra practice session, I was a little disappointed with John's performance and mine as well on the first public performance – though the reviews the next day were all excellent. But the second night went very much better: and in spite of my nerves, I have never enjoyed playing orchestral concerts as much as I did in Houston with André.

André Previn looks witty: but at first sight, Sir Georg Solti would not strike most people as the lightest of all personalities. But his eyes soon give him away: they are wonderful eyes – alive, very humorous, and bright.

John has played with him on many occasions, but one appearance in Jerusalem with the Israel Philharmonic particularly sticks in our memories.

On the morning that they were due to play, an official-looking note was shoved under the door of John's hotel room. "By Order of the Chief Rabbi" John read, "all beards are to be shaved off on this Most Holy of Days".

An alarmed John was going to ring down to the hotel lobby for confirmation when he remembered the date – it was April Fool's day.

He had no doubts as to the culprit's identity: and he resolved to get his own back. The concerto he was playing that night was the Liszt E Flat major – and when the time came for the cadenza, John went instead into one from the Tchaikovsky First. Solti swung to look at him, pale with surprise and alarm, before John returned triumphantly to the one Liszt had written.

Afterwards, Solti was very good about it. But I wonder what the musical Israelis made of the transposed cadenza. In any case, no critic so much as mentioned it the following morning.

In the summer of 1970, John was invited, together with Janet Baker, to be a soloist with the New Philharmonia Orchestra on its visit to Japan for the Expo '70 celebrations: and as the plane taking everyone out there was chartered, I was able to go along too at no extra expense.

We were both looking forward to the trip. John loves Japan, with its many contrasts – the flashy Western exterior and the hints of a different culture beneath: the modern conveniences and comfort and the delicate and stylised ancient rituals: the noisy bustle of the streets and the serenity of the old temples. And of course, it was exciting to be travelling there with fellow artists of so high a calibre.

We liked Janet Baker from the start. She is an unpretentious Yorkshirewoman, and during the night hours of the endless flight, she thought nothing of going to sleep stretched out on the floor of the cabin. She travelled with us in the first class compartment of the plane, along with her husband Keith and the tour's two conductors, John Pritchard and Ted Downes: and she never got fussed or more than humourously upset by the delays which plagued the long trip.

The first hold-up was in Rome, when we had to refuel. The next was in Bangkok, where we waited for five or six hours. By the time we finally took off again, we had been on the trip for almost a night and a day.

...Time seemed to be passing incredibly slowly. The plane tilted slightly and straightened: beneath us there was nothing but cloud stretching from horizon to horizon. In the economy section behind us, the air was getting thicker and steamier; smoke drifted over the seats, and most of the people not fast asleep were now tipsy. In our section of the plane, Janet was dozing – so was John and almost everyone else. The plane tilted again, more steeply this time.

Something was not right, I was sure of it. I thought of waking John, but looking at his curly slumped head, I had not the heart. I got up and walked down the aisle to where the orchestra's personnel manager, Chris Yates, was sitting. "What's happening, Chris?" I asked.

"Now don't worry, Brenda" he said. "Our pilot's never flown over this region before, and he's not certain of our position. That's all."

"That's all!" I yelped. "What do you mean by 'this region' anyway?"

"Well . . . we're somewhere over Vietnam."

"Vietnam!" I gasped at him.

"I said Vietnam." He smiled slightly, spreading his hands.

I went back to my seat very shaken. The war was still in full swing: I found myself searching the clouds below for a squadron of enemy fighters, for signs of a rocket piercing the clouds . . .

Eventually we landed in Tokyo, many hours later than scheduled. There we were to learn that I had not been alone in my alarm.

Soon after our arrival, we were at a superb party thrown for us all by the British Ambassador, Sir John Pilcher, when the wife of the first clarinettist, Jack Brymer, came up to join John and me. "I've just been to a reception on a British ship" she told us, "and the officers were all commiserating with me over our awful experience. I asked them what they were talking about, and they answered 'When your pilot got lost.' After all, they said, it's not often that the British navy is put on alert to watch out for a plane that's gone missing!"

I wondered if Chris had known about that – if so, I was glad he had spared me!

After the Japanese tour was over, John allowed himself only a short holiday in Spain before resuming the crazy pace of his career. By now, the strain had at last begun to show – he was smoking almost non-stop, and drinking more heavily than in the past.

I remonstrated with him, I tried to persuade him to slow down. But John was not only getting more assertive with each month that passed: there were moments of a dark and smouldering irritation that kept my protestations at a safe distance.

From August 1970 and well into 1971, the concerts never let up for a moment. Typical of his schedule is this one from mid-March – and it included many changes of repertoire as well as the socialising he loved. He gave a recital in Malvern on the 11th, and another in Yarmouth next day; on the thirteenth he gave a live broadcast from the Royal Festival Hall in London. The following night, he starred with Larry Adler in a gala concert of Gershwin music, held at the Phoenix Theatre in the presence of Princess Margaret. The 16th and 18th saw him playing concertos in Switzerland: on the 20th he was back in England to play the Rachmaninov Paganini Variations in Manchester, and on the 21st in Leeds. 24th March was a recital date in Lambeth; 27th March was an engagement in Croydon's Fairfield Halls. And at the beginning of May, we went to Russia again.

There was no one at Moscow airport to meet us, and we found ourselves stuck in the customs hall in the middle of disorganised crowds. Anyone who has experienced that cold and cavernous place, with armed soldiers, dour officials and rough shoving queues, will know very well how we felt. But fortunately, another uncanny ability of John's is for memorising telephone numbers; and he was actually able to remember that of Sir Duncan Wilson, the British Ambassador. So after an urgent call to his residence, it was not long before an Embassy official appeared; and with confidence and convincing panache, he extracted us from the unfriendly chaos.

He took us straight to the Metropole Hotel. We had barely stepped into our luxurious room on the top floor when the official said "All right, lets find the bugs" – and started to look for them on door frames, behind pictures, and under the bed.

"You can't do that" John said – adding naively "They'll hear you!"

"What's the point of pretending, John? Everyone knows what's going on." Smiling wickedly, he continued "If you only knew what we say to the Embassy bugs when there aren't any women around!"

The next morning, our Russian interpreter, Nina, turned up at last; to John's unconcealed delight, she was blonde, rather beautiful, and unexpectedly trendy in her style of dress. She stayed with us for the entire tour, which in addition to Moscow included Kiev, Vilnius, Riga, and Leningrad.

But for both of us, Tbilisi in Georgia was the most exciting place that we visited. It combines a gaudy Eastern atmosphere with a sunny and mountainous setting; women are rarely seen on the streets, and the men have a dark Tartar look. With my blonde hair and fair skin, I was gaped at wherever we went: but the people were very hospitable, and we were taken out into the country for feasts of lamb on skewers, which we ate crouched at very low tables, and which lasted for several hours.

The most depressing point of the entire trip came right at its start. We had arrived from London without knowing exactly what the schedule would be, which is normal on Soviet tours. Nina told us that the first engagement was to be in Lvov, near the Polish border.

We could not believe it when we saw the aircraft that was to take us there; it was an ancient propeller plane of a make unknown to us – to me it looked almost home-made. And incredulity turned into amazement when we saw our travelling companions – they were mostly peasants dressed in black, doggedly bringing into the cabin everything that they possessed. Babies suckled, chickens with tied legs looked round with darting eyes, cheeses, fruit and sausages bulged out of string bags, and cases were piled along the aisle as though this was some kind of travelling warehouse.

The flight itself turned into a three-and-a-half-hour nightmare. The pressure system in the cabin was inadequate; we all felt giddy from lack of oxygen, and our ears were popping continuously. As the plane bounced drunkenly over the clouds, babies screamed, chickens squawked, and over-ripe fruit spilled into the aisles. John held tight to the arms of his seat, snorting nervously the while, and even Nina looked pale.

But at last the ordeal was over, and we disembarked at Lvov airport. A representative of Gosconcert greeted us distractedly before turning to Nina and launching into a loud stream of Russian. She replied with equal animation, suddenly very pink-cheeked.

For ages, it seemed, the argument went on; our pleas for an explanation were ignored. Then Nina swung round to face us: she said "We have no concert here in Lvov!"

There was no plane back to Moscow that day. We were taken to an ugly modern hotel: apart from an unsprung bed, the room was almost unfurnished, and the plumbing was worse than unspeakable.

No one apologised to us for the débâcle; but in what we took for an unspoken atonement, we were presented with tickets for the Lvov Ballet Company that evening.

What the ballet was called, I do not know; but the costumes were hideous, the corps undisciplined, and the prima ballerina was fat. Towards the end of the last act, the unfortunate lady raised herself on one point, tumbled against her partner, and in a froth of frills and shaking flesh, collapsed in a heap on the floor. It was the last straw for John and me: I sat in an agony of barely stifled giggles, while his bulk shook the row of seats like an earthquake.

Next day we went back to Moscow on an equally dreadful flight; and some time later, an official at last had the grace to admit that there had been a misunderstanding over the dates. And I must give the Russians due credit – they did pay John's full fee for the non-existent concert, which would not have happened in all other countries.

And whatever the drawbacks of the tour, it was still a marvellous experience. John and his Russian audiences continued their passionate love affair: each time he performed alone or with orchestra, he was given a reception of such spontaneous rapture that he could not help but be moved to the heart.

Life with John in those years was demanding, lonely and exhausting; it kept us apart too often, and by that I do not mean only physically. But it was unpredictable and changing, and it was never less than exciting. I wanted nothing better from Fate than to go on being Mrs. John Ogdon.

17

If John had to name his favourite pianist, I have no doubt he would choose Vladimir Horowitz.

In 1966, this legendary artist made his return to the concert platform at Carnegie Hall after an absence of almost twelve years. Excitement in the music world reached fever-pitch: queues stretched round the block from the box-office for days in advance, and even for established soloists, tickets were rarer than gold dust. John, to his delight, had been offered a seat, though he was due to perform in Washington DC on the same day. As luck would have it, however, Horowitz's recital was to take place in the afternoon, while John's was not until the evening. So in the morning, he flew to New York, listened to the master's performance, and then rushed back to Washington just in time to give his own recital.

Horowitz's programme included the Bach Busoni C major Organ Toccata, the Schumann Fantasie, and Liszt's Danse Macabre – and his interpretation of these works lived up to John's expectations, and more. It is fair to say that this one recital was an inspiration to John musically for years.

Horowitz is a technical master who can do whatever he wants at the keyboard: his tone and his line can be magical. But his interpretations too can be demoniacally driven: the astounded listener is carried away on a journey of exhilarating danger. Sadly, like John, Horowitz has paid for his demons.

During much of his time away from the platform, this lean and sensitive man did not want to leave his apartment, and he showed little interest in playing. But even someone of his world-wide reputation has not got endless financial resources; and it is said that when at last he was forced to sell the Picasso "Blue Boy" he owned, he told friends "Now I have to earn money for the groceries." And so he returned to the platform with that superb Carnegie Hall recital.

Since then he has been playing with increasing regularity all over the States – though he almost always insists on performing in the afternoons, so that he has less time in which to get nervous. He has other idiosyncracies too – for example, he refuses to fly, and travels with his personal cook.

Happily for John, he enjoys meeting talented young pianists, and one day we were taken to his Manhattan apartment by our agent at the time, Harold Shaw. The room we were ushered into was dark, with a silk sofa, heavy curtain drapes, and beautiful bibelots everywhere; it was a luxurious cocoon of a place. We were greeted by his wife Wanda, daughter of the great Toscanini: but we had to wait a few minutes before being joined by the maestro himself. The long, thin, beak-nosed face was ashen pale, and as usual, he wore a dark suit, white shirt and a large, brightly coloured bow tie. He looked just like what he is in fact: a living legend.

But the legend soon proved to be jokey and charming – and before long, he and John were deep in discussion about composers and interpretative problems. He asked John to demonstrate a point on the piano – John obliged, and at once Horowitz joined him to play a few measures. Soon they were both playing in turn – Schumann, Liszt, Rachmaninov . . . "The line," Horowitz would say. "I base it on listening to singers, the human voice is the best teacher of all." And so they continued – excited, oblivious, lost to the everyday world.

We returned to the apartment more than once after that, and the story was always the same. I think that if you had told John in his Royal College years that one day he would be playing with Horowitz, he would probably have passed out in shock; and even now, with his own name firmly established, he still felt like a disciple at the feet of the Master.

The same year that John went to the Carnegie recital in New York, we heard Artur Rubinstein at the Festival Hall – in my case, for the first time. I was as stunned by the eighty-year-old pianist as John had been earlier by Horowitz. When he started to play Chopin, the tears literally poured down my face – I had never before heard anything quite so exquisite. John was profoundly moved too; for us both, it was a memorable recital.

There are no driven demons in Rubinstein. His playing is

unmannered and pure; and he has mastered the hardest of lessons – the art of total simplicity.

It never ceases to amaze me that some people – even some third rate musicians – can state that there is an artificial mystique about the great soloists, that the only thing that is really required is a sense of rhythm and an ability to hit the right notes. They might as well say that all an actor needs to play Hamlet is a feeling for poetic metre and a capacity for remembering the lines. It may sound obvious, but in my experience it still needs to be said: the force of personality colouring a performance is as varied in Horowitz and Rubinstein as it is in Olivier and Brando.

It is sad that failing eyesight has at last forced Rubinstein from the platform. But by all accounts he remains open and expansive, a brilliant raconteur and wit: his own stories can reduce him as well as others to tears of the purest enjoyment, as we have found out for ourselves in Spain, and as John learned in Japan and New Zealand as well. In New York, his apartment looked well used and lived in: so too, of course, does his face.

One thing he does have in common with Horowitz – and, for that matter, with John – is physical stillness at the keyboard, though he was not averse to a little dramatic arm-lifting in the final few bars of a piece. He has said that too much bodily movement is often a compensation for inadequate ability: "When I see a pianist waving about in the slow movement, staring up into the air" he told us. "I wonder what is the matter with him. He is looking for a fly on the ceiling, perhaps?" With a malicious twinkle, he adds "You notice in the last movement he only has time to look at the keys!"

Another of John's idols is the Russian Sviatoslav Richter – who in some ways reminds me of John. Both are utterly immersed in music, often seeming in another world from the rest of us; both are socially gauche, and neither is naturally articulate.

Richter is a big man, balding and with a strong jaw. Having been familiar with his photographs alone, I was amazed when I first saw him on stage – he sidles in from the wings, looking as if he is going to trip over, with his head held deferentially to one side. Off stage, he is the only man I have met who can walk

131

towards you while giving the distinct impression that he is scuttling backwards towards the horizon. Indeed, on tour in America, he *has* been known to vanish from sight, once for several days – to the panic of the agency representative who was supposed to be looking after him. Later, I do not think anyone ever found out exactly what he had been up to.

He is the most gentle of men, but he can be temperamental as well. Several years ago, for example, he was due to give a televised recital from the Festival Hall with the great violinist David Oistrakh. In rehearsal, he claimed that the television lighting was blinding him; at his insistence, lamp after lamp was switched off, and only when the hall was darker than it would have been for an ordinary concert did the pianist profess himself satisfied. The television recording had to be cancelled, the audience sat enveloped in gloom – and Richter played like an angel.

Though John was not jealous of the older generation of pianists, he used to be competitive to the point of resentment with many of his contemporaries. But even in his early career, there were some young pianists whom he openly admired. Stephen Bishop – later, Bishop-Kovacevich – was one, and John was to dedicate his Second Sonata to him. John has always been impressed by the exactness of his friend's rhythmic sense; Stephen is also the most honest of pianists, never faking or taking short cuts.

When we first knew the pugnacious-faced expatriate American, he used to be notorious for his changing romances with woman and with vintage cars – in the latter case, the bigger the better! In those days too, he was almost as sloppy as John. His room in London's Music Club was shambolic; scraps of food festered between magazines, and sandwiches somehow managed to crawl inside the piano to curl up and die on the strings. Quite when and how Stephen turned into the glamorous man of today, I am not sure; but now his surroundings are comfortable, he is invariably well dressed and neat, and his thick head of hair always gleams.

One of the greatest of all John's contemporaries is his former rival in Moscow, Vladimir Ashkenazy.

Like Stephen Bishop-Kovacevich, Volodya has changed

almost out of all recognition since we first knew him as a friend. That was the year after Moscow when – still the pride of the Soviet Union – he rocked the political and musical worlds by deciding to make his home in the West. In those early days of asylum, when he was living in London, he was retiring, pale and frail looking, hardly saying a word – though of course he was held back not only by shyness, but by a limited knowledge of English. It was a delight for both of us to see him open up and flower in just a few years – to discover his warmth, his wit and intelligence. Small and by no means conventionally hand-some, he is, to my mind, irresistible: when he is amused, his dark eyes sparkle, and his wide smile is immediately infectious ... I remember particularly the times when he would come to our house in 1966, to rehearse the Theme and Variations which John had composed for him – John was so large and docile and lumbering, Volodya so spare and so quick.

The two men are different in so many ways. Volodya is less tolerant of fools, and more uncompromising in his standards. Also, unlike John, he tries to avoid the constant socialising when he is off on a tour, preferring the company of a few close friends, and of his wife and children who usually travel with him. He bears out an apparent paradox that I have noticed throughout my life – that articulate and inquisitive people often seem happier in intimate groups, whereas the less socially gifted, like John, prefer big parties and a stream of new faces.

One innovation Volodya has made on the concert platform is to wear a dark suit and white polo necked sweater, which not only look good but are more comfortable than tails. But other-wise – apart from their musical interests – it is probably in matters sartorial that he and John are most alike. Volodya's suits ignore all the dictates of fashion – box-coated and narrow lapelled, they look as if he had brought them with him from Russia. Oddly enough, his attractive Icelandic wife Dodie is every bit as clothes-conscious as I am.

The most publicised winner of the Moscow Competition, or of any competition anywhere, was, of course, the Texan Van Cliburn. Four years before John and Volodya competed, he had returned to the States to be greeted like a conquering hero: he was idolised, feted and mobbed everywhere that he set foot. Such treatment could easily have gone to the head of an unwordly and very young man – but Van survived it completely unspoiled.

We met him originally at the Stratford Festival in Ontario, Canada, and both of us fell for his charm. Very tall, slim and snub-nosed, he still looks the epitome of the corn-fed all-American boy; he remains religious and conservative in outlook, and he is one of the very few people we have come across who is totally without any malice. He can be emotional too; in 1978, John sat on the jury of the Van Cliburn Competition in Fort Worth, Texas, and was touched to notice how involved Van became with the contestants and with their progress.

His generosity is matched by his modesty. I remember once hearing him give a recital in Philadelphia – after a slightly shaky start with a Bach Prelude and Fugue, he went on to give stunning accounts of the Barber Sonata and Ravel's "Jeux d'eau." But when we went backstage to see him, we found him full of apologies. "What a mess!" he told John. "The trouble was Eugene Ormandy phoned up to tell me you were going to be in the audience. It threw me – I was as nervous as hell!"

It is very much Britain's loss that Van refuses to play here. He has never completely recovered from the unwarranted savaging he received from some London critics not long after his triumph in Moscow. He thought then, and with reason, "With my career, I can easily do without England;" and he has almost never been back.

Critical blessings and bashings are all part of a musician's life, of course, and must be accepted as such. Only in one aspect do John and I believe that national papers are sometimes irresponsible – and that is in the case of young artists who are trying to start their careers. The London recitals at the Wigmore, the Purcell Room and the Queen Elizabeth Hall are usually paid for by the artist himself, often at considerable sacrifice and at a guaranteed financial loss: but a recital in one of these halls is the only way to get the national reviews, without which he has little chance of launching himself. But too often, some newspapers ignore such a recital as not being important enough.

But whether an artist is famous or not, his sensitivity to unfavourable criticism rarely diminishes with time. Even the most distinguished musicians can be very upset. Benjamin Britten was actually made ill, and in the mid-fifties his doctor forbade him to read his reviews.

Sir Georg Solti takes a more positive approach. One day he took John and me into a room in his London house, the walls of which were covered with awards, prizes and plaques. "If ever I get an unfavourable review" he told us, "I come here into this room to remind myself of what I have done – and right away I start feeling better."

Horowitz was not so easily comforted. At the time of his retirement, he is reputed to have said "The critics have exhausted their praise. If I were to keep on playing in public, I would only disappoint them, that's all." And in a way, those words proved prophetic. When he made his 1966 come back, the reviewers hailed him as a God returned among men: but with each successive appearance, their ardour has slowly cooled down. Not that they do not acknowledge that he is a phenomenon of our time; but now they see him again as a mortal, and so – as one more fine but fallible pianist.

John too can be hurt by a carping review. And naturally he feels threatened as well, because a nagging fear always persists that "what the man said" might be correct – even when the critics disagree amongst themselves. For example, in 1969, his pleasure in reading that the *Daily Telegraph*'s Peter Stadlen thought his performance of Beethoven's Sonata Op. 111 was "the strongest, truest and most penetrating I have ever heard" was overshadowed by his deep disappointment that the *Financial Times* critic "disliked the performance intensely". It is true of John and most artists, I think, that the reservations, not the praise, are remembered.

Even though John has mellowed with time, he does not get along with every musician he meets: but for the most part he revels in the company of his fellow soloists. And because he is generous with those whom he likes, they in turn also like him: because he is not by nature a back-biter, he is almost never bitten himself. In the bad years to come, the good will he had built up was to prove its worth in the support that was given him by so many colleagues.

135

18

As John's career had improved, so, dramatically, had our life-style.

In January 1965, we had left Isleworth for a larger, detached house in Golders Green: only two years later, we were out house-hunting again. With the children growing up fast, we already needed more space: and very important as well, we wanted a drawing room large enough to hold our two pianos, so that we could practise our duo recitals together.

At the end of 1967, we discovered the house of our dreams.

Anyone who knows Britain's capital must agree that the Regent's Park terraces designed by John Nash are amongst its most elegant sights. Pillared, pedimented, and cream coloured, dating from the 1820s, they ring the vast area of parkland like a succession of magnificent palaces, though each in fact is made up of individual houses. And one of these houses, we learned, was for sale.

Chester Terrace stands on the east side of the Park, separated from the public ring road by a long strip of garden and a small private street. The façade is embellished by Corinthian porticos, while identical floor-length windows open on to a balustraded balcony running the length of the building. This exterior had recently been repaired and repainted and the inside gutted and modernised, while retaining the handsome Nash style. There were five floors, counting the basement: three luxurious bathrooms: an intercom system throughout: and a lift as well as the staircase. The ceilings were high, the proportions spacious, the views over the Park breathtaking – and the most important advantage of all, the drawing room was forty two feet long. For me, there was only one snag – the house was Number Thirteen: but in such a beautiful place, surely nothing could ever go wrong!

At the end of 1967, our offer of £40,000 was accepted – we could hardly believe in our luck. The Golders Green house was sold with no problems: and in May, 1968, the Ogdon family moved into its stately new home.

But incredible though it may seem, when we made up our minds to buy the house, it never occurred to us that we were, so to speak, moving up in the world. Success of that kind had not been our aim – beautiful and convenient though the place was, it had been above all the space for the pianos that had decided us. But our ignorance could not last long: friends' reactions helped it to dawn on me rapidly that I was mistress of one of the more desirable – and enviable – houses in London.

As for John – he revelled in his grand new surroundings. But his pleasure was not caused by pride – it was simply a joyous acceptance of his mounting fortune and fame.

Even before undertaking the move, we were spending every penny we earned – for one thing, anyone as successful and hard working as John needs a large staff to look after him. We had to hire typists and the occasional secretary to help cope with the flood of his mail – with fan letters, pleas from composers: correspondence with recording companies and agents world-wide: and of course, unending travel arrangements. There were lawyers and accountants to pay – and also the childrens' school fees. All this financial pressure was on top of the house, and the people we paid to help run it.

I was still as determined as ever not to become the "little woman": so though I supervised the nannies and household meticulously, I tried not to be tied by them. I still wanted to travel when possible with my husband; and more importantly, our duo piano team was thriving by now, and I had to spend hours a day practising. But the fact that I was consistently busy meant that for the childrens' sake and my own peace of mind, our domestic staff had to be experienced and reliable – the best.

For a while, we thought our prayers had been answered when we hired a handsome young Spaniard. He was temperamental at times, but that was a small price to pay for a fastidious cleaner and valet who was in addition an excellent chef. For almost two years he pampered and spoiled us – until he took a holiday to visit his boyfriend.

He came back deeply depressed. He was touchy and consist-

137

ently rude: he did not want to stir from the basement, and he began using foul language with Richard. Soon, he refused to take orders from me – John was his master, he said. The whole household became perceptibly infested by his simmering anger and gloom; in some ways, he was harder to cope with than if he had been one of the family. So when one day he gave in his notice, we had no choice but to accept.

But I was sorry to see him go. We hired a married couple instead, but they seemed barely able to get through the work he had so effortlessly done on his own. And a couple – and the couples who followed – were doubly expensive to hire: what is more, their salaries, as well as their keep, always rose faster than John's concert fees.

Practical considerations aside, though, it must be admitted that John revelled in the idea as well as the fact of people being paid to look after him: I am convinced that he could ask nothing better of life than to recline on cushions of silk, being wined and dined by a harem responsive to his every whim. But though he was generous with our employees, few found it easy to cope with him. His habits remained as erratic as ever, as did the hours he kept: he always left the bathroom in a towel-soaked flood, cigarette butts reached mountainous heights, and coats, gloves and shoes lay about the place wherever he had taken them off.

He was demanding of the help in another way, too. He had always enjoyed convivial company; and now he could afford to play host whenever he felt in the mood. After concerts at the Royal Festival or Albert Hall, it was normal for us to invite up to fifty people for a standing buffet at home – or, as an occasional alternative, we would give a sit-down dinner for ten. The Christmas period when John was not away on tour was usually a lavish carouse – though John had an ability to combine play with work that was totally beyond my capacity. I remember once practising with him throughout Christmas Day, much to the childrens' disgust – he was coaching me through my part in Messiaen's "Vision de L'Amen", the idiom of which I found difficult at first: and yet he still had the energy to celebrate well into the small hours that night.

Sophisticated hostess though I was becoming – almost in spite of myself – my assurance was shattered one day when our friend, John Dankworth, rang up. He was arranging a gala at the Phoenix Theatre, he said, and he wondered if I would give a reception for Princess Margaret after the show. Because I adore John and his wife Cleo Laine, I agreed: but I put down the receiver in a panic. How did one entertain royalty – what on earth was the form? Suddenly, in spite of my house and my clothes, I stood revealed to myself as still being, at heart, that shy middle class student from Hyde. It was a deflating, if salutary, experience.

In the end, Princess Margaret decided to go home to Kensington Palace. Such was my relief at being let off the hook that I threw a big party in any case, and – no offence to Her Royal Highness intended – I had an unusually good time.

Often, on social occasions, John would shed his gentle, inhibited manner, and hold the floor like an orator, not only expounding brilliantly and probingly on music, but on literary matters as well. For him, socially, there was no middle ground, which is where most of the rest of us communicate: but he would make an impressive if Dickensian figure as he paced up and down, his powerful shoulders hunched high and his beard jutting outwards imperiously. Yet sometimes these articulate bouts disturbed me in a way that I did not show publicly – they seemed caused not only by innate excitement, but by something altogether less abstract.

William Walton was the first person to express my fears in words. In 1967, even before we had moved to Chester Terrace, we had gone to stay near his home in Ischia, and one day he had taken me aside. "Brenda," he had said, "John's drinking rather a lot, isn't he?"

"Well . . ." I had adopted a defensive approach. "He never touches a drop on days when he's playing, you know. He's letting himself go a bit because he's on holiday."

William's shrug was slight. "Maybe you're right. But people are beginning to notice."

I had done my best to make light of it: but later, I plucked up my courage and told John what William had said, adding that I agreed.

John looked at me directly, and through his lenses, his eyes were murderous. But when he spoke, it was quietly: "Mind your own business" he said.

139

And so the drinking went on. He was never reeling, his words were never slurred, and it was true he never drank on the day of a performance – but as the years passed, he pushed closer to the borderline between "a little too much" and excess. His smoking was too heavy as well – by the end of the sixties, he was up to thee packs a day. So though he was naturally strong, he was also out of condition; while the pleasures of the affluent life added inches to his waistline.

The affluent life, for all its advantages, was also driving us further apart. I am gregarious, but I resented the fact that the place always seemed crowded with guests on the rare occasions when John was at home. In fact, in our early days at Chester Terrace, he would often bring friends back for drinks and dinner without letting me know in advance. It did not take long for me to rebel, and things began to improve – but still the place was too often full of barely familiar faces. Worst of all were the completely unknown hangers-on, from whom John could not or would not protect himself.

So once again I found myself cast in the role of an ogress – though in these cases my conscience was clear as I showed them the way to the street. All the same, it is not easy to cope with the resentment one causes – as the husbands or wives of other people in the public eye will understand only too well. Dodie Ashkenazy, Volodya's blonde wife, is someone else who has had to use an icy cold stare on occasion.

The trouble was, there were times when I felt sorely tempted to get rid of some of the people John liked. Always happiest in the company of men, he developed a bias towards older composers, few of them clever or amusing to my mind; and they would loll about the dining and drawing rooms, often into the early hours of the morning, like irresponsible students. Mostly I put up with them in silence for John's sake – except on rare occasions when I could bear it no longer.

"It's like ... like an intrusion on our marriage" I would protest. "John, we're never alone any more!"

"But that's because I'm away touring most of the time..."

"That's not what I meant, and you know it."

"Well, we're alone now. And we are when we go to bed..."

"... When we're always too tired to talk!"

He would scowl at me in that savage way that had become

too familiar for comfort since our move. "I'm going to have my friends in my house when I feel like it, Brenda!"

"Brenda" by this time was a warning sign – it meant that I was out of favour. But whatever our distances or differences, the bad patches in our relationship – at least, until 1972 – were still far less frequent than otherwise. Mostly John called me an affectionate "B", or in his best moods, in private, "Buntiks". And of course, I realised in my heart that even if we had been alone together more often, he would not have known how to share his more intimate thoughts. After all, so far as I knew, he had never yet shared them with anyone...

And socially, the elderly composers took up only a part of John's time – we entertained, and were entertained by, many friends whose company we both enjoyed equally. Surprisingly, perhaps, some of the people who were closest to us had nothing to do with the world of professional music. Ben Worthington, who with his wife Valerie had shared our confusion over Legnano, is a stockbroker: so too is Sheelin Eccles' husband Simon, with whom we have spent many a happy occasion.

If we were not entertaining at home, we would often take people to restaurants – usually to Tiberius, the Savoy Grill, or Annabel's. John spent his money with glee – he had no interest in it as such, he understood it only in terms of the pleasure it gave. His attitude had come to affect even me – money was far less real to me now than in my penny-pinching years as a student and as a young wife.

John was lavishly extravagant with everyone – and to nobody more so than me. He showered me with clothes and with presents – I learned to bite my tongue if I saw something I liked in a shop, because if he were to suspect that I wanted it he would be certain to buy it for me.

And yet, except where cigarettes, food and drink were concerned, he almost never spent money on things for himself. Cars, clothes, expensive accessories – personally they meant nothing to him. True, he enjoyed the accoutrements of our existence with all the innocence of a child; but in spite of the nannies and servants, he remained Dorothy's scruffy, incapable genius, totally and blithely indifferent to the social impression he made.

And so we continued to live for the day, with hardly a thought for tomorrow. Perhaps I should have worried and protested more – but I knew John would refuse to discuss his spending with me. In any case, there was no need to worry about his career and the way it was developing: and we were paying an accountant good money to look after our financial affairs, and he was giving us no words of warning.

But with the start of the 1970s we were drawing all too close to what proved to be our final extravagance.

19

The idea of our building a second home somewhere in the Mediterranean was not exactly a new one to us.

In the summer of 1965, when we returned to Rome after our abortive attempt to join the rain-sodden Spoleto Festival, John had said "Brenda, I've just remembered that William Walton lives in Ischia – let's phone and see if he's home."

William was at home, and immediately invited us to lunch.

We flew to Ischia by helicopter – a twenty minute flight from Naples – and we watched awed as the island came closer, rising from its halo of translucent green. On landing, we found that it more than lived up to its promise: orange and lemon trees were heavy with fruit, clouds of bougainvillaea spilled over walls, and the coastline was spectacular and steep. As for La Mortella, the Waltons' house – it took our breath away.

Designed to William's own specifications, it clings to a hill high over the sea; the garden, which is built in a series of terraces, has a collection of rare flowers and shrubs. A fountain is controlled from the house; a swimming pool basks in the sun; a steep path leads to the beach; and round every corner one comes to, there is always another visually dazzling surprise.

We had eaten lunch outside, on the largest terrace of all. While John and William had chatted about music, I had told Lady Walton – Susana – how much we love Italy. "In fact" I had said "next year we're hoping to take a holiday house on the Adriatic coast."

She had glanced across at her husband, engrossed in his discussion with John. "It would be fun" she had answered me quietly, "if you rented one of our houses instead – we have several on the estate. Think about it, why don't you?"

Sitting on that great sun-drenched terrace, looking out at the view of gardens, cliffs and blue sea, I had known there was no need to think. I had accepted her invitation at once.

So August 1966 saw us and the children installed in Casa Drina, a charming three-bedroomed house belonging to the Waltons; it was set in a tree-shaded garden, and came with a maid and a cook.

Here, for the first time in ages, John managed to relax completely. He had brought his silent keyboard with him as usual – he uses it for practice on tour and on holiday – but most of the time it stayed closed. He seemed more aware of other people than he usually was, and more perceptive of the beauty around us: I remember finding him on the patio one night, standing with an entranced and childlike delight as a galaxy of glow-worms span round him. The many stairs that wound through the terraces gave him some much needed exercise, and twice a day, and sometimes more often, he would go down to the beach for a swim. In the evenings, William and Susana would quite often join us for dinner, usually in the local Trattoria Romantica: they were recognised and greeted wherever they went, and seemed very much part of the local community.

But, as we soon learned, they were not cut off from the world. All the latest magazines, newspapers and records were sent out to William from London, and friends from all over Europe came to stay in the guest houses – Terence Rattigan was one regular visitor. People, most of them English, flowed in and out of La Mortella, keeping William and Susana in touch with gossip and trivial matters as well as important events.

It was a heady experience for John and me to be welcomed into such cosmopolitan company as this. Caustic, original and witty, William held court at its centre: and we found life at his home was as stimulating as it was relaxing.

Sitting on the Waltons' terrace one day, staring out at the wide sunlit view, John said to me quietly "B, how nice it would be if we had a place of our own where we could lead a life something like this . . ."

"Yes." I looked at him, tanned and clear-eyed in the sun, healthier than I had ever known him. "One day perhaps . . . If we can ever afford it."

John did not mention the matter again: but the seed had been planted . . .

We returned to Ischia in both of the following years; but after that, much as we loved it, we decided we ought to try other places as well. At various times we had holidays in Majorca and the Algarve – but it was Spain with which we both fell in love.

The auguries for a relaxed few weeks' holiday in the summer of 1970 had not been good. My father had died suddenly from a brain haemorrhage in January – and much as I had always adored him, I was not prepared for the terrible void that opened up in my heart. It must have taken me almost six years to adjust to the fact of his death; and the first five months of 1970 have been all but obliterated from my consciousness except for the memory, blunted now, of a once unbearable pain.

For my mother, the loss of her husband was a blow so shattering that we feared for her mental balance. All her life, she had managed to convince herself that tragedies could be overlooked if only one was sensible enough; but for once emotional escape was impossible, and she had no experience of coping on which she was able to draw. Watching the cracks appear in the usually immaculate facade, I decided to take her away with us on our holiday later that year. A change of climate and scenery might do her good, and there would be the children, whom she loved, to distract her.

The problem was, where was the best place to take her? Friends urged us to go to Marbella, which had mountains and beaches and guaranteed good weather; and in the end I was persuaded to rent a house for a month on an estate not far from the sea. My mother and our French au pair were to set up residence there first, with Annabel (now almost nine) and Richard (an exuberant three). John and I would be joining them after a week, straight from a tour of Japan.

We arrived in Marbella to find my mother's state of mind a little improved – for one thing, her familiar frugality with the housekeeping money had reasserted itself, driving the poor au pair almost berserk. But inevitably, with my arrival, much of the responsibility was taken away from her, and before long she was regressing into a state of confused realities. Her one consolation was to make charcoal sketches of the town and the spectacular country surrounding it.

145

I was grateful to Marbella for stimulating my mother to this new interest at least – and we found ourselves as impressed as she was by the beauty and grandeur of the mountains as they swept the horizon down to the sea. The weather, as promised, was perfect, and the happiness of the deeply-tanned children did wonders for my morale. Rather to my surprise, I enjoyed the food too; and I shared with John a love of Spanish music, from the haunting rhythms of Albeniz and Granados to the haughty fire of flamenco. If I could not yet be happy, I was still happier here than I would have been anywhere else.

One evening, sipping ice-filled drinks and watching the sinking sun turn the sea into gold, it occurred to me that John was being unusually quiet, even by his standards, "What are you thinking about?" I asked.

He took a breath, and was silent a moment longer. Then he said "B, it's as nice as Ischia here."

I caught his glance. "Yes" I said, and began to talk about something quite different. But in that moment, we had again shared the dream expressed on the terrace of La Mortella. We had understood each other...

Our tacitly accepted plans hung fire for another year, during which, to our infinite relief, my mother slowly but permanently returned to her recognisable self. Then, one Sunday in the early autumn of 1971, I looked up from the *Sunday Times* I had been reading. "John" I said.

Something in my tone persuaded him to come across to me at once. I smoothed the paper over my knees and pointed. "Look".

I was showing him an estate agent's advertisement. It contained a couple of pictures of mountainous landscape a few miles away from Marbella – and it announced that plots of land were up for sale in a development called El Madronal.

'Hm...' John frowned slightly.

'It might be worth looking into" I told him. "I mean, it couldn't possibly do any harm..."

We both had a few days free in late October; we used them to go back to Spain, taking Annabel with us.

We were driven from Marbella to El Madronal by the seller, a man called Paco Parladé. "I think you will like it" he said. "It is very beautiful."

El Madronal, when we got there, turned out to be more than

beautiful. The countryside was blooming and unspoilt, shaded by pine trees and olives – hills and mountains, subtly changing colour as they receded, stretched far away into the West, while five miles to the East we could see the Mediterranean's bright blue expanse. It was, we agreed, the most heavenly view that either of us had seen in our lives.

We already knew that the asking price for the land would be £12,000, and also that we would be able to raise the money without any difficulty against the value of our Chester Terrace house. Now that the time for decisions had come, John did have a moment of doubt – even so, there and then in the bright Spanish sunshine, we agreed to buy the plot of land on which we were standing.

Paco Parladé told us that – subject to our approval, of course – his brother, Jaime, would design a home for us in the style of an old Spanish farmhouse: and soon after our returning home to London, the first drawings arrived in the mail. They were perfect: the house looked traditional yet spacious, in character with the region yet with contemporary luxuries as well – and it boasted a vast south-facing terrace overlooking that breath-taking view. We were thrilled.

Two months after seeing the land, we sent off the first of our payments. The next and final instalments were paid in March 1972; and Plot 32, El Madronal, became the sole property of John Ogdon.

In a flurry of mounting excitement, we started trying to give a more concrete form to our plans. We hired an English architect, Eddie Gilbert, to make the practical interpretation of Jaime's design; then a Spanish architect had to be brought in by law to oversee the construction itself. A builder was approached and contracted; and the overall estimate for finishing the house was given as only £18,000, which was safely within our budget. Things could not have worked out any better.

Or so we thought. At first.

Building had not started when, in August 1972, we rented a villa that had already been built on El Madronal.

The holiday, in some ways, was not one of unalloyed harmony. Our friends the Worthingtons stayed with us for the first two weeks; but there was only one small four-seater car between all of us, including the au pair and the children – which might not have mattered so much except that we were five miles away from a shop and even further from the nearest good beach. To make matters worse, the road was exceptionally bad, rutted and pitted with rocks, and punctures were not infrequent. So on occasions, however good the intentions, tempers did run rather high.

I was worried, too, by John's drinking and smoking, and by his apparent inability to relax as he had done on most other holidays. Not that he seemed morose or depressed – on the contrary, he was overweeningly confident, apparently convinced that whatever he wanted was his for the asking. He was becoming ever more dogmatic, refusing to tolerate any discussion, above all with me. And although he was rarely deliberately unpleasant, the walls of assurance he was raising kept me at a much greater distance than the diffident vagueness had done.

One day while we were in El Madronal, John received a telegram from Wilfred Bain, Dean of the Music School at Indiana University in Bloomington in the mid-West of America. It asked whether John would consider a meeting to discuss the possibility of his joining the faculty, and on generous terms.

We had not heard of Bain, the University, or Bloomington, and John was not about to discuss anything. We decided to ignore the whole matter.

A couple of weeks later, a second, similar, telegram arrived. John left the room as he was reading it, and soon came back empty handed.

"What have you done with it?" I asked.

"Thrown it down the mountain" he said.

And that – so we both thought – was that.

Everything being equal, and in spite of the tensions, the holiday could still be called a success – one that boded well for our future in Spain. The villa was charming, the children were healthy and happy, all of us were soon tanned glowing brown, and we spent many hours in and around the large swimming pool: while to make things better still, after we had been there a fortnight, we were joined by my beloved cousin Helen Bullock and her two children. We had an English au pair and two Spanish dailies to look after us; and so, apart from the shopping (which earlier I had shared with the Worthingtons) and preparing evening meals whenever we did not go out, my responsibilities were minimal.

And far from least in the holiday's assets was Plot 32 itself. We visited it far more often then we needed to, simply to indulge our proud sense of ownership and to show off the place to our friends. Never mind – or not too much – that not a piece of earth had been turned, that as yet not one stone was in place. And Paco Parladé's hint that the building estimate may have been marginally on the low side was not worth getting *too* excited about. No – any faint doubts or worries were as nothing to our pleasure in just standing there on our plot of spectacular land, draming of the gorgeous new house that one day would be a reality.

Oh well, we told each other: If not this year, next year . . . Sometime . . .

20

As 1972 came to an end, we were blithely unaware that dangerous cracks in the edifice of our lives were already widening, unseen.

There was no way that we could have known. In the past ten years, few other musicians anywhere had known a success such as John's. There was not a country that had a vestige of musical culture in which he did not perform; he played with all the world's great orchestras, and with conductors from Giulini to Ormandy: and many reviews extolled him so highly that it would be immodest for me to quote them.

But even in those years of triumph, there had been some professional set-backs – particularly after John had made the decision to leave Ibbs and Tillett.

During a 1964 tour of Rumania with the LPO, the conductor John Pritchard had introduced John to a tall slim and blue-eyed friend of his called Basil Horsefield. It turned out that Basil was a musicians' agent; and after only one or two meetings, John began toying with the idea that he should take over his representation.

At that point in his life, John felt that he was playing too many run of the mill dates in Britain at too low a fee. It was not that he thought himself too grand for the bread-and-butter engagements – but they were so plentiful still that they were taking up all the time he could have used for composing, for studying new works, and for helping other composers. And understandably, he did want more of the prestigious dates that all those "bargain basement deals", as he used to call them, were often obliging him to refuse. He had discussed the subject with Emmie to what he felt had been little avail: on the other hand, John believed that Basil could, and would, handle his career in the way John wanted.

For me too, things had not been going smoothly with Ibbs and Tillett: in fact, the agency by this time no longer represented me. I had been summoned to their offices soon after a Wigmore recital which I had given in September 1964; straight backed and bluntly direct, Emmie had told me that in spite of my favourable reviews, it would be a waste of her time and mine if I were to remain on her books. "Give up, Brenda" she had said. "There is no demand for women pianists in this country – they don't bring a penny into the box-office." Our duo piano team she also thought was of minimal interest: "Find something else to do," she advised me – "concentrate on John and the family."

I will never forget the desperation I felt. It was one thing to decide for myself that the family had to come first; it was another thing altogether to have that decision imposed from outside. Besides, I had never intended to abandon the piano, only to get my priorities straight. After all those years of struggling and dreaming and living nothing but music – after all those years! – to hear that there was no possibility of work, no chance of a career, was an almost unbearable blow.

At first I had to nurse my bruises alone, as John was away in the Soviet Union. On his return he was full of expressions of sympathy, though in his heart of hearts, I suspect, he was pleased that Emmie had advised me to turn into a devoted young housewife. But what John did care about were the prospects of our two-piano team – and here, he would have welcomed encouragement from Emmie. And so it did no harm to Basil in John's eyes when he expressed enthusiasm for our team.

What could go wrong if Basil were to represent him, John wondered? We both liked him as a person and he was sympathetic to John's aims. In any case, John was already world famous – the problem was not finding engagements, he believed, but keeping them to manageable proportions.

So late in 1964 – entirely on his own initiative, and unprodded by Basil – John informed Ibbs and Tillett that he would not accept any more dates from them after his outstanding engagements had been cleared. In a year, he had honoured all his commitments, and in September 1965, Basil officially became his representative.

It was not Basil's fault that things did not turn out as we had hoped. John's fee was immediately upped, and he got many excellent dates. Our duo team did better than it ever had in the past: we played Mozart's Double Concerto in E flat with the Northern Symphonia Orchestra all over the North West of the country, the tour concluding in a concert we gave in the Queen Elizabeth Hall. But in those days at least, Basil's experience and contacts had been mainly in managing singers, a rather different field from an instrumentalist's, added to which, his net was not spread as wide as Emmie's – nobody's was. So the concert dates began to grow scarcer.

As for Emmie Tillett – she felt that she had been betrayed. After all, she had had faith in John long before Moscow: she had sponsored his second Wigmore recital, and she had fought ruthlessly for his early career. Surely, she thought, such belief had merited his loyalty! She made no attempt to conceal her displeasure and hurt. Socially, if we were at the same London concert, she cut John and me publicly dead.

Other changes in John's career were to come. Soon after he left Ibbs and Tillett, we heard from Elsie Illingworth of the Hurok office in America. A no-nonsense Yorkshirewoman and an old time associate of Emmie's, she had been looking after John's career in the States: now, with no explanation, she informed John that Hurok was no longer interested in him, and that he must look for American management elsewhere. This came as a terrible blow to John, because things had been going so well in America – it is bad enough to be kicked when you are down, but it is almost worse when you had thought you were up.

Well, we thought, there were plenty of other agents – and indeed John had no trouble at all in finding himself a new one. He signed with Fritz Steinway of Judson, O'Neil, Beal and Steinway: and Fritz proved to be charming and helpful.

But all too soon, we found worrying parallels with the situation on this side of the Atlantic – Fritz's hold on the American concert scene was not as all-powerful as Hurok's. No longer did John's US tours consist of twenty or thirty concerts – now the maximum he could expect would be ten a visit, sometimes considerably less. The engagements themselves were first-rate – but crossing the Atlantic more often for fewer engagements did

152

not make good sense financially. In America, as in Great Britain, the butter was no longer so thick.

John was still in demand, by most standards he still had an enviable career; but by 1967 the drop-off in concerts was becoming too evident for comfort, in that it was no longer a question of choice. The time had come for John to decide between a less demanding professional life with a drop in his overall earnings, or a return to the unending treadmill – and to more money.

The issue was not long in doubt. John was still as ambitious as ever, and though in theory he had longed for the pressure to ease, in reality Slogger Ogger was once again eager for more. Further, John was loth to lower our standard of living and, I have to admit, so was I.

So one day in the summer of 1967 – less than two years after John had broken away – I made an appointment to see Emmie Tillett in her Wigmore Street offices: John did not come with me, as ever leaving the coping to me . . .

Walking into that office needed every last ounce of my courage. I remember opening the door and seeing Emmie at her large desk, while photos of Ferrier, Moiseiwitsch, Baker and Boult looked out at me from the walls. Her smile was slight, but her eyes were not unkind.

She waved me to a chair. I sat down and wasted no time. "John would like you to take him back on your artists' list" I said.

The little smile broadened but that was all: Emmie could not have handled me better, behaving with the most kindly professional tact. Yes, she said, without hesitation, she would be delighted to welcome John back, as soon as it could be arranged. And of course, his fee would remain at the level which Basil had been charging for him. It was a polite and civilised meeting, but both of us were keenly aware of the emotion the other was feeling.

In the particular circumstances, I think that Basil may have been glad to get rid of us: but he has remained our good friend to this day.

Not long afterwards, even Emmie Tillett learned how the mighty can be shaken, if not actually felled. In 1969, two of her brightest young men, Jasper Parrott and Terry Harrison, suddenly formed an independent agency of their own, and not only did it prosper, it became a most formidable competitor. Ibbs and Tillett remained influential, but its virtual monopoly was ended for ever.

After the break had been made, Terry approached John to find out if he was interested in signing with Jasper and him: but John's answer was in the negative. After all, by 1968 John was again playing as hard and as often as he ever had. Which was too hard, of course, and too often.

There were some other disappointments as well. For example, in October 1969, John played the Brahms D Minor Concerto with Leopold Stokowski at Carnegie Hall – a combination that wrought a rare magic. At a smart New York restaurant afterwards, the 88 year old maestro took time off from his cultivated flirtation with the beauty seated next to him to tell John that he was determined they should record the Brahms together. John was thrilled at the prospect – but when, later, attempts were made to turn the intention into reality, it transpired that he and the old man were committed to different recording companies, and a collaboration could not be arranged. It was a loss not only for John, but for music lovers everywhere.

On a more personal level, John had been concerned for some years because his brother Karl's life was not getting happier with time. And then, in 1972, when he was only forty one years old, Karl died alone and in virtual poverty. John was profoundly distressed by the news, which visibly added to the stress he was already under by that time.

We were both of us also upset when Alistair Londonderry and Nico divorced. In our minds, their names had belonged together as romantically as Romeo's and Juliet's; each of them had had such an influence on our lives, and on so many levels ... At least, though, that unfortunate ending did give way to a happier story: because in March 1972, Alistair married the ballerina Doreen Wells, and they are now the proud parents of two strapping sons.

There were two connected episodes within the decade which at the time seemed to me unimportant and petty.

The first occurred in the late sixties. A man who lives some distance outside London phoned John at home and asked if he would give a recital for a particular charity. John, who had long been indefatigable at putting his services to the aid of good causes, at once agreed.

'What about a fee?' the man asked.

'Well...' John was nonplussed – money was something he preferred to leave to his agent. Hesitantly, he suggested £75.

There was a moment's silence at the other end of the line: then the caller hung up.

John was upset and puzzled. "What did he expect me to say?" he asked. "I wouldn't have thought about money if I hadn't been put on the spot!"

That seemed the end of the matter: but in 1972, an acquaintance approached John at a party: "I hear" he said, after mentioning the man's name, "that a few years ago he invited you to play a charity concert and that you insisted on a substantial fee."

John flushed. "Tell him that if he'd wanted me to play for no money, he should have said so directly!"

Sure enough, the charity organiser was soon back on the phone; but this time it was I who picked up the receiver. John's schedule, as usual, was crowded, but we managed to settle on an evening that was convenient all round.

"About the matter of a fee..." the man began.

"No fee as such, but he'll need £50 for expenses" I said quickly. I saw no reason why John should give not only his energy and time, but suffer a financial loss into the bargain. I explained: "As you know, my husband can't drive – and as I won't be able to come, he'll have to hire a car and chauffeur for the day."

This time, there were no stated objections. I informed Ibbs and Tillett, and they sent a letter to the organiser noting that £50 expenses had been agreed.

But a day or two later, the man phoned again – and this time, he again spoke directly to John. Apparently he said that anyone who lived as well as John did should be ashamed of himself for expecting expenses which the charity could not afford. The implication appeared to John to be that he was getting too big for his boots, and he was so completely taken aback that he told the man to forget about the £50 completely.

The comments, however, had drawn blood, and painfully so – and they prompted John to an extraordinary and impetuous

155

gesture: he took a copy of his father's personal description of his nervous breakdown to the recital – and gave it to the organiser to read.

It was an unsettling episode, of course, but not, one would have thought, of shattering importance. But a strange thing happened during that evening, which John did not mention to me at the time. As his father's precious confessions changed hands, John felt something go snap in his brain: it was a tangible, physical sensation. And from that moment, an obsession was born.

In the weeks and months after the concert, the organiser's comments continued to haunt him. Did not the man understand, John thought, how very busy he was – how much all this playing took out of him? Did he not realise that John would have earned £600 for a normal concert anywhere else in England? How *could* the man convey that he was too keen on money – and who was it who had actually done the favour, who was it who had put himself out? And anyway, was John worth £50 for a whole damn recital or was he not? . . .

He did not confide these thoughts to anyone else: not even to me. I wish he had – who knows, talking might have helped put the matter in a balanced perspective before it was, tragically, too late . . . But probably that is just wishful thinking.

So, in hurt silence, John brooded, turning the matter over again and again in his mind.

So much suffering and over so little – not even the agreed £50! The charity organiser took John at his word, and the expenses never were paid.

By 1972, John was getting more obviously unstable emotionally – more dogmatic, more impatient, more ill-tempered. I put it down to professional pressures, as did everyone else. His family and his friends tried to reason with him, begging him to slow down; but John remained deaf to their pleas.

I found myself by necessity increasingly devoted to the more mundane matters of our existence – the paper work, accounts, legal matters . . . . things which John now impatiently refused to consider. In fact, I was at last getting close, as I ruefully realized, to the "little woman" Dorothy had hoped he would marry, and whom John had also once said that he wanted. Of course, from the start we had had a tacit agreement that I

156

would take care of our practical problems: but for the first time, it was becoming virtually impossible to combine that role with a life of my own.

Yet whatever the demands he was making on me, John was still basically the man I had known from our college days – a man who in any case had never been "normal". He was still just as generous as ever, he still enjoyed the company of his friends, he laughed about the same kind of things. And it had been his own choice to work at this pace. He had tried an easier life and had failed: and if now the tension was showing, that was the price his nature exacted.

Concerned for him though I was, I was not as yet really worried.

The decade included only one or two incidents that portended what was to come.

In March 1968, just before we moved to Chester Terrace, John returned home from New Zealand in a very strange and unsettled mood. He was stony faced and remote; he refused to embrace or even touch me.

I thought he must be over-tired – after all, true to form, he had refused to make any stop-overs in a flight that had taken a good thirty hours. But after a very short time, I realised that not even exhaustion could wholly explain such a coldness. "What's the matter?" I asked him. "Why are you acting so strangely?"

For a moment he remained silent, but I could feel the tension crackle between us. And then suddenly, he let out a terrible roar, and picking up a Danish porcelain figure, hurled it against the wall.

The impact was such that it exploded, the pieces scattering over the floor. John swung back to face me: his fists were clenched threateningly, his face was flushed and distorted, and the violence that blazed in his eyes is something I shall never forget. I stood rooted to the spot in sheer panic.

Somehow I managed to summon up words: I talked to him – about what I no longer remember – as softly and gently as my unsteady voice would allow. Slowly the tension gripping his body began to lose its frightening hold, his shoulders relaxed, falling slightly, and the tight fists began to uncurl. Finally, he agreed to lie down.

In the days that followed, John started to behave very much better, though I dared not question him again: and he offered me no explanations or apologies.

Only many years later did he tell me that he had met a girl on the New Zealand tour and had fallen in love with her. He has mentioned her only the once, and he has always refused to discuss her: I do not even know the girl's name. I was shocked, and saddened for both of us; for all our trials, we had been very devoted, and I am sure that before this, for John there had never been a woman other than me ...

But whatever the misery and resentment he may have been feeling that day, his eruption of uncontained violence was a terrifying thing to experience. Even at the time, without having the wisdom of hindsight, I thought there was something unnatural about it: as though the demon that sometimes took possession of his playing had at last appeared in our everyday life ...

In August that same year, we took our last holiday in Ischia; and this time we rented the Waltons' own fabulous house. The weeks we spent there should have been perfect – and certainly, in terms of surroundings, the holiday was one of the loveliest we have spent in our lives.

And yet, for the first time in our marriage, I felt inconsolably lonely. John was working obsessively in William's music room most of the time, completing a piano Sonata: he felt, he told me, nothing less than inspired. But though I could admire his diligence, I could not accept that throughout the whole month, he hardly spoke to me once.

I tried to occupy myself with Annabel and Richard, and as always they rewarded my attentions threefold. But I remember looking away as I played with them on the terrace, and seeing John's big bearded figure as he brooded over his shadow in the brilliant Ischian sun. He seemed so very alone as he stood there.

I felt a shiver run through me. Though I did not know it then, it seems to me now that it was a shiver of cold premonition.

Part Three

The Years of Breakdown

21

1973 began well enough: certainly with no indication of what it was holding in store.

John was more approachable than he had been for months, and was brimful with energy and purpose – two qualities he was going to need in a year that was to bring him almost two hundred concerts. And professionally speaking, it was a promising start to the year for me too: because early in January, at St. John's, Smith Square, in London, I made my first appearance as a soloist in over eight years. I played Mozart's piano concerto K595 No. 27 in B Flat with the Hertfordshire Chamber Orchestra under David Measham: unfortunately, John was playing in Windsor and could not be there, but Alistair Londonderry and many other friends turned up to lend me support. Afterwards John – who had rushed back to London – hosted a celebration dinner at Mr. Chow's restaurant in Knightsbridge, where everyone was generous with compliments. It had been a profound pleasure for me to play again on my own: I was very happy that night.

There were other good times as well in the first few weeks of that year. After my concert, the whole family, including my mother, flew to Arosa in Switzerland for the first skiing holiday of our lives. For me and the children, the sport was to become an addiction – although, to no one's surprise, it did not prove to be a forte of John's. As we improved and became more adventurous, he remained on the lower slopes with Class One; whenever possible, he would detach himself from the lesson to light up yet one more cigarette. I could not really blame him – when he was made to participate he would soon be flat on his back; he would lie spreadeagled and helpless in the snow, while the instructor and several giggling students struggled to prop his bulk upright again ... All the same, he seemed to be enjoying himself: so much so that – guilty because of the expense – we extended our fortnight's holiday by another full week.

At the end of the month, with the children both back in school, I flew with John to Texas, where he gave the American première of his own Concerto with the Houston Symphony conducted by Lawrence Foster. Larry – a clever man with a wit that can be rather too acid for comfort – had also conducted the concerto's first London performance, and the recording for the Angel label: and as before, he provided John with an immaculate and sensitive accompaniment. The reviews were all very good, and John could not hide his delight.

But delight perceptibly changed into arrogance; and only a matter of days after the concert, he began to order me around like a maid whose sole purpose in life was to wait on him.

Throughout February, and the usual non-stop succession of concerts, his mood of overbearing self-confidence continued – even surviving a memorable journey which we made together at the end of the month.

We had been engaged by the Amigos de la Musica Association in Marbella – our new home town, as we liked to think – to give a two piano recital on a Monday night. So on the Sunday we caught a flight from Heathrow, which left on schedule at noon. The French air controllers, however, were on one of their depressingly predictable strikes, and some time before we were due to touch down, we were re-routed via Tangier. After a short wait at the airport and some fairly good-natured grumbling, we took off again for the short hop over the water to Spain – only to find ourselves making interminable circles high above the Atlantic. Finally, after more than two hours, the pilot's exasperated voice came over the intercom to tell us that the traffic from France was so heavy that the Spanish airports could no longer cope: and so we were forced to fly back to London.

By this time, the erratic scheduling caused by the strike had made its mark on Heathrow; and in the resultant chaos, all our luggage was mislaid. For almost three hours we waited in the throng of bad-tempered passengers before our cases were finally found: then we took a cab home through the cold winter's night to catch up on a few hours' sleep.

The next morning we took a taxi back to Heathrow, and boarded a flight for Madrid. But this plane did not even take off: and two hours later we were back inside the departure lounge.

By now the joke was beginning to wear rather thin – and amid mounting anxiety and clockwatching, we managed to get seats on a plane that was leaving for Brussels. But in Brussels too, contrary to all the airline's predictions, the delays were as bad as in London: and after several more hours on the ground, we had to give up all hope of making our concert in time.

I sent telegrams or made phone calls to all the interested parties in Marbella, expecting we would be told to fly home: but instead, to our surprise, we were asked to continue our journey.

We landed at Malaga airport at last under a star-studded 4 a.m. sky and were driven to Marbella and a warm if sleepy welcome at the house of our friends Harry and Jackie Digby.

Meanwhile, the previous evening, hundreds of people – many of whom had made long journeys to hear us – had turned up at the Hotel Andalucia Plaza only to be told at the entrance that the concert was not taking place. But with admirable Latin aplomb, the organisers blandly announced that the performance had been rescheduled, and would take place the following night.

And so we played after all – astonishingly, to a full house. I was tense because not only was this my Spanish debut, but we were offering a particularly taxing programme, including a Mozart Sonata, the Suite No. 2 by Rachmaninov, the Brahms-Haydn Variations, and Milhaud's "Scaramouche". Also we were playing from memory – a nerve-wracking experience for two pianists, because if one of them should have a memory lapse, there is no possibility of improvising so as to conceal the mistake.

We made our entrance on stage to a stamping and whistling reception, with congratulations being shouted on our having finally made it. Perhaps helped by the adrenalin still lingering after our crisis, we both played very well, and were rewarded with a standing ovation. Suddenly, as we stood on stage taking our bows, hearing the repeated bravos and seeing the rows of smiling faces in front of us, the whole mad hassle of the last couple of days seemed worthwhile after all.

First thing the following morning, John was off once again to

163

begin a Scandinavian tour. I was to catch a different flight, to London, later that afternoon.

In the morning, a wealthy and aristocratic Spaniard whom both John and I knew quite well phoned and offered to drive me back to Malaga airport. Gratefully I accepted.

In the car, he glanced at me sideways a moment – and in his lightly accented English, he said "Brenda, I would like to have an affair with you."

I did not know what to say – my father's daughter, as ever, I laughed and tried to make light of it.

Unperturbed by my outwardly flippant reaction, he told me that I looked exactly like a woman he had once hoped to marry, but who had turned down his proposal. Not that he did not love his present wife very much – he did not intend to cause her or John any pain: but he did passionately want this affair ... He was persuasive, insistent, and charming, while I remained smilingly tongue-tied.

At the airport, he saw to everything for me. I found myself looking at him with new eyes: he moved with an athletic and military authority, and he was every inch a man of the world ... And oh – it was so *pleasant* to be fussed over by an attractive, intelligent man! I could not remember the last time such a thing had happened to me ...

As I said goodbye to him outside the emigration hall, I was experiencing a long-suppressed yearning – the yearning to be helpless for once.

John returned from Scandinavia more demanding and dogmatic than ever: and he refused to discuss anything with me, however important – or trivial – the subject. But I had little time to dwell on his moods, because he had hardly come back before he was off again – indeed, these days he was rarely at home.

And as well as the unending concerts, he was busier than ever recording. Between 1970 and 1973, he made eleven records for EMI alone, including most of Scriabin's works for piano and the entire Rachmaninov Etudes Tableaux; also, at the company's urging, he made a disc of popular solo piano pieces, and during one of the politically-motivated cultural stoppages that occur between the East and the West, he stood in at two days notice for Emil Gilels to record the Grieg and

164

Schumann concertos with the New Philharmonia Orchestra under Paavo Berglund.

As if that were not enough, the two Rachmaninov Sonatas, the Alkan Concerto for Solo Piano, a collection of Nielsen's piano works, and Beethoven's Hammerklavier Sonata all appeared on the RCA Victor label; while his twelve recordings for Argo included solo and concerto performances as well as some duo pieces with me. In addition, we made four recordings together for EMI, including works by Schoenberg, Britten, Messiaen, and Milhaud.

But well received though our two piano recordings had been, they were the subject of an ugly row between us – the first time that John was openly, unrelentingly unpleasant in front of somebody else. We were having dinner at home with a friend, Richard Croucher; John had drunk rather too much, and suddenly, without any warning, he launched into a vicious attack on me, on my playing, and on the idea and the very existence of our two piano team. He was so verbally abusive that I jumped from the table, the tears pouring down my face for the first time in years. "I won't listen to you – I won't stay and hear this!" I protested, before running, shocked and humiliated, to the privacy of our bedroom.

Evidently Richard – who is a striking and, under different circumstances, a very amusing man – gave John a severe ticking-off. I hoped that as a result John would explain or apologise; but instead, he behaved as if he had not said a word.

My mood was not made any lighter when I learned from a sincerely apologetic Paco Parladé that the estimate on El Madronal had risen by twelve percent. At once I suggested to John that he should not authorise a start to the building; but of course he would not listen to me. "Twelve percent isn't much" he insisted. "We can afford it with no trouble, you'll see."

But far from all the news from Spain was depressing... Ever since my return to London from Marbella, the man who had driven me to the airport there had been sending me passionate letters and making romantic telephone calls; and shut out as I was by John, I soon began to look forward and even to rely on them.

In May, John was due to make a tour of South Africa. Two or three weeks before his scheduled departure, he said

"Brenda, I want you to come with me. And both of the children as well."

"Not the children, John – they'll still be in school."

"Then take them out."

"But..."

"Take them out! And book us first class all the way."

"No!" – it was a small shriek of horror. "We can't afford it – it'd cost us a *fortune*! Not just the travel – all the hotels for three weeks..."

He leaned forward, staring at me with a frown. "First class, I said – all the four of us!"

It was an order, not a request. So reluctantly, tearfully, I obeyed him.

The trip, when it did take place, turned out to be an unusually happy one for the children – then aged eleven and eight, they still remember it vividly. On the flight, we were treated like royalty, and we were hospitably received everywhere we went in South Africa. So much of that country is stunningly beautiful, and all of us felt physically better just for being there. But the constant evidence of racial repression did undermine my enjoyment.

John seemed to be much more his good-natured self again – or perhaps this was an early example of my capacity for self-delusion, because most of the time my attention was focussed not on him so much as the children.

At the end of the South African tour, John went on to Kenya, where he was giving more concerts. The children and I flew to Spain, where a villa in the grounds of the Marbella club had been arranged for us by my wealthy Spanish admirer.

In some ways it was a strange relationship I shared with him during that holiday in Spain. I am sure we both entered it casually, if somewhat tentatively on my part: and the affair's outward conduct was certainly conventional and cautious enough. And yet – though I was by now well aware that he was an experienced womaniser well used to keeping his head – there *was* an element of emotional danger... But in the end I think that no-one was hurt – and that includes him and me.

He was attentive: he did look after things for me, and make me feel attractive and wanted. It was a luxurious and strengthening episode that did wonders for my flagging self-image –

and I was not ashamed, or sorry it happened.

One familiar worry marred my brief escape – according to Paco Parladé, the estimate on Plot 32 was still rising, and fast. And the more he explained to me in his frank way, the more appalled I became: it was starkly obvious that the house would cost far, far more than we had envisioned – that is, if it was ever going to be finished.

Back in London, I found John still in a mood of intransigent arrogance; but even though I knew my pleas would fall on deaf ears, I begged him again to veto the building. But he was adamant that everything should proceed according to plan.

Later that year, in the summer, we went with the children to Shawnigan Lake Summer School, on Vancouver Island in Canada; John had been invited to teach there, giving the first master classes in his career. He also gave three recitals – one solo, another with the violinist Ruggiero Ricci, and finally a third one with me.

The setting of this famous boys' school, with its old buildings, and the surrounding water and trees, was beautiful: and to John's delight, the food for the faculty was excellent. But where our accomodation itself was concerned, no one could say we were privileged: we were housed in a primitive wood cabin – Richard bluntly called it a shed – which was very uncomfortable indeed.

But again the children had a marvellous time. I spent my days with the two of them at the club down by the lake: they both learned to sail and to water-ski, and they would swim and splash about by the hour. I would have enjoyed myself too if only it had not been for John.

This was the first time we had been together continually since the three weeks spent touring South Africa: and the change in him was much for the worse. He was able to teach, and so far as I know he taught well: but otherwise he was unapproachable not only by me, but by the children and everyone else. He was nervous, irritable and tetchy: and nothing except possibly food would persuade him to stop working for a moment. He practised, he taught, he composed, hour after hour after hour – relentlessly, obsessively, non-stop. He was chain-smoking all the time, too – at least sixty cigarettes every day.

167

On one occasion, as I was about to get into our hired car and drive off for a morning's swimming and sun with the children, I implored John to come with us. "Or if not now" I said tentatively "please take just *one* morning off sometime soon. You haven't even been down to the club yet – and it would be so nice for Richard and Annabel..."

He scowled at me. "I haven't come here to have fun: they've brought me all this way to teach."

"Not only to teach! You know they're not paying that much – the club and the lake and the boating, they're all meant to be part of the package!"

He turned away.

"Please John..."

He swung back abruptly – "I hate you, Brenda!" he roared. His eyes blazing, he hurled a string of abuse at me.

I got into the car and drove away fast, with the children white-faced in the back.

Down at the lake-shore, I did my best to act normally; but my heart went on beating too fast. It doesn't make sense, I told myself, I don't understand, I don't *understand*! Is is my fault? What can I have done?

The children were chasing each other at the edge of the lake, the incident already forgotten. I watched them, dark against the sparkling water, and instinctively hugged my elbows closer against me. Oh God, what can be happening? What is going so dreadfully wrong?

22

Shattering though John's outburst had been to me, we did not so much as mention it during our remaining few days at Shawnigan Lake. He continued to work as obsessively, he was just as remote and withdrawn – and sometimes he would stare at me in so threatening a way that I abandoned all thought of reproaches.

But in spite of his ominous mood, John played well at Shawnigan Lake. He particularly enjoyed the recital he gave with Ruggiero Ricci, experiencing an immediate musical rapport.

Over one of our excellent dinners, Ricci mentioned that he was on the faculty of the Music School of Indiana University at Bloomington. I knew I had heard of the place, but for a moment was uncertain where: then I remembered the telegrams from the Dean, Wilfred Bain, which John had received in Marbella the previous summer – indeed, since then, Bain had approached John again in London, by letter. I asked Ricci what he thought of the School.

"One of the best in the country" he replied. "Probably *the* best, I think."

John roused himself from his silence to say that he too had been approached with a view to joining the faculty.

"If you enjoy teaching" Ricci smiled, "and if you can put up with beautiful countryside rather than with a big city, I guess you might find it OK."

But even if John's schedule had allowed time for a university job – which it did not – he had no desire at that point to teach on a continuing basis: and so again, we forgot about Bloomington.

From Vancouver Island, we flew to Wyoming, where John had been invited to play Richard Yardumian's Passacaglia, Recitative and Fugue – known for short as his Piano Concerto –

at the Grand Teton Music Festival in Jackson Hole, a famous skiing resort. The scenery was utterly breath taking, and we were given a luxurious condominium to live in – the height of indulgence after Shawnigan Lake.

John was still dictatorial with me in private: but in more public terms, his behaviour began to improve. In part, I put down the change in him to the presence of the Yardumians themselves. Dick is an open, warm man, and one of our dearest friends in the music world; Armenian by ancestry, he is musical director of the Swedenborgian Church in Bryn Athyn, Pennsylvania, and his attitude to life and to music is profoundly religious. Gregorian chants, music from the Armenian liturgy, a scholarly knowledge of ancient modal systems and American regional music all combine in his compositions with an element of inherent mysticism. John finds his works eminently pianistic, and admires them as deeply as he likes their creator.

John played the concerto superbly – as he invariably does. In fact, he has also recorded it twice – once for RCA in the sixties, and again in 1977 in a prize-winning version for EMI with Paavo Berglund and the Bournemouth Symphony Orchestra.

Dick's fellow Swedenborgian and long-time benefactor, Theodore Pitcairn, was also in Jackson Hole for the Festival. He was tall, distinguished, eighty years old, and a multimillionaire: and when he learned that John had ten days free right after the Festival, he insisted that we spend them at his Cape Cod home as his guests. What is more, he adamantly refused to let us pay either our own plane fares or those of the children.

The Yardumians came to Cape Cod as well. Dick's Mass was soon to be performed in Boston; and while we were staying at Theodore's house near to a shingle beach and an icy-cold sea, some of the singers due to take part came out to rehearse the work under Dick's guidance. John would accompany them on the piano – and when he was not taking part in these sessions, he seemed quite happy in protracted discussions with Dick. I occupied myself with the children: and if John and I did not exactly communicate, at least a temporary truce had been called.

The short holiday over, John returned to the usual round of

170

international concerts: while much of his limited time at home was devoted to a piano concerto which the Dutch composer, Gerard Schurmann, was writing for him. Though John had played one completed movement earlier that year in Ireland, the work as a whole was still in its development stages – it was being composed with John actually sitting at the keyboard, suggesting, experimenting and rehearsing under the composer's sure guidance. But to my dismay, I soon learned that Gerard – a solidly handsome and approachable man with pouchy eyes and a tough set to his jaw – is by nature a night-owl like John; and these free-wheeling yet concentrated sessions would often go on well into the early hours, either at the Schurmanns' house in Finchley, or, more usually, at our home. On the latter occasions – worried as I was by the unrelenting demands of John's performing and travelling schedules – I would sometimes brave the fumes from Gerard's old pipe, and ask the composer to leave; fortunately he was usually good-natured about it, though John, predictably, was not.

I wish my concern had been limited only to Gerard; but in between the bouts of hard work, we were throwing more parties than ever. On these purely social occasions, however, John had now dropped all pretence of active involvement; hardly bothering to acknowledge his guests, he usually sat smoking alone in a corner, and he spoke only when he was spoken to. Indeed, he appeared to be so much out of things that, later, I was to discover that some of our friends were convinced that it was I who was foisting these parties on to an unwilling John.

Nothing was further from the truth – though, of course, being the hostess, I did try to see they went well . . . On returning home from a concert trip, John's first words would too often be "Brenda, I want a party": if I hesitated, he would give me that familiar scowl from under his brows, and accuse me of neglect, of stupidity – of hating him . . .

His drinking had reached alarming proportions by this time – and he was smoking at least four packs every day, littering the house with his stubs. Friends continued to express their concern to him over the way he was driving himself – but they might as well not have troubled. John said that he knew what he wanted from music and life, and what he wanted he would get in the way that best suited him.

And I must admit that in spite of his tempers, his demands and his distances, and in spite of my own fast-fading confidence, his periods of self-certainty could be contagious – even, by moments, exhilarating. How could one doubt such a total conviction – who would dare question such faith? And so, confused, overwhelmed and obedient, I mostly went along with it all.

But John's belief in himself could not reassure me about Plot 32. By the autumn of 1973, building had started at last – and to my horror, I now learned from Paco Parladé that we might find ourselves paying out as much as £2,000 every month! Alistair Londonderry shared my alarm when I told him: "John must slap on an injunction – stop the work as soon as you can!" he advised me. Even an accountant had at last voiced concern: he warned us that many people had got their fingers burnt badly in Spain, and that John was risking running up a very large debt. But John insisted that the work should continue.

One night, in October, the matter came up at a dinner party we were giving for some close friends at home. "The dollar premium has gone up" I told them. "Our costs go on soaring each month."

"John, don't you think you ought to hold back?" someone ventured. "The international monetary situation . . ."

"We've got to start building for tax reasons" John interrupted. He glowered down at his plate. "Besides, I can meet the demands."

The friend dared a second time – "But John . . ."

"No!" John looked up again, his expression deceptively calm. "I have plenty of concerts coming up and I am able to meet the demands!"

In the uncomfortable silence that followed, the tears again rose to my eyes.

John crouched slightly lower in his seat. "Stop crying, Brenda" he snapped at me. "There are thousands of people in this world who are very much worse off than you."

That was when I first realised, I think, that there was a growing warp in his logic. But still I continued to tell myself that this was no more than a difficult phase, due above all to overwork . . .

November arrived – and another aspect to John's erratic behaviour was beginning to get more pronounced – his apparent determination to shock me. It was as if he was becoming two people: the eccentric and absent-minded genius whom everyone wanted to mother, and an obstinately challenging vulgarian.

November was also the month when I found him in front of an open top-storey window, staring out over the park. As I reclosed the window against the cold winter air, he complained to me that he could not breathe – but he resisted my suggestion that he should see a doctor. I did not dare to insist; his rages, which were sudden and frightening, could be triggered by the least show of will on my part.

And still John allowed nothing to interfere with his preparations for the Schurmann Concerto. Though the piece is a very difficult one which few pianists since have dared to attempt, he was determined to play it from memory rather than with the aid of a score: he continued to spend hours at a time closeted at the piano with Gerard, and, when he was alone, he would work on it with the same single-minded and unbalanced obsession he had shown at Shawnigan Lake.

It may well seem incredible, in view of all the warning signals, that I did not realise how ill John already was. I could perhaps attempt to excuse myself by saying that I had been brought up, and had lived, in total ignorance of mental illness and breakdowns; I could also claim that I was far from unique in this – that in our society, in spite of so many claims to the contrary, we are not encouraged to face up to the distress signals of the mind as we are to those of the body.

But my failure to realise what was happening is not explicable in terms of society and background alone; in matters of the unbalanced brain, it is I believe, a sad paradox that it is often our love for the victim that blinds us to his true condition. Quite simply, it is virtually impossible to grasp that someone we are very close to – someone to whom we talk every day, someone we sleep with, and play with, and work with, and who is an integral part of our very existence – it is impossible to conceive or to grasp that this person may be going out of his mind. We attribute the erratic episodes to overwork, too much drink – what we will: in fact, we worry about almost everything except the inconceivable truth.

And the story in such tragic cases is almost always the same.

173

Husbands, wives, close relatives, lovers – like me, they look at the symptoms without comprehension; and when they are left with no choice but to act, the breaking point has already been passed. The psychiatric hospitals are filled not only because of the mental illnesses themselves, but because those of us who care most and have most at stake dare not recognize the bare truth in front of us.

Several days after finding John standing breathless at the window, he said over breakfast one morning "You know you mentioned seeing a doctor . . ."

"Yes."

"I want you to make an appointment for me. But with a psychiatrist, not an ordinary doctor."

"A psychiatrist! Why?"

"I don't know."

"But you must have a reason!"

"Um . . ." He looked away. "Well, in books, sometimes it seems to me that the texts are being altered. And music . . . my scores occasionally change, I think."

"John, that's nonsense!" I felt a chill of alarm – and a new possibility occurred to me. "You haven't been taking anything, have you? I mean hard drugs or anything like that?"

"No." He looked at me, frowning, his eyes puzzled behind the thick lenses. "Get me a psychiatrist, Brenda."

I did as he told me, at once: after making a few discreet inquiries, I phoned a doctor who had been recommended to me as one of the best in the country. Unfortunately, though, John's immediate schedule was so heavy that the first appointment I was able to make for him was not for another twelve days.

For the first time in years, I began asking myself serious questions about John's father and his tragic illness. John had a copy of his father's book, describing the breakdown in detail – and often over the past months I had found him reading it with a grim concentration . . . Could breakdowns like that be hereditary? – I was sure I had heard that they could. But then, his brothers and sisters, if in some cases a little eccentric and liable to bouts of depression, had always been totally sane. So why should John be any different from them?

No, I reassured myself silently, such thinking had to be on the wrong tack.

174

On November 20th, we were due to play in an important Royal Concert, at the Festival Hall in front of the Queen and the Duke of Edinburgh. The London Symphony Orchestra was to accompany us in the Mozart three piano concerto, and once again, André Previn would be playing with us.

But as in Houston five years before, I was becoming increasingly worried because John had not practised the work with me – nor, to the best of my knowledge, had he done so alone. The rehearsal with the orchestra had been called for the pre-concert evening – and as John was not due home from some south coast concerts until the same morning, the only chance we would have for a private run-through together would be during that afternoon.

But the morning passed with no sign of John. After lunch, I phoned the hotel where he had been staying, and was told that he had checked out hours before. The clock ticked on, it seemed to me ever more slowly – it was three o'clock ... four ... five ... not a phone call from John, not a word. Six o'clock ... I sat in the dining room with my mother, who was staying with us at the time: "Where can he be?" I asked her pointlessly. "We'll have to leave for rehearsal in less than an hour!"

"Calm down, Brenda," she said, though she was even more agitated than I. "I'm sure that he's going to turn up."

"I'm nervous enough as it is, without having all this on top of it!" I got up, and began to pace the room restlessly. "I hope he's alright, that he hasn't had some kind of accident. Why doesn't he call? Where *is* he?"

At six thirty, we heard the front door slam; moments later, John strode into the room. Both my mother and I were momentarily dumbstruck – his eyes were wild and unfocussed, his hair was all over the place, and his clothes were a dishevelled mess.

"John ..." My first reaction was that he must be drunk; but I swallowed my reproaches and questions. If John felt like explaining, he would, without any prompting from me – if not, nothing I could say would persuade him. Besides, the situation was so urgent that I risked provoking a scene – "You're not fit to be seen on the street, let alone go to rehearsal!" I noticed the stubble was thick on his cheeks. "Change your clothes and shave and, John – hurry! We'll have to leave the moment you're ready!"

175

To my relief, he went upstairs without protest.

It was not so much alarm as anger I felt – he is more impossible than ever, I fumed ... But when he came down to the
room again some twenty minutes later, looking better but still
rather tousled, I only said "Right – we'd better get round."

The rehearsal was held a short drive away, at Cecil Sharpe
House in Regents Park Road – one of the many strange out-
posts where London orchestras have to rehearse. On the way
there, we exchanged hardly a word; and as John sat brooding
beside me, it occured to me he was not smelling of drink ...

I was as tense as a board as the orchestra launched into the
tutti, having no idea how John would acquit himself: but after I
started to play, my months of preparation paid off in an easy
and fluent performance. To my astonishment, though, it was
matched in all aspects by John's; and afterwards – an honour
indeed – the orchestra applauded us warmly. Our conductor
and co-soloist, André, was most complimentary to us: and as
we left for home, I was feeling quite reassured. So what if John
had spent all the night at some party, or whatever it was he had
been up to? There was not much to worry about if he was
capable of playing that way.

The concert itself went very well. But only a day or two later,
there was another distressing episode.

The evening before John was due to première the Schurmann Concerto in Portsmouth with the Bournemouth Symphony Orchestra, he announced that he would not be playing
after all – the omens for the performance, which he said he had
found in the newspapers, were all unrelentingly bad.

I was so upset by this new turn in events that I was almost
ready to give up and let him have his own way; but Gerard, of
course, with his new work at stake, was nothing like so resigned. It took every ounce of his powers of persuasion to get
John to change his mind, but he did succeed at long last. Even
so, not until John actually walked onto the platform were we
completely sure he would play.

But play he did – and superbly.

That night in our hotel bedroom, John began behaving so
aggressively with me, and talking so incomprehensibly about
matters unrelated to our mutual experience, that I went to the
room Gerard was sharing with his beautiful dark-eyed wife
Carolyn, and persuaded them to let me spend the night on a

chair. By this time, I was half-expecting that they would suggest that John should go to a doctor at once: but if the thought had occurred to them, they did not express it to me. And so I persuaded myself that if they could take things this calmly, then maybe I was being hysterical.

And indeed, the following day, John seemed much more reasonable. There were no more problems about the second performance in the orchestra's home town of Bournemouth; and the London première, at the Festival Hall, took place with John in fine musical form.

But at long last, I was getting scared.

Only a week after the performance in front of the Queen – and having played Gerard's Concerto three times in between – John took part in his fifth charity concert that year in London alone: this one had been arranged by our friend Peter Andry of EMI Records in aid of the building fund of his son's school, The Hall, which Richard had also attended. It was held at the Guildhall, and we played our Mozart Concerto in E Flat for two pianos: musically it went with no untoward incident, but off stage, John was again being aggressive and mean.

The next evening, the 28th November, we had been invited to dinner by our friend Brian Masters, along with the actress Barbara Leigh-Hunt. We had got to know Brian – a writer, biographer and critic – through Alistair Londonderry: in fact, it was Brian who had introduced Alistair to his second wife, Doreen Wells, and was best man at their wedding. A lively and witty young man with a razor-sharp edge to his mind, he was an enthusiastic admirer of John's, and we had always enjoyed ourselves in his company; but on this occasion I was so confused and upset that I did nothing at all to help him make the evening the usual success. I remember following him into the kitchen – leaving poor Barbara to cope with my sullen and unresponsive husband – and telling him I could not go on living with John if he continued to be so unpredictable.

After dinner, John, who had been drinking heavily all evening, asked Brian if he had any dope in the house – he wanted to get stoned, he said. Again, it was a deliberate attempt to shock me rather than a serious request; and he succeeded in his intention, though Brian, successfully, made light of it.

We left Brian's home about midnight. As always, I drove; John sat beside me, his shoulders hunched, staring silently out of the window.

As we entered the hall of No. 13, John slammed the door viciously behind us. Startled, I turned to look at him. He was staring at me with hatred – indeed, I am not putting it too strongly when I say as though he wanted to kill me.

"What is it??" I managed to stammer.

He went on gazing straight at me, breathing deeply; beads of sweat stood out on his forehead. There was a violence in his powerful body barely poised on the edge of release.

Trying not to look scared, hoping not to provoke an attack by too sudden or unnatural a movement, I turned to walk from the hall.

At once he lunged – I jumped sideways in panic, but it was a heavy wall mirror that took the brunt of his rage. He smashed the glass – quite how, I do not know: but the crash was deafening, and silvered splinters sprayed over the rug. Again those murderous eyes were fixed on my face; he said hoarsely "This charade has got to stop!"

I had no doubt that I was in danger – somehow I managed to dodge past him and to run outside into the street. He chased after me, but I still had the car keys in my hand – I literally threw myself onto the front seat and immediately started the engine. I accelerated in a loud scream of tyres just as John grabbed for the door.

I made no conscious decision about what I was going to do next – it was instinct that prompted me to go back to Brian's. He was already in bed; but, seeing the state I was in, he was wonderfully soothing and kind. He sat up with me for an hour and more as I described to him what had happened, and as I repeated my anxieties and fears. Tearfully, I confessed I was too scared to risk going home; at once Brian made up a bed for me, lending me a pair of pyjamas.

At 2:30 am John phoned, to find out if I was there; he was sounding quite calm, Brian told me, but I refused to speak to him, as he wanted. In his diary, Brian recorded "John remained affable, but suggested a rare touch of irritation in his voice. 'Oh well, if that's how she feels' he said." Brian also noted that he felt sorry for John, and he wondered if I was over-dramatising my story – and who can blame him for that?

By the next morning, after a sleepless night, I realised that I had no alternative but to return to Number 13. Everything I possessed in the world was there – nor had it crossed my mind seriously that I could ever leave John for good. By this time the maid would be up and my daily help would have arrived – besides which John was off to Ireland that afternoon, so we would not be together for long . . . But I was still apprehensive as I parked the car and walked to the front door.

John greeted me with contrite affection; he must, he said, have had too much to drink. For the first time in several months, he seemed almost his old self again.

I had been hurt by John too often during the last year and more to expect that our troubles were over; but he was so calm, so sweet, so repentant, that I did find myself actively hoping that on his return home from Ireland, things might at least start to improve.

Briefly, that morning with John, I think we both knew an echo of happiness.

On Saturday, 1st December, John came back from Ireland. I heard the taxi pulling up at about eleven o'clock in the morning. I went down to the hall to greet him – and stood rooted as he came through the door. "Get the psychiatrist", he said as he rushed past me; he ran straight up the stairs to the drawing room.

The glimpse I had had of him was brief, but it had been more than enough. It had been not only his extreme agitation, nor the wildness of his expression, that had scared me – it had been the bleeding wounds on his face and hands, the razor-cut crosses on both his temples.

My knees gave way and I sank down on a chair in the kitchen; for five more agonised minutes I just went on sitting, frozen in shock. Above me I could hear his footsteps, pacing round and round, on and on.

Suddenly the spell that was gripping me snapped. I phoned the number of the psychiatrist whom John was due to see the next week; he was out, and as it was a Saturday, it was not easy to trace him – but eventually I did track him down. He promised to come to the house as soon as he could – sometime within the next hour.

179

Then I phoned Brian Masters once more; he too said he would be round right away.

I sat at the kitchen table again; above me, the relentless footsteps continued. Still I could not understand what was happening, still I half believed that this must be a nightmare from which I must very soon wake. But at the same time, somewhere inside me, I knew that I could no longer run from the truth.

23

The psychiatrist and Brian arrived at the same moment. To my alarm and astonishment, John came down the staircase to greet them – but he seemed to behaving almost normally again. He appeared to be unaware of the crosses cut into his temples, of the blood that was trickling down his cheeks; I suspected that he might be surprised if we were to point out that they were there . . .

The psychiatrist went upstairs with John while I stayed with Brian in the dining room. We could hear John talking volubly, but were unable to make out the words. "What can he be saying?" I asked – "Brian, will he be all right, do you think? Surely he will get better soon?" Brian did his best to be comforting – but I was completely unreachable in the icy aloneness of fear.

After about forty five minutes, the doctor came back downstairs; Brian left us, going, with the doctor's permission, to talk in his turn to John.

I asked "What is the matter with him?"

"Well . . . his mood is quite optimistic – but there is serious thought disorder, and I'm afraid that there is some evidence of aural hallucinations as well."

"What does that mean?"

"That he should be in hospital – the sooner the better."

"Oh." Stupidly, I had been hoping I could keep him at home. "Will he be there very long?"

He smiled – the professional non-commital smile of a doctor. "The first thing is to get him there, isn't it?"

He phoned the hospital with which he was associated, and arranged for John's admittance that afternoon. He replaced the receiver and turned back to me. "Have you got a car?"

"Yes."

"Good. I think it would be best if you drove him to the hospital yourself."

"No!" I protested, "I'm scared! You've seen how he is . . ."

"I am sure you have no reason to worry – I wouldn't let you take him if you had. That friend of yours – can't he go with you?"

"I suppose so . . . I haven't asked him."

"Your husband tells me he has no objection to a spell in the hospital, and I am certain he means what he says." And then, politely, the doctor bade me goodbye, assuring me as he went through the door that John would soon be on the road to recovery.

Later, I learned more about that session between John and the doctor. Amongst other things, John had given him an obsessively detailed account of his brush with the charity organiser, who, the previous year, had conveyed he was getting too big for his boots by demanding £50 for expenses. Over the past few weeks, John had confessed, he had become convinced that messages from this man were being concealed in the newspapers, as well as in radio and television transmissions, and that he – John – was constantly being put to all kinds of tests. In addition, he had recently started to feel electric pulses playing all over his body, through which, he had thought, he was receiving the man's direct instructions – one of which had been to cut the ritual cross marks on his temples.

John had further believed that he was destined to re-live the same breakdown which his father had suffered before him, and which he had been reading about so intently; and it was for this reason that he had been willing to accept that he was ill and should have hospital treatment.

This single forty minute session had been enough to convince the doctor that John was the victim of an acute schizophrenic illness, probably of the paranoid type – but he did not tell me as much at the time. Not that I would have understood if he had . . .

While I had been with the doctor, Brian had been talking with John; once more, his diary records what took place . . .

'He keeps looking at his hands, at the palms. "I must have flunked something" he says.

'"What?" I ask, "something long ago or just now?"

182

1a Brenda in 1956

1b John with his parents in Cornwall, 1951

1c Wedding day, Hyde, Cheshire, 1960
In background Peter Maxwell Davies, the best man

2a With Sir Malcolm Sargent, rehearsing
the Shostakovich Concerto No. 2 in F, 1961

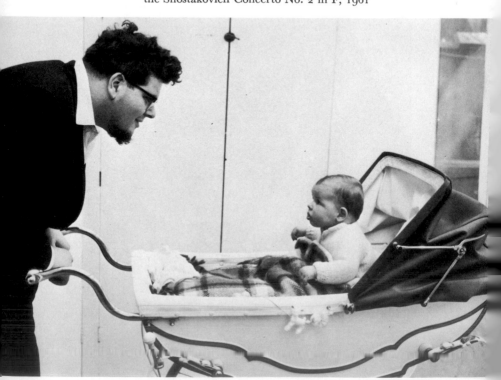

2b John with Annabel

3 Joint winners of the Tschaikovsky Prize – Vladimir Ashkenazy (left) and John, with Khruschev in Moscow, 1962

Великому русско
композитору
Петру Ильичу
ЧАЙКОВСКОМ

4 With Mstislav Rostropovich and Natasha Chaikovskaya, Moscow, 1962, outside
the Conservatoire building

5 During an American tour, 1964

6a John with Denis Matthews – a favourite pastime

6b In a London restaurant, 'Old Vienna', 1967

7a John and Miss Houseley, his early piano teacher, Mansfield, 1974

7b Brenda and John at Bloomington, Indiana, with Michael Kerr, August 1979

8 With their son Richard, London 1980

'"Just now, I should think" he says vaguely, still staring at his palms. "Look, they have gone red. I wish I knew why. It must signify something quite different, but I haven't seen the significance yet."

'"I can tell you, John, Brenda is pretty frightened."

'"I am very frightened myself at the moment."'

John then mentioned the charity organiser again, telling Brian that the man was "the only one to make the correct interpretation". When asked what that was, he said the man had understood why John's father, brother and sisters were in a conspiracy along with Hitler and the Moors murderers. They all saw a new explanation for the universe, he said, but it was an explanation not based on words.

Poor darling vulnerable John – so torn apart, so lacerated with guilt, identifying himself so completely with the forces of evil – and all because he had not given his services to the charity free!

'At this point', Brian's diary goes on, 'we are called down to lunch. John is still perturbed, restless, worried. "Would you like to eat alone, darling?" asks Brenda.

'"Yes, is that a bore?" he says, distractedly.

'"No, sweetie, of course not."

'He goes upstairs, the maid takes him a tray. I am touched and impressed by Brenda's deep love for him, and his dependence on her, which I had doubted at times . . .'

As so many other people have doubted, before and, particularly, since.

During lunch – which I could do no more than pick at – I asked Brian if he would come with me to the hospital, and without hesitation he promised he would.

I went upstairs to tell John we should soon be leaving. By this time, the blood had dried on his cheeks, but since I had last seen him he had daubed his face with white powder, and was wearing lipstick as well. Determined at all costs, somehow, to cope, I packed him an overnight bag with no comment, and persuaded him to come downstairs again.

Up to this point, Brian had not actually seen the incipient violence in John – so few people have, so few even today are

183

able to believe it existed. But now, on walking into the hallway, John paused by a large, hand-painted Danish vase and stared at it with such slit-eyed fury that we were both of us certain that he was going to attack it. As I tried to coax him out of it, I was all too aware – as was Brian – that his target could easily become me: but I had the courage of sheer desperation, and eventually, by one means or another, distracted him from the vase.

By this time, his willingness to leave with us had weakened; he walked from one room to another, going anywhere but to the front door. But finally Brian persuaded him to put on his coat, and together we half-cajoled, half bullied him outside on to the street and into the car.

It was a long drive to the hospital, and one that the doctor had been wrong in letting us undertake on our own. There was heavy traffic for most of the way because of a football match; and apart from one silent and near-tearful episode, John was getting ever more agitated. Suddenly he started trying to strip off his clothes, and every time we pulled up at a traffic light, he did his best to open the door and get out. Brian was marvellous with him, restraining him not by physical action, but by constant, even light-hearted talk. It was a terrifying drive; but somehow we got him at last to the hospital.

Once there, John's agitation became still more extreme – he could not keep still for a moment, but kept on pacing in circles. I vaguely remember talking to the admitting sister, and, with the help of some nurses, getting him into the bare room where he was to stay.

Brian wrote later that John suddenly announced . . .

> '"That's it! I've seen it!"
> '"Seen what, John?" I ask.
> '"The answer. In six hundred and sixty six years, the old people will murder all the babies, to give themselves an extra piece of life" . . . Shamelessly, he undresses, fantasising. I am near to tears myself. It is pitiful and awesome to see a great man reduced like this.'

At the time, we both thought that John's stripping was a form of desperate exhibitionism, a matter of forcing us to pay him attention. But now I know that in fact it was a sense of inner imprisonment, of suffocation, quite common to the deeply disturbed; the same sense that had made him throw open the top-storey window in Chester Terrace only a couple of weeks before.

We spent two hours with John before a doctor even turned up to see him. For the first thirty minutes or so, the excited ramblings continued; and for all of that time, we were both still frightened of him – of what he might be capable of doing to us, or perhaps to himself. But then gradually he began to calm down, and started talking wistfully, even poetically – as Brian said, in terms of childish discovery: "Water is wet, grass is green, the water under the mountains is beautiful."

"Yes," Brian said softly.

"Women are beautiful," John whispered. "Their hair is like silk."

"Yes," Brian soothed him. "Yes, it is."

In this quiet and trusting state, John was almost unbearably touching. And for the first time I was struck at how thin a line divides madness from so-called reality. After all, John was still making sentences, stringing words together in sequence; he remained recognisably himself, unmistakably John . . .

At last he mumbled himself into sleep, lying like an exhausted bear on the bed, and when a doctor eventually turned up, it was time for Brian and me to leave.

It was a silent drive back into town. Profoundly grateful, I thanked Brian for all he had done, saying goodbye to him at the front door: And once in the house, I sat motionless, too drained and too empty to cry.

I had not been at home very long when the phone rang. It was John.

He sounded his everyday self. "I want to get out of here" he said. "I'm coming home."

I stiffened. "John – you *have* to stay in the hospital!"

"No I don't." Before hanging up, he said "I know my rights!"

I was concerned, but not deeply worried. Though it was true that no commital order had been signed, and that legally he could leave hospital whenever he felt like it, I did not seriously believe that his call was more than bravura.

At about 8.30 pm, I heard a taxi pull up outside the house; I got up to look out of the window in time to see John step into the street.

I tried to appear unperturbed as he walked into the drawing room. The moment that I set eyes on him, I realised that there was no immediate danger – he was calmer, and obviously drugged. But he still looked very unfocused; and his suitcase, which he had been aware enough to bring with him, was half-open with its clothes tumbling out, while its leather straps trailed on the floor.

I let a few minutes pass before calling up the psychiatrist; I did not want to provoke John by taking too premature an action. I had fully expected, though, to provoke the doctor into taking immediate steps of some kind; and I was surprised and also alarmed when he promised to come to the house, not at once, but the following morning.

Though the maid we employed at the time had her own room in the house, I did not feel safe with just her there when John was in so unreliable a state; so I turned to Brian Masters yet again. A brave and true friend to both of us, he was soon ringing the doorbell.

Still it was the charity organiser who dominated everything that John said: he was, we were told again, unique in perceiving the unspoken truth. But eventually exhaustion overtook John once more, probably helped this time by the drugs, and he dropped off into sleep.

Up to now, I had been unable to see any further than the situation that faced us immediately: but during the interminable night, the larger implications began to dawn on me for the first time. It was not only John himself who was so suddenly and dramatically threatened – it was the children, his career – the whole way of life that we led. I remained wide awake until dawn, fighting hard to convince myself that very soon, all must be well again.

And indeed, next morning, John had apparently made a miraculous recovery, and over breakfast he chatted to us with an unbroken lucidity. My hopes began to soar fast – clearly the crisis had passed... But my optimism was dashed when the doctor put in his belated appearance. "You've got to get him back into hospital", he insisted – adding with what seemed an inapposite urgency under the circumstances "And at once!"

Again he contacted the hospital and once more it agreed to accept John – provided that this time he was put in a more secure ward. I was afraid that after dismissing himself, he might well refuse to go back – but he was even more willing to obey the psychiatrist's instructions than he had been the previous day, conceding with a rational matter-of factness that he did need medical help.

'A realm of Bedlam, like Dante's *Inferno*' Brian wrote about the ward into which John was taken. 'Women crying, women stripping naked, women fondling us ... John is not in that state at all. He sits down to lunch with them for about two minutes or less, but one of the mad women hits him on the head, and he gets up ... A woman throws coffee cups all over the floor, while another woman castigates her. It is a vision of torment.'

Seeing our horrified reaction, the doctors insisted that it was in John's best interests to remain there. But I agreed wholeheartedly with Brian – John was not like the others, next to the others he was docile and sane! On and on the argument raged, four doctors against Brian and me ... John was famous, a great pianist, we told them – he had experienced a brief schizoid fantasy, that was all, he must not be left in this place!

Finally, Brian cut the argument short – John had not been committed, he said, and there was no law to force him to stay. Swearing he would find an alternative hospital, he helped me take John outside to the car.

Back at home, over lunch, John was quiet, almost totally withdrawn; he seemed hardly aware of our presence. But little wonder his condition had worsened, Brian and I both agreed in our ignorance: the experience he had just undergone would have been enough to drive the sane mad!

By now I too felt stunned into helplessness; but Brian was a dynamo of energy, phoning the psychiatrist, anyone and everyone he could possible think of who might be able to help John.

Eventually it was arranged that John would be admitted as a private patient by the Priory Hospital in Roehampton.

The Priory, which is set in its own large and immaculate grounds, is a rather luxurious place, yet reassuringly cozy in atmosphere. John was given his own pleasant room, and there was an attendant posted outside his door every hour of the day and the night. And there were no bars, chains or heavy pad-locks of the kind we had seen at the other hospital.

We met the doctor who would be in charge of John's case; his manner impressed both Brian and me, and I told him as much as I could about John and the circumstances of his breakdown. Afterwards, as if my talking so freely might have reduced the problem to less awesome proportions. I half-asked, half-pleaded "Doctor, he isn't insane, is he?"

"Temporarily insane" he said gently.

John, who had been heavily drugged on arrival, was still able to make an attempt to get dressed, insisting that he wanted to go home with me. But after some gentle persuasion, during which the drugs increased their effect, he announced that after all he was willing to stay.

During the drive back to Chester Terrace from the second hospital that day, I felt an upsurge of relief. John would be safe and well-looked after at the Priory – and why get hysterical, after all, when he was only temporarily insane? "Temporarily" was the only word that mattered, and I hugged it closely to me. "Temporarily" meant John would get better, and that our lives would soon be normal again.

24

My sense of relief was short-lived.

I went back to the Priory early next morning: indispensable Brian came with me. We found John in bed, half asleep under heavy sedation, and so he remained all the day.

The doctor told us that John was even more ill than he had appeared to be on the surface. Bluntly, he said that there could be no hope for him without a course of electric shock treatment, for which he would need my permission.

The prospect terrified me and frightened Brian as well; we knew very little about such a course, but to both of us it had a threatening ring. The doctor insisted, however, that John would suffer nothing worse than a temporary memory loss – surely a small price to pay for restoring him back to himself.

Something within me went on resisting: I asked for a day's grace to make up my mind. Reluctantly, the doctor agreed.

I felt the burden of deciding was too much for me alone – John was not only my husband, he was a public figure and an outstanding artist. So when I got home, I phoned a few of our closest friends and asked them for their advice. Most of them were against permitting the treatment, but for reasons as vague and superstitious as mine: whereas the two or three who were in favour all appeared to be better informed. They pointed out that shock treatment was in common use all over the country – it was nothing strange or underhand or shameful.

All the same, after hours of agonising, I decided to refuse the doctor permission.

My decision was not well received. I was told that unless I permitted the treatment I must take John home with me again.

By this time, I was up against more doctors than just the one officially in charge of John. An admired and successful Harley Street teacher and practitioner had also seen John professionally, along with a practising psychologist of the highest repute: and both of them supported the proposal for shock treatment.

But that morning, when I visited John in his room, he had seemed calm and quite rational again. "He's behaving almost normally today" I told the doctor defensively.

"Mrs Ogdon!" the reply came, exasperated, "please accept my word that his condition is very serious indeed, whatever he may look like to you! It would be dangerous for him and possibly for you if we continue to withhold the treatment." The threat was repeated – "Do as I ask or else take him home with you!"

I could not make up my mind if he was bluffing or not; but obviously I could not risk John's dismissal from hospital. All the same, I asked for, and won, another twenty four hours to think.

Back at Chester Terrace, Brian, as always, lent his support. In purely emotional terms, he too was opposed to the shock treatment: but the decision, as he pointed out, had to be a matter of logic. And logic dictated that, having already tried two hospitals in only four days, there was no reason to suppose that a third would disagree with the Priory. And anyway, it was ridiculous, not to say foolhardy, to imagine that we could know better than reputable and experienced doctors who were unanimous in their opinion that the treatment was vital for John.

On Wednesday 5th December, after two days of doubt and delay, I gave my reluctant permission.

From that moment, though I did not realise it then, knives were drawn and sharpened against me in certain cliques in the music world.

It might appear strange that I should have been under attack for allowing a respectable and still-common method of treatment; but the objectors insisted that John's case was an unusual and special one. He is a pianist, an artist, a genius, they stressed, as indeed, they still stress today – his talent might well have been affected, not to mention his physical co-ordination. . . . The first reservation, I am sure, is unjustified. The second, about his co-ordination, had not even occurred to me, and alas, it did prove to have some validity – if only for a very short time. Even so – better a thousand times a clinker or two in performance than perfect facility denied of expression!

190

And an artist, however outstanding, is also a man – and a million times better a sane healthy man than a great talent locked in a cell!

The decision may or may not have been the right one, but I stand by my reasons for making it.

All that being said, John's spell in hospital gave me my first experience of what I thought then – and what I think now – is the excessive secrecy of the medical profession, not just at the Priory, but in general.

How could I have been allowed to believe that John would be so easily cured?

In time, I was to learn that there had been a general agreement that the clinical picture was that of a paranoid schizo-affective psychosis – which, in layman's terms, means very big trouble indeed. But, in the early days of his illness at least, nobody told me as much. Nobody prepared me for the fact that the drugs John was currently taking were not guaranteed to be the best ones for his condition, that his treatment was likely to be one of experiment and possible error, and that even if the right course were found, the strength of dosage, and the balancing of one set of pills with another, might be a protracted and delicate process. No one prepared me for the fact that less is known about the treatment of mental illness than about that for most physical ailments. Nobody prepared us for the probable side effects inherent in so many drugs – blurred vision, severe constipation, or perhaps sudden shivering attacks. And though the doctors must have been aware that a long struggle might lie ahead of us, not one of them gave us a warning.

Who knows? Perhaps they were trying to build up our confidence. And if I had asked the right questions, doubtless I would have been answered. But I did not know what questions I ought to ask.

So I took John's imminent recovery for granted.

Peter Andry did not share my fool's paradise; and he asked the doctor in charge directly "Will Brenda have to take all the responsibility for John?"

"It is none of your business" the doctor said. "You are not even one of the family!"

But neither did he answer Peter's question for me...

During the time he was in hospital, I visited John almost

191

every day; and soon, some of his friends were allowed to see him as well. He was mostly uncommunicative with me: but when I was not there, in the first three or four days, I am told he would talk about the charity organiser endlessly, as well as about the conspiracy in which he believed they were both taking part. But later, as his mind began to run on less bizarre channels, he turned his verbal resentment on me – though never once when I was present myself.

Apparently, during his more depressed periods over the next two years or so, John was liable to repeat these attacks on me, if with rather less vehemence than in the Priory. Alistair has told me that he and other friends used to ask John "If you feel like that about Brenda, why on earth don't you leave her?"

"Oh no, I couldn't do that" he would reply. "No, I don't want to do that!"

Perhaps stupidly, under the circumstances, I was very hurt when I found out what he had been saying. Richard Croucher – the friend who had been our dinner guest when John had been so rude about me and our piano team – has tried to put things in perspective for me. "Of course, his illness made him irresponsible" he said: "but apart from that, you must never forget that however brilliant he is, he is still in many ways a child – and that when he married you, he was in a sense going from one mother straight to another. And any child, if it feels insecure or threatened or that things are not going well, is liable to tell the world how mean Mummy is. But he doesn't mean it, you know."

Even so, some people apparently believe that John did mean just what he said.

John had stopped making accusations against me by the time he left the Priory. Alas, almost everything else about him had either stopped or slowed down as well.

In the three weeks he had been in the hospital, he had been given six courses of shock treatment, and they had indeed had their effect. He was drained of energy, and showed little interest in anything or anyone; and if he had lost his obsession with the charity organiser, he had also forgotten a great deal else in his recent life, the good things as well as the bad. His coordination, too, was not all that it should have been.

And quite apart from his reaction to the shock treatment, he

192

was still very heavily drugged – I had to administer huge and elaborate concoctions made up of stabilisers and strong anti-depressants. I was convinced that the dosage was excessive by far (though I now realise I may have been wrong) – but in any case I had no choice but to do as the doctors instructed.

When the children came home for the Christmas holidays, John was still in hospital: and I did my best to prepare them in advance as to what they ought to expect. Even so, for the twelve year old Annabel and the eight year old Richard, it was an awesome and sobering experience to see their father in so zombie-like a state. But they both behaved wonderfully to him, treating him with an unself-conscious love and great gentleness.

Christmas was of necessity a very quiet affair – but perhaps surprisingly it was not unhappy. However slow John was, or however overdosed, we were experiencing some peace at last – the peace, as I believed with all my heart, that follows after a storm has blown itself out. For the entire family, I think, the year ended on a note of high hope . . .

What were the reasons for John's breakdown? I wish that there were easy answers.

First of all, what is a nervous breakdown? Most people think of it as a kind of opting out – as a time when things become too much to bear and one goes to bed and refuses to get up again. Probably that is the most common kind – but of course, there are many variations included in the overall heading of a "breakdown". For example, far from opting out, the patient can be so convinced that humanity's fate rests squarely on his shoulders that he becomes afraid to make the smallest of movements for fear of the consequences world-wide. Belief in elaborate conspiracies, similar to John's, are by no means uncommon; prevalent too is a desperate search for meaning, a need to understand and make sense of the universe . . . Such mental illnesses carry labels, of course, with any number of qualifications and sub-headings, which need not concern us much here. Suffice it to say that to the friends and the family of the sufferer, such manifestations usually come as a cruel surprise – again, I presume, because to talk of such experiences frankly is still considered – though dangerously – taboo.

So – if breakdowns can have many and varied expressions,

193

can we be sure what causes them to happen? Stress, of course, and bereavement – there can be a multitude of obvious pressures. Some people consider that heredity may play a part; or the patient may be the victim of an illness that strikes for no apparently logical reason.

But how can these generalities be applied to John's individual case? In face of my experience over the years. I can only say that, in the particular as in the general, I do not believe in any one cause for the breakdown. True, for a long time he had been driving himself much too hard: but far from being a cause of his condition, this may well have been a symptom. Some of our friends believe that the final contributory factor was the effort he put into the Schurmann concerto, which he premiered in the week before his crack-up – and yet, John actively enjoyed the long hours he spent on preparing the piece.

The charity organiser's criticism of John's moral responsibility was most certainly of overwhelming importance. (Its shattering effect, of course, was something the man could not possibly have foreseen). For years the mixture of guilt and indignation connected with that episode returned to haunt John again and again, until everybody who knew him feared it could never be exorcised completely. But a catalyst, however powerful, is not the same thing as a cause.

And there is me.

I will not stoop to pretending that I am the ideal partner for John. But few matches between us mortals are ever made, or continue, in heaven; and, for reasons I will discuss later on, I defy any blanket condemnation.

But all these possibly contributory causes do not *explain* why the breakdown took place; many people drive themselves too hard, suffer criticism and stress without mentally falling apart. So another and most vital reason must have lain within John himself.

I have already mentioned heredity, and some experts do think that there is a chemical imbalance to which John's family is prone. Who knows, according to them, it is likely that in the most ideal of possible worlds, John might still have suffered a breakdown.

But psychological illnesses may be no more the result of heredity, circumstances or stress than are those that attack other parts of the body; in short, they are just what they are said to be

– illnesses. Just as a diabetic keeps a supply of insulin for use in a possible emergency, so must a psychotic keep pills available in case of a sudden attack. Manic depression is no more anyone's or anything's "fault" than the onset of crippling arthritis; while schizophrenia is as much of an illness as, say, multiple sclerosis.

Of the labels used by the doctors over the years for John's condition, the most common was "schizo-affective" – which means, in general terms, a condition which may have schizophrenic, schizoid or schizophrenia-like features, but which is indeed qualified – and modified – by the addition of strong emotional influences such as depression, excitement, or fear. Such emotions are often lacking, or blunted, in true schizophrenia, and their presence – thank God, in John's case! – greatly improves the prognosis (or medical forecast).

The doctor at the Priory told me that John was also almost certainly a manic depressive; he described John's God-like self-confidence in 1973 as the manic phase, and warned me, rightly, of future depressions. But oddly enough the words "manic depressive" hardly figured in any of the British diagnoses that I was shown then or any time up to 1978. In the light of what we have learned about John, I wish that more stress had been laid on them.

Yes, friends in the past have told me, they understand what I am trying to say about the intricacies of mental illness. But five minutes later, these same friends might very well comment "If only John had never played that charity concert", or "Of course, he drove himself into it, working as hard as he did." And one realises that, still, a vast number of people simply cannot or will not break away from straightforward and rational explanations.

I suspect that this must be because to abandon such explanations would necessitate the unsettling admission that any one of us, at any time, could be vulnerable to some form of insanity. So attempting to make sense of the senseless is one way of distancing that fear.

But so self-protective an attitude does not advance understanding: and meanwhile, we, our families and our friends remain, as much as ever, at risk.

I do believe, however, that willingness to accept the facts of mental illness is at last beginning to show some improvement; for one thing, the increasing effectiveness of drugs, though by no means guaranteed, is lessening the menace of madness. As the menace recedes, people are prepared to be considerably more honest: and it is through honesty, and never through evasions and veils, that we – the victim and his loved ones alike – can find the strength that helps us survive.

But the day when ignorance no longer rules is still a long way in the future.

Meanwhile, when John came home from the Priory in 1973, my ignorance rivalled the best of them.

25

Most of John's concerts for January naturally had to be cancelled. But early in the month, he started to practise again – at first only for about half an hour a day, but the sessions grew rapidly longer, and soon his co-ordination problems appeared to have vanished. He was still quiet and very remote, but I was feeling ever more optimistic.

On Saturday, 19th January, he was due to play a recital of his own compositions at the Wigmore Hall. I was tempted to cancel it: but John told me he wanted to play, and, as many friends and his doctor believed, a return to performing in public might prove to be positive therapy – especially so as the works were his own. And so he kept the engagement – and to everybody's overwhelming relief, he acquitted himself in more than adequate style.

Encouraged, and with the doctor's continued approval, I again let him keep a commitment a week or so later at the Festival Hall, where he was to perform the Delius Concerto from the score. But this time, of course, he had a responsibility not just to himself and the audience, but to the orchestra and conductor as well: and as the day of the concert approached, so did my doubts and tension increase. On the evening itself, Peter Andry, his brother and their wives came with me to lend me – and John – their moral support; and as things turned out, the performance was far from being a disaster. But the familiar fire was missing – the demon had vanished completely.

What else could we have expected, I thought, with all those drugs being pumped into his system? Once more, I challenged the doctor: if John was indeed getting better, could we not *please* cut down on his dosage? No, not just yet, he told me: soon, perhaps. We would see . . .

"But he *is* getting better?" I asked.

"Oh yes" he said, "just be patient. It is mainly a matter of time."

In the first weeks of February, John gave two or three more selected concerts in England – his playing, although often good, did prove to be variable overall and the old excitement did not reappear. At home, too, the expected improvement stubbornly refused to take place: John seemed in a private world of his own, and he would often look through people, myself included, as though for him we did not exist. He was incapable of the smallest decision, of doing anything at all for himself – and as he would not respond to my coaxing, I had no alternative but, when necessary, actually to order him around.

His strange condition began preying on my mind all the time. I was living with a fear I did not want to acknowledge but from which I could never escape: it was unyielding inside me, like a bone-hard, tightly-clenched fist. Not even the kindness of friends could ease its grip for more than a moment.

And most of our friends did rally round and give us support – Brian Masters, perhaps, above all. Alistair and both Andry brothers were unfailingly thoughtful and kind: while Gerard and Carolyn Schurmann were not only sympathetic to me, but unstinting in their devotion to John. Ben Worthington, when he came down to London from Northumberland and Simon and Sheelin Eccles as well, were no less willing to help. I shall forever be grateful to all of them – and I was touched and impressed to realise how deep a love John had inspired.

Suddenly, in the middle of February, John became less remote – he was even occasionally quite talkative, and everything he said was totally sane. Immediately my spirits took flight – the worst was over at last!

He was due to make a tour in the States at the end of the month, which I had feared he might have to call off: but now that things were looking so different, I asked the doctor's advice.

"Yes" I was told. "Let him do it."

I went with John, of course; improved though his condition might be, there was no question of him travelling all that time on his own. The first stop of the tour was in Denver, where John played Shostakovich's Second Piano Concerto in F Major, with the Denver Symphony Orchestra under the English conductor, Brian Priestman. We discovered that another British musician had flown to Denver as well – the composer Richard Rodney Bennett, whose Concerto for Orchestra was being premiered in the same programme.

After two appearances in Denver, at both of which John performed well, we all flew on to New York, where the programme was repeated a third time, at Carnegie Hall. Once again John played successfully – our only real disappointment being the lukewarm critical reception that was given to Rodney's outstanding new piece.

All this time, John's condition was continuing its belated improvement – so much so that I actually felt safe in letting him travel on his own for two or three short concert trips while I stayed behind in New York.

The final concert of the tour took place in California; from there, we flew back to London. And only days after our return, to my incredulity and my dismay, John lapsed into a mood of black introversion.

This was not meant to happen, I told myself and everyone furiously – he had been well on the road to recovery, so how *could* he have a relapse? But I tried my best to rationalise the reversal – he had been through a lot, after all, and I could not expect any overnight miracles. The tour had been a little too much, too soon – he was tired, what he needed was rest . . . Yet even as I tried to bolster my optimism, my irritation at his brooding passivity increased – it seemed to me that he was making no effort to help himself, that he was not fighting towards a recovery. It was difficult for me to believe that he had no choice in the matter, particularly as I was not told as much: and so I confess that I needled and badgered him. But that was also my way of trying to side-step despair.

On 7th May, John played Mozart's Concerto in B Flat, K.450, with the London Philharmonic Orchestra at the Festival Hall. In the interval, the leader of the orchestra, Rodney Friend, drew me aside. "John is very strange, Brenda" he said: "Very strange."

I had always respected his blunt Yorkshire honesty; so I found his comment deeply upsetting. But I was as determined as ever to believe in the imminent recovery – and perhaps innured by

199

this time to the degree of John's odd behaviour, I did my best to forget the ominous words.

Later that month John played at the Bromsgrove Festival, and also in our home town of Manchester at the Royal Northern College of Music, the new buildings of which had just opened. I was cold with apprehension before this latter recital because it was going to be broadcast – but in fact he played superbly, and his performance drew excellent reviews. Relief prompted me to over-reaction: "Really, he's right back on form again" I told everyone brightly, myself almost convinced by the words. "Soon we won't even remember his breakdown!"

But however much I tried to be positive, my body would not be deceived. The fist inside me retained its cruel grip, and I was already visibly thinner.

June came, and with it a visit to Switzerland, where John had been invited for the second year running to give master classes at L'Institut des Hautes Études Musicales in Crans Sierre, not far from Montreux. The Institute's co-founder was the conductor, Daniell Revenaugh, one of the most colourful personalities either of us have come across in our lives. Florida-born, and about the same age as John, he is too blunt and exuberant for some people's taste; I remember that when he entered the EMI headquarters in London, some of the staff would leap from their desks and make a mad dash for cover. But John has always been particularly fond of him, and with very good reason. For all his brashness, Daniell is attractive, brilliant, and full of ideas, and he has proved one of John's most loyal and positive friends from the time they first met to the present.

The two men had originally been drawn to each other by their shared enthusiasm for Busoni – in fact, Daniell was largely responsible for getting EMI to record the concerto with John, while he himself conducted the orchestra. And to bring them both even closer – he had been henchman, student and confidant to Egon Petri (under whom the youthful John had studied in Basle) during the pianist's last years of life in California.

John's first visit to the Institute the previous May had been one of 1973's happier experiences – and now, with so good a friend with whom to spend time, and the advantages of the towering scenery, a charming town, and the delightful apartment that Daniell had found for us, things should have boded well once again for our time in Crans Sierre.

But John, in the week or so before our arrival, had been so quiet, so slow, so – it seemed to me – over-drugged, that I did not see how he would be able to teach, let alone play as well as he should. And so I took a difficult decision; entirely on my own responsibility, I cut down on his medication.

In terms of his playing, my action appeared to be justified. In Crans Sierre itself, he performed very well when occasion demanded; and a trip to Berlin with the school orchestra saw him on excellent musical form. Equally, I am convinced that his ability to teach was greatly improved – and though his students undoubtedly found him eccentric, they seemed to enjoy their classes with him.

But John's state was in some ways even more worrying than it had been before our arrival. His eyes, which for months had been lifeless, began looking disturbingly wild; while, although he was no longer continually silent, what he now said was not always logical, and the name of the charity organiser was starting to crop up again. But, still, I searched for the bright side: at least he's not going on about the man, I thought – it just means that he's getting his memory back...

Daniell must have been very perturbed – but perhaps, like me, he wanted to believe that John's recovery, though slow, was assured. In any case, the pretence went on as before.

On the way back to England – with John on full dosage again – we stopped off at Geneva, where my cousin Geoffrey had an apartment. His wife, Gill, is a nurse; and she was one of the first people anywhere to talk to me frankly about our situation.

"John is very ill indeed" she said. "Brenda, surely you can see that for yourself!"

"Other people don't say so!"

"Because they're scared" she told me. "People are!"

She asked me how I would cope if John were to break down completely again; would we be able to manage financially? What about the children and their education? Was I prepared to look after John – and if so, did I know how grim, how frustrating, how draining it is to care for the mentally ill?

Though the prospect Gill's frankness presented was undeniably stark, she did make me realize that ours was not an isolated case, that there were uncountable precedents in the world, that other people had known pain and fear and that somehow they had survived. She helped me realise as nobody else had that John and I were not alone.

If only a few other people had been half as honest as Gill! If I had been made to face up to the fact that John might be regressing instead of improving, I would have been more understanding and patient with him and, as a consequence, kinder.

But as Gill had said, most friends were scared to be honest, and hers remained a voice in isolation. Ignorance continued to carry the day – "His condition is only temporary" I kept on insisting. "Our doctor has promised us that!"

All this time, the building of our house at El Madronal had been continuing – very slowly indeed, but nonetheless surely as well. And of course the work had to be paid for, which – with the dollar premium as high as forty five percent at the start of the year – was proving very expensive indeed. In three payments between late January and the middle of April, I sent Paco Parladé close on £10,000, which I had to borrow from the bank against the value of No. 13.

To make matters worse, the property market in Britain was going into a dramatic slump – and houses in Chester Terrace, which only a year earlier were being sold for upwards of £200,000, were now being valued at less than half that amount. Our bank manager, alarmed at seeing the value of our collateral dwindling in so spectacular a fashion, while John's earnings were less than they had been, began putting increasing financial pressures on us. I was becoming reluctantly, but increasingly convinced that even if – or rather, *when* – John returned to a full-time performing schedule, we would be forced to sell one of our houses if we were to repay our fast-mounting debts.

From early July to September, I had arranged to rent a house near San Pedro de Alcantara on what seemed to me reasonable terms. Very extravagantly in the circumstances, I arranged for John's Model A Steinway Grand to be shipped out to Spain so that he could practise while we were there: I was convinced that the chance to play as he wished while leading a relaxed and pressure-free life, would do him all the good in the world.

The house, Puerto de Cortes, white-columned and with a generous balcony, was charming, if primitively equipped inside; there was a swimming pool, and only the previous year the garden had won a prize as the best on the Costa del Sol. And far from least in the holiday's assets, there was my friend and daily help from Chester Terrace, Bridget Reynolds.

Bridget was beautiful and bright, and to me, by this time, indispensable. At home in London, she would arrive early in the morning and, after a discussion with me, do the shopping, make our lunch, and leave a delicious dinner behind in the 'fridge: then, her tasks impeccably done, she would leave again at 2:30. Now, in Spain, the dinner parties she did for me made her the talk of the Costa del Sol. The wealthy widows who dominate the social scene there tried to persuade her to remain and to do meals for them as a freelance – but fortunately for me and our family, she opted to come back to England and us.

The sun shone, friends came to dinner or lunch, and we made return visits to them – we spent hours at the beach and the club, we used the swimming pool constantly, and only John and I were not addicted to croquet on the immaculate lawn. Richard and Annabel were lively and happy, and occupied most of my time. We were all of us active and busy.

All of us – with the exception of John. He was again almost totally introverted: he sat through meals in an unbroken silence, even if he was spoken to. He never touched the piano that I had imported, and he would not join us at the pool or the beach. He spent most of his time in his bedroom, smoking continuously while he stared at the ceiling.

At first I tried to chivvy him either into spending some of his time at the keyboard or else into joining us in just having fun. But I soon realised my efforts were useless, and I had no choice but to leave him alone. "He's resting" I told myself and everyone else. "That's why we came out here, isn't it? He's getting his strength back again; we must all be careful not to disturb him."

And still not a soul contradicted me, or discussed John with me directly – though who knows, perhaps, albeit unwittingly, I did not encourage them to. I remember that a friend of ours who was also a practising psychologist and who had come to stay with his wife and family for a few days, did say to me one morning on the terrace "This is a very worrying situation". I waited, half fearful, half hopeful, to see if he would add something more; but he kept silent, and I asked him no questions. If the situation had been truly serious, rather than just "very worrying", then surely he would have told me, I thought.

But repressed doubt still ravaged me physically: I was by now hardly more than a skeleton.

One of the reasons for renting Puerto de Cortes had been to give me the opportunity of.finding out for myself how building was going on Plot 32, and to assess our situation and prospects more accurately. To my delight, I discovered that the house was taking a recognisable shape. It promised to be just as we had envisioned it to ourselves, and as always, the view of mountains and sea took my breath away with its beauty.

Paco Parladé, when I explained our problems to him, was very good about not pressing hard for money – and even though he knew I had wanted the construction work stopped, our relationship stayed cordial and good.

In the middle of August, towards the end of the holiday, John left Spain to keep two engagements in Britain – one was to be in Glasgow, the other was a Promenade Concert in London.

He did not venture a word on the drive to Malaga airport, indeed he seemed hardly to hear what I said to him; but he did not seem to be strange enough for me to consider cancelling the trip. So I kissed him goodbye at the departure lounge, and wished him good luck for his concerts.

In Glasgow, he was met by Gerard Schurmann, whose concerto he was going to play. John's condition, I am told, had deteriorated during the flight, and he was confused and disorientated. Gerard was very concerned, both for John and the performance he was likely to give – and, as it turned out, with reason, because John did not play at all well.

After the concert, Gerard had to go on to Edinburgh – and there was some alarm when John did not turn up on a flight he was supposed to have taken to London. Gerard, alerted by Ibbs and Tillett, was preparing to go back to Glasgow to find out what had gone wrong when word came through that John was staying in his hotel room because of a stomach complaint. Everyone sighed with relief – and three days later, John turned up at No. 13.

Very soon afterwards, on a Sunday morning, I was lying by the pool in the hot Spanish sun when Bridget came onto the terrace. "There's a telephone call from London" she said. "It's your sister."

"My sister! Are you sure?" What on earth could she be calling about? We liked each other, but we had never been close, and contact between us was rare.

I went inside and picked up the receiver. "Janet?"

Her voice was unsteady and tense. "I'm very sorry to have to tell you, but John is in hospital again."

"Oh no!" I cried. "Why? What's happened?"

"He's taken an overdose of pills. Brenda, he tried to kill himself!"

26

I caught the next flight from Malaga to London.

Carolyn Schurmann met me at Heathrow. It was too late to get out to the hospital, and so she drove me to Chester Terrace: on the way there, she told me what had happened.

She and Gerard, she said, had arranged to drive John out to Henley-on-Thames for the day; however, when they had called to pick him up from Chester Terrace in the morning, the front door had been locked and no one answered the bell. Gerard then tried telephoning John from a phone booth, but the ringing tone had gone on and on.

Certain that John must be in the house, Gerard wasted no time in contacting the police. They arrived at No. 13 in a matter of minutes, and broke a window to get into the place. They found John in a coma upstairs.

John owes his life to Gerard's prompt action. He had swallowed a huge number of pills: he was taken at once to the Priory, where a stomach pump was used.

Meanwhile, because the police had been called, the press caught wind of a story, and reporters turned up in force at the Priory. But Wilfred Stiff, of Ibbs and Tillett, handled their questions with consummate skill, and nothing on the subject was printed next day.

Early on the Monday morning, I drove to the Priory expecting to find a pale and weak John: but I walked into his room to discover him sitting up in his bed, and what is more, looking positively cheerful. He had been given a very strong dose of new drugs, mostly, I think, of an anti-depressant named Parstellin: and the second he saw me he said – with more animation than he had mustered in months – "Right, let's leave this place and go home!"

My reaction to this was mixed. Following hard on a shattering relief came resentment and personal hurt. How could he sit there so blithely – how could he not show any guilt for the anguish he had put us all through?

There are moments when to say "Of course, he did it because he is ill" does not seem explanation enough, however true it may be. This, for me, was one of those times.

The doctor was concerned by what John had done, but not, to my eyes, unduly so – in fact, the general attitude was one of encouragement and even of optimism, as if John had been very remiss but now he had been taught a lesson.

I was uncertain what to do next. At some point soon, I would have to return to Puerto de Cortes; it was my responsibility to close up the house, and I had to bring our car to England as well as to get the children back in time to start school (I had left them in the care of Bridget and her brother, who had come to stay with us too). I explained my dilemma to the doctor; to my amazement, he made no objections to my leaving at once, if I needed to.

I was not altogether happy about going back to Spain so soon – but better leave now, I thought, with John still in hospital, than after he had been released to come home.

Closing the house and then making the trip back to England took us several days – I drove across Spain to Biarritz, where we put the car on the train to Paris. At this point Annabel and Richard had only the vaguest conception of what all the fuss was about – and witnessing their spontaneous curiosity and involvement in everything happening around them, I felt painfully protective towards them. For their sake – and I must be honest – the emotions I felt towards John included a growing resentment and anger.

Unknown to me, John had been released from the Priory on 1st September, after spending only five days there altogether; and as I was still not back from Spain, he had been put in the care of the Schurmanns.

The children and I arrived back in London at 2 a.m. a day or two later, after an extremely rough Channel crossing, to discover that the first floor balustraded balcony outside No. 13 Chester Terrace had collapsed in a very bad storm. It was obvious to me at once that it would be a building problem of major proportions: and emotionally it was the last straw.

When John came home from the Schurmanns his good mood of the Priory had evaporated, and he was as depressed as before. I too was gripped by a sense of despair, all the deeper because earlier hopes stood revealed as total illusion. I had to get the children to school, I had a fight on my hands with the Crown Commissioners about rebuilding the balcony, I was worried to death about our debts, I was skinny and physically drained. John was no help at all – not, of course, that I expected him to be; but on top of everything else, I could not accept his lack of concern. I was unable to reach him; he was almost like some inanimate object that only existed so that it could be cared for. It is a sad but commonplace fact that one cannot always find strength in misfortune: and I could not summon the patience to deal gently and lovingly with John, which of course meant that I was no help to him. And so, after only a matter of days, I let him go back to the Schurmanns in Finchley.

Years later, Gerard confessed to me that as long ago as December the previous year, some of our friends and even a doctor had urged him to take as much responsibility for John as he could. After all, he and John had been friends since the late sixties, and the months they had worked together so closely preparing Gerard's piano concerto had resulted in a special rapport. Gerard himself is of the opinion that John has probably confided in him more freely than in any one else in his life.

Gerard so believed in his mission, and was so profoundly convinced that he had a good chance of helping John, that for nine months or so he accepted no new commissions which might have interrupted his ministrations. In the meantime I remained unaware of his sacrifice – and while I obviously realised that he was giving John a great deal of time, I had not yet fully appreciated that he hoped he might prove a healer in addition to being a friend.

Now he and Carolyn were to have John all to themselves for a while . . .

But in his way, Gerard was almost as ignorant about mental illness as I; whereas I had done my best not to see it in the hope that if ignored, it would go away, he still believed that his sincere support would itself prove a life-line enough to haul John to the shores of recovery. Plans were discussed without me at Finchley, not only for the immediate future, but for the long term as well. It was agreed that Gerard would soon accompany John on a Mexican tour, where his concerto was going to be played. There was also a suggestion that John should assert his own independence and get a flat by himself – pipe dreams, of course, for a man who had never looked after himself and who was at the moment more helpless than ever. But I am sure the dreams were well-meant: Gerard was attempting to remove him from the pressures of our life together which were, even now, crushing me.

Sadly, Gerard and Carolyn must have thought then that I was a bad influence on John. I hope that time, and my loyalty to him, have shown that in the long run, they were mistaken – but as I have said, I cannot deny that for that short period, I was far from a help to him . . . Yet perhaps it should also be remembered that the fabric of the Schurmanns' lives, their family and their future were not inextricably bound up with John's. We all had the privilege of loving him; but I am not denigrating their efforts when I say they could not share the heavy practical burdens, their existence was neither threatened nor falling apart – and they did have the luxury of choice.

But in any case, it is undoubtedly true that during his first days back in Finchley, John's mood did appear to improve; he even, in a desultory way, kicked a ball about in the garden.

Meanwhile I was continuing to cope as best I could with the builders and bills, with the bank manager, and with the music agents, all of whom were naturally asking me if John's engagements and tours should be cancelled; I was worrying myself silly about what to do concerning our houses with so much less money coming in, and I was even more concerned about the children. Never before in my life had I been so frightened or so alone.

One day, after John had been back at the Schurmanns' for about a week, I could bear the unshared tensions no longer. And so I made a phone call to John. I cannot pretend it was unselfish or kind, or that I was justified in making it – but after all the months of his constant remoteness, it was my own cry for help, an instinctive, uncontainable need to provoke him into some kind of emotional response. At this point, the way I was feeling, any response, even insults, would have been better than none: awareness, whatever its form, was what I wanted from John. To get it, I went as far as to threaten divorce – but still, although he protested, I felt that I had not got through to him.

I put down the receiver every bit as alone as before, except that now I felt unbearably guilty.

Next morning, Carolyn found John sitting up in bed with his glasses on, apparently asleep. She could not wake him up.

After the last suicide attempt, his medication had been changed by the Priory, and the Schurmanns had charge of his pills; so they did not at first suspect another overdose. They called their GP, who, unbelievably, told them not to worry, he was sure John would eventually wake up.

Unconvinced, they phoned John's doctor at the Priory. He demanded they get back to the GP at once and insist that this was an emergency.

And an emergency it proved to be. John, it transpired, had hidden the remainder of the pills which he had been taking in Spain in both his suitcase and sponge-bag – and again, the dose he had taken was huge.

He was rushed to the nearest hospital, Barnet General, and for the second time in less than a month, the drugs were pumped out of his system. Only a man of his unusual strength, the doctors said, could have had any hope of survival.

During the four days he remained at Barnet, my sister Janet, who is a professional nurse, put constant pressure on me not to send him on to the Priory, but to put him instead into one of the great teaching hospitals, the Maudsley, in Denmark Hill in South London. I asked our friend the psychologist what he thought, and he supported Janet wholeheartedly. And so, on 20th September, John was transferred to the Maudsley.

In terms of both luxury and privacy, it certainly was not the Priory, but it was pleasant enough. The day ward where John was to stay was called the Villa, and as well as being a locked ward, it was mixed. For the most part, the staff was made up of young men, who, reassuringly, wore ordinary clothes rather than uniforms; but they were of course trained in controlling patients if there should be any violence or trouble.

Under his new Maudsley doctors, John was give no medication, in order to clear his system completely; then, after being re-examined in his undrugged state, he was put on a new course of pills – altogether a less heavy regimen than he had been living under up to this point.

I remember telling the psychologist that I was disturbed by the way John's medication was being altered so completely and often. "It's a difficult problem," he told me. "Everyone is made differently from everyone else, and responds to drugs in different ways. What they are trying to do is find exactly the right cocktail for John."

"Then let's pray" I said "that this time it's it."

He smiled faintly. "Yes. Let's."

There was one hour's group therapy every day in the Villa – and as a result, John began to experience a sense of camaraderie with the other patients. Sick as many of them were, they shared a common awareness that they were all in the same boat together; also, whereas the sane visitors to the ward tried to carry on sensible conversations with them, and did their best to make sense of the answers, they themselves had a more relaxed attitude. As a rule, if one of them interrupted another, or a second replied in non-sequiturs, no one felt threatened or hurt: if a third walked away in mid-sentence, no one took any offence.

If, to a layman's eyes, psychiatric nurses can appear off-hand or indifferent to the patients under their care, it is because they have learned from experience that normal social communication often does not apply. But compassion is usually there; and if it is not, many patients are instinctively aware of the lack. It is astonishing what a difference just one nurse can make to the atmosphere of a ward.

John was allowed to come home for weekends and the occasional afternoon as well; and after two and a half weeks, he was released altogether. This time, I realised I had to be strong: both his suicide attempts had been made when we were physically apart from each other, and it was my duty to look after him now. Also, however devoted the Schurmanns might be to him, the responsibility was not fair to them – the fight, as they too were realising, would not be quickly or easily won.

And alas, it was very soon obvious that his new cocktail was no more the right one than its predecessors had been; depression cloaked John again.

Things were not made any easier by a blister that had developed on his heel – probably caused by the overdose of drugs. A

211

nurse, in trying to treat it, had inadvertently lanced it – and as a result it had festered. Throughout the month of October, it showed no signs of starting to heal.

John was due to go to the States again for two weeks at the end of the month. The doctors in charge of his case at the Maudsley were in favour of his making the tour: and they found an ally in our friend Ben Worthington, who had come from his Northumberland home to lend us support after John's second suicide attempt.

So John and I flew to America as planned.

By this time his blister was in such a bad state that after only a day in New York, I had to take him to seek medical help for it; as a result, I found myself bathing his foot three or four times every day, and treating it with a variety of powders and ointments. It was an unpleasant chore, and sometimes agonising for John – but at least the blister soon began to get better, which is more than I can say for his mood. Virtually confined to our room by the pain, he would sit all day long on the bed, smoking and not uttering a word. I even had to cajole him into giving each of his concerts; fortunately, most of them were centred around New York, and – considering the circumstances – he played remarkably well.

We flew direct from New York to Manchester, where John was to perform the Britten Concerto with the Hallé. Rather than staying with relatives, we checked into the Midland Hotel – the scene of our care-free spaghetti dinners all those long years ago – which was near to the Free Trade Hall, where the concert was going to be held.

Our flight landed late in the evening, and next day I felt exhausted, both from jet-lag and the New York experience. John's rehearsal had been scheduled for two o'clock that afternoon; normally I would have gone with him, but on this occasion I excused myself, feeling as I did in need of a rest.

John smiled at me as he left for the Hall – that sweet, gentle smile of his that I had not seen for so long. It was a pleasant surprise, reminding me of the old John: he was still there somewhere in the pall of depression, I realised, and I was struck by how much I loved him. I blew him a kiss, and wished him good luck for the rehearsal.

Half an hour later, as I was luxuriously dozing, the bedside

212

telephone rang. It was the orchestra manager calling. "Where is John?" he asked tetchily. "Everyone's waiting for him."

"But he should have been with you twenty minutes ago! He must be in the hall somewhere!"

"He's not, Brenda. We have looked for him and he is not in the building!"

A search for John was embarked upon. I had no idea where he might have gone to: there was little I could do but wait. I lay back again on the bed; I had not the energy to move, but I remained tense and awake...

After two hours, the phone rang again – I sat up and grabbed the receiver. "Hallo?"

It was the wife of the charity organiser. "Brenda," she said, "John is here!"

They lived, as I knew, a great many miles away from Manchester. "Here? What do you mean – where?"

"At our home!"

"What – but he can't be!" Stunned, I told her "He's meant to be at rehearsal..."

"He's saying he must see my husband." She was, not surprisingly, distraught.

I asked her if her husband was home.

"No, he's away for a day or two."

That at least was lucky, I thought. "Tell John he must come back here immediately!" Another alarming thought struck me. "But I'm afraid I still don't understand – how has John got all the way to your house?"

"He's come by taxi" she told me – and added "and he hasn't got the money to pay for it!" She went on to say that the driver refused to return with him unless I guaranteed to pay the fare in cash.

I had no alternative but to agree. So after another couple of hours, John and the taxi arrived, and I handed over £70.

I was too upset to discuss the matter with John, and anyway, discussion would have been useless: yet he was humbly and sadly contrite, like a child when it knows it has done wrong. Fortunately, there was another rehearsal the following day, to which, of course, I went along: and both it and the actual performance went without further mishap.

From Manchester, we returned home to London. John retired to his dressing room, and for several days I saw little of him as he lay by himself, forever smoking.

His next engagement, a recital, was to take place less than a week after his Hallé engagement, in Oakengates in Shropshire. On the morning he was due to leave, he refused to get off his bed. "I don't want to go to Oakengates" he told me.

"John!"

"I don't want to!"

Obviously I could not force him. "All right" I said – "but you must phone Ibbs and Tillett now to say you feel ill and are cancelling, so they have time to find a replacement.'

"No" he muttered. "You do it."

"John – can't you do just *something* for yourself for a change?" Somewhere, somehow, a line had to be drawn – if I could not help him to help himself in even so simple a matter, I might as well give up all hope. "Just pick up the receiver and call them! *Please*, John – it's the easiest thing in the world!"

I left him and went downstairs to our basement office. Once there, I decided that after all, I had better call Ibbs and Tillett myself; I was put through to Beryl Ball, Emmie's long-time and efficient assistant. As I was speaking to her, I heard the lift coming down from John's floor.

It stopped outside the basement, close by the office. I turned to look at John as he came through the door.

"Beryl", I managed to stammer. "Oh my God – John's cut his throat!"

27

The blood was everywhere, it was running down John's chest and soaking his pyjamas: white tendrils hung from two deep slashes on either side of his neck.

I hung up on Beryl immediately and dialled 999. John sat down on a chair. Why he was still conscious I do not understand; it must have been a superhuman effort just to drag himself from the bathroom on the top floor and into the lift. . . It is a wonder that I did not faint either – but I knew that if I could not manage, then John would be very soon dead.

The ambulance came in a matter of minutes; so too did Wilfred Stiff, who, alerted by Beryl, had rushed from his office and caught a taxi to our house. With siren wailing, we set off for University College Hospital; the ambulance men did their best to look after John, to staunch the flow of his blood. I remember crying out "I can't look at him – I can't!"

"Then don't," one of them said to me gently. "You don't need to." All those men were so selfless, unruffled and dedicated, and I cannot praise them too highly.

We were rushed from the ambulance and into the Emergency Entrance – things happened fast and with unfaltering precision. Every one was totally dedicated to the task of saving John's life.

He was given a massive transfusion of blood: and for the third time, remarkably, he survived.

I remember being at a hospital when another attempted suicide was admitted, suffering, as in John's previous attempts, from a drug overdose. "Oh Lord, here we go again" I heard a doctor say with harsh irritation. "Get out the stomach pumps – let's go!"

In my experience, most doctors have little sympathy for

215

those who try to end their own lives; fighting to save a would-be suicide is regarded as a chore and a cruel imposition. And when John was recovering this time, a doctor making the rounds of the wards suddenly lectured him with a bitter and frustrated savagery on the enormity of what he had done.

For me too, it was once again difficult to summon any deep sympathy: and for a long time afterwards, I was guilty about the anger I felt. Only recently, in America, has John's psychiatrist assured me that my response was a natural and healthy one. Suicide, he pointed out, is an act of major aggression: to have pretended otherwise and to have suppressed my defensive reactions could have had potentially dangerous consequences on my own fight to survive what was happening.

For me – even remembering that John was a manic depressive unable to master his moods – each of his suicide attempts was an insult and a personal blow; the feeling of desolate rejection is not transferable in words... Not, I should add, that I berated and scolded him as the doctor had – I did try my best to be kind. But neither did I stroke his forehead and murmur lovingly "There there, never mind, it's all right." Frankly, I think few people do act that way in such circumstances, outside popular fiction.

John stayed in University College Hospital for a week; then, on 11th December, was transferred back to the Maudsley and the same Villa ward. For the first time since his breakdown a year before, he was admitted under certification.

As after earlier crises, both his mental state and his mood soon took a sharp swing for the better; so sometime in the Christmas period, I asked the doctors how soon I could expect him back home.

In six months at the soonest, they told me – probably not for a year.

I was appalled. What could I expect when he eventually came out, I asked – could they promise me he would have recovered? No, the doctors said, with more frankness than I had met with up to now – they were not prepared to guarantee anything.

The whole pattern of John's treatment was making no sense to me, even allowing for experimentation: just five days in hospital after the first suicide attempt (though admittedly that had been at the Priory), less than two weeks after the second, and now suddenly they wanted it stretched to six or even twelve months! If he came home, I protested, he could still be treated as an outpatient, he could still see the doctors three or four times most weeks. But they were adamant that he should remain under certification in the hospital.

John, too, was upset at the prospect of so long a confinement. There was a recital that he was due to give at the end of January in aid of Moorfields Eye Hospital; "I want to play it, Brenda" he told me. "I want to get to the piano again. Take me out of here. . ."

A friend of ours who was a Minister in the government heard about our dilemma and offered to use his influence in securing John's earlier release. Convinced that being at home with constant access to his piano would be be better for John than so many months in the Villa Ward, I accepted the offer; and so, in the end, the doctors gave way. John came home on 22nd January, having spent five weeks in hospital.

The charity concert went well. But a recital he gave at the Wigmore Hall only two weeks afterwards was a disappointment of major proportions.

Peter Stadlen, of the *Daily Telegraph*, long a supporter of John's, noted sadly that he was not his admired self. David Murray, of the *Financial Times*, was deeply offended; of the Brahms Paganini Variations, he wrote. "He set about it with the impersonal destructiveness of the proverbial bull in the china shop. He did it without apparent malice. Indeed, he gave no sign of any feelings about the music at all." Joan Chissell of *The Times* was kinder, but no less puzzled and upset.

I should not have allowed John to play – either then or maybe not at all during the first three months of 1975. And it is possible that the doctors at the Maudsley had been right – no-one can be certain, of course, but in the light of what was to happen, perhaps he should have stayed on in the hospital under continuous and close observation.

Anyway – after the Wigmore, the daggers already being aimed at me were sharpened more keenly than ever. Behind my back, I was accused of not really caring for John, of forcing him to play because I wanted the money. After all, people said to each other – isn't that what Brenda has *always* done?

217

It is a sad and ironic fact that in addition to having to care for the mentally sick, we who are closest to them must also carry the stigma of blame. Almost every breakdown, every suicide, is said to have happened because the mother was too domineering or the wife too cold, or the husband ineffective or selfish; almost every crack-up is supposed to be the fault of somebody else. But the truth is rarely so simple and everyone, before pointing the finger, should pause to consider that they might be only increasing an already intolerable pain.

In my case, rumour has it that I laid extra stresses on John by spending most of his money. And it is true that in John's years of unbroken success, I did indeed spend a great deal of it; we had been healthy, carefree and young, and the prospects for his future career and his earning power had seemed unlimited to us... But when it came to spending with reckless abandon, even I could not begin to keep up with John himself...

Well, the accusation continues, I still forced him to take on too many engagements in order to make all that money we squandered. But it was not I who was finding the concerts! – it was his agents who were getting them for him, and, as is perfectly natural, they were expecting him to fulfill them. Music is a business as well as being an art, and John was making money not just for himself, but for the agencies too. As for me – never on any occasion did I drive him to accept a date that he did not want.

But what about the years immediately following John's breakdown, when I encouraged him to fulfil his commitments? Was that not because I was eager for money?

For most of 1974, when I had tried to hide my head in the sand, there had seemed no better proof of his recovery than to see him maintain his career; and even later, when I realised that the road back to health would be chequered, I still believed that it would do him more good to play – and I must stress, usually in good form – than to sit around doing nothing at all. I continued to believe I was right.

But yes: it *is* true that I wanted the money.

It is too easy to say that right after the breakdown at the end of 1973, I should have sold up all our belongings, taken the children out of their schools, and moved into a cheap apartment somewhere; such action would only make any sense when viewed with the wisdom of hindsight. And besides, we were in

218

debt even then; and being as ill as John was is not only very distressing, but also alarmingly expensive.

I could have gone out and worked of course – taken a teaching job if I could have found one. But that would not have solved financial problems of the magnitude of those facing us. And then who would have looked after John? No fairy godmothers offered themselves. And how many of our friends would have been able to take responsibility for so sick a man, and over an indefinite period, when even the devoted Gerard and Carolyn had eventually felt obliged to give up? .. Or does anyone seriously believe that I should have abandoned him in some Health Hospital or other?

Yes, we needed the money – and "we" included John!

Looking back on my relationship with John, it is not so much the financial problems over which I question myself; what concerns me far more is whether, on a much wider basis, I have always been as understanding with him as I should have been. Human guilt being what it is, I have to say "no, not always." But I must also be fair to myself . . . For example, even before we were married, it was understood and accepted that my task was to look after John, at least on a personal level: he expected and wanted me to organise him and tell him what he ought to do next (except when he made one of his own irreversible decisions, which I would still have to put into practical effect). So if at times I may have seemed domineering, it was because he has tacitly asked me to be.

As for being unsympathetic to his illness ... Through ignorance, I was for some periods less supportive than I might have been, and I have not always been a model of patience. But it is hard to see your whole life collapsing around you; it is difficult not to resent nature's injustice in stealing away so many years which otherwise should have been happy ...

And make no mistake about it: it is not easy to live day to day with someone who is mentally ill. I remember waking up one night to find I was screaming at John in my sleep to stop his diatribes of several weeks about the charity organiser... And almost worse were the depressions: it is indescribably dispiriting to have no feed-back at all, no contact or natural response. I confess there were times, and many of them, when I thought I could not summon the strength to go on – and to go on for who knew how long?

219

There is another important obstacle which is all too rarely discussed. During John's most disturbed periods I had to learn how to treat him with the dispassionate efficiency of a professional nurse, because any heartfelt emotional involvement would have been sure to drive me mad as well. But then, when he was improving, I was expected at some undefined moment to revert to being a wife, sharing, committed, and warm – until the next relapse happened, when I would have to re-harness my emotions... People cannot be robots, however, controlling themselves with a switch: and the adjustments were not only difficult, they were sometimes impossible to make.

The medical profession, at last, appears to be taking a more concerned and overdue notice of the very serious strain suffered by everyone close to the mentally stricken – the Maudsley even had a commendable policy whereby social workers advise the families that are affected... But by the time I came back from Spain after John's first suicide attempt, I had still received almost no personal counselling – and I was in so bad a state that a friend suggested I seek psychiatric advice.

The doctor I consulted wanted to put me into major analysis, delving first of all into my childhood. But surely he should have realised that I could not reasonably have been expected to embark on a long and difficult self-exploration on top of everything else! What I wanted was immediate guidance on how to get through day by day – how to deal with things positively, in the best way not only for me, but for John... But the psychiatrist stuck to my past; and so I left him, and continued to cope on my own.

But if, in some ways, I have failed John, I can honestly claim that I always continued to care for him according to my best abilities: and I stood by him consistently throughout the years of his illness. And however angry or miserable I was, I have never doubted my love for him: neither, I believe, has John doubted me.

After his disappointing recital at the Wigmore, John entered one of those periods when he was exaggeratedly obsessed by the charity organiser, and his silence gave way to a torrent of words. "He wanted to put me down" he would say, agitatedly pacing the room – "the £50 was just an excuse, it was not enough to count one way or the other! I like money, of course, but I wouldn't have said I was greedy for it – cut-price deals have been the story of my life! No one could say I had the wrong attitude because I asked for expenses – no, I *wasn't* getting above myself! It only shows how these self-important organisers get above *them*selves!"

He would grind out his cigarette and light another immediately. "With all this talk about the ethics of charity work, you notice that the ethics of approaching an artist correctly through his agent were conveniently ignored. And afterwards, he didn't go back to the agents to say he couldn't afford £50 – he called me direct on the phone to tell me I was getting above myself! Presumably he knew he was talking to a dedicated musician whose gifts were truly irreplaceable? Didn't he know what people hoped from me, how much they expected? If so, he showed no sign of it, no sign at all! Anyone who knew my schedule would have respected it! People expect too much from artists – why do they have no consideration for the pianists they invite?" He would glare at the person he was lecturing. "What I wanted, just sometimes, and what Brenda wanted too, was fun and laughter as well!"

A moment later, he would relaunch his tirade. "I would like to see *him* give something in return! But *I* was supposed to come floating down all that way – without making problems for anyone! Just let anyone try asking the organiser to come up to London to get me to play! . . ."

And quite suddenly, the guilt would take over: "Yes, but people should do charity work" he would cry. "Still one should do charity work!"

And then he would go back to the beginning, and the whole obsessive cycle would be repeated again – and again and again.

Poor darling John: at the same time that my exposed nerves were aching for him to let up, my heart would be bleeding for him. . . But my crying would be no help to him; and I was beginning to wonder if after all, he should return to the Maudsley.

But now the doctors there were no longer as eager to keep him confined in the hospital as they had been a couple of months earlier: now they believed, on the evidence, that he would probably do just as well staying at home. And so John remained there with me.

Meanwhile, with infinite regret, I had put No. 13 on the

221

market. John, when I told him, was much opposed to my selling it, but he was in no condition to give considered advice. With his future still a question mark, our creditors were pressing us yet harder. The Midland Bank was making very threatening noises; and even Paco Parladé – who had instigated a series of "letras" with his bank in Marbella, which had allowed John to borrow for up to three months at a time – was now telephoning me constantly, asking always for money, more money. With a clearly genuine regret, he told me that there were yet more unforeseen expenses at El Madronal for central heating, tiling, and so on; and in spite of a stream of letters between us, our solicitor, and our attorney in Spain, disputing the small print of our agreement, the estimate for the final price continued to rocket.

Our solicitor, our accountant, our bank manager, in fact every professional adviser I turned to, insisted that No. 13 must be sold. So alas, when the doorbell rang these days, it was less likely to be one of our friends than some prospective buyer or other.

In spite of all the pressures and worries, there was one concert we played that both of us really enjoyed. We gave it at the Dome in Brighton, in April, 1975, for the Jubilee Season of the Brighton Philharmonic Society; and we performed Poulenc's Concerto in D Minor for Two Pianos for the first time together. The conductor, Massimo Freccia, was a delight to work with; and it was a pleasure indeed to hear John playing so well again.

But mentally, he was still in a dubious state as the time approached for him to leave on an American tour that was scheduled for May. The itinerary included concerts in Baton Rouge, Louisiana; White Plains in New York; Fort Wayne, Indiana, and San Antonio, Texas, where he was to play Richard Yardumian's Concerto.

In my opinion, he was in no condition to go on his own – which he would have to do if he did not cancel, as I could no longer afford to go with him. I, John, and a doctor who had recently taken over his case, had several long discussions before the doctor decided that not only was he fit enough to make the trip by himself, but that it could do him good.

It was true that previous spells on the road seemed to have

222

had a positive influence – but I had always been with him, and I was very dubious indeed about accepting the doctor's decision. But John himself was eager to go; though when the time came to see him off at the airport, he suddenly implored me to accompany him after all. As to do so was out of the question, I almost cancelled the tour there and then; but with all his concerts so imminently due, and his US agent expecting to see him in a matter of hours, my nerve failed me, and I let him go.

Four or five nights later, the phone woke me in the early hours. The voice at the other end of the line was American, and it belonged to a nurse in San Antonio, Texas. John, she told me, had been brought into hospital by the police; he was the victim of serious hallucinations and delusions, and for the time being he was being kept in a psychiatric ward. Harold Shaw, his agent, she continued calmly, had arranged for him to be flown first class to New York, from where an agency representative would put him on a plane back to London.

John told me later that when he had arrived at his San Antonio hotel, he had been seeing huge glowing crosses suspended in the sky, and that everybody around him appeared to be wearing crucifixes on their necks – these did not frighten him, however, nearly so much as they tired him. He had gone up to his room on the sixteenth floor – and there he had heard voices summoning him on to the ledge outside the window. He had obeyed their command.

He had been spotted almost immediately, and the police had been called. But John insists that he had had no thoughts of suicide at that point; and when he had heard the police coming into his room, he had climbed back at once through the window... He had been upset when he had discovered that his concert appearance would have to be cancelled, particularly as it was to have been the Yardumian Concerto; and he still believes that he could have played it. And what is more, he is probably right: one of the astonishing aspects of his illness used to be that in some – if not all – of the crises, he was capable of playing most beautifully.

I went to meet him at Heathrow airport: he was very heavily drugged. I drove him straight to the Maudsley.

There were different doctors in charge of him now, and they

223

told me they were in favour of shock treatment. But after John's earlier experience, I was not prepared to give my permission again. The doctors argued furiously with me, but this time, whatever they threatened, I simply would not be budged. I remember sitting in a consulting room the afternoon after John had been admitted, and thinking "If I just stay here and keep on opposing them, they'll get tired and eventually go home." So I held out for more than three hours: and I won.

If only, from the depths of my misery that day, I could have seen that there would soon be reason for optimism! True, the years to come would know difficult periods, the climb back to stability would see brief relapses – but in truth, the very worst was now over.

28

The Maudsley is a showplace amongst psychiatric hospitals; it is one of the best places of its kind anywhere in the country or even the world. At the same time, though, I believed John was the victim of a major curse of the National Health Service, particularly where mental health is concerned – the fact that the doctors assigned to his case were constantly changing.

But at least John's fame ensured him careful medical attention – which, as I have learned from the experience of others, is more than can be said for some lesser known patients in less famous NHS establishments. In many of those, the inmate is lucky to be seen by a doctor for as long as ten minutes each week; and as soon as he has been drugged into some approximation of sanity, he is released to manage as well as he can – even if, as can too often happen, he has been deserted by family and friends.

But if hospital treatment can be perfunctory, out-patient treatment is worse, with the still-convalescent patient often sitting for two hours or more for his fortnightly or monthly consultation, only to be faced with a doctor he has never seen before in his life. On the strength of the one hurried interview, and a quick shuffle through the case papers, pill levels are cut down, maintained or altered, and then everyone hopes for the best . . . Little wonder that many ex-patients suffer from a relapse.

The inadequacy of the Health system is rarely the fault of the doctors themselves – the staff in most psychiatric hospitals is overworked and invariably too small. How the problem can be solved, I cannot imagine – because dramatically improved financial and professional incentives for working with the mentally ill will never be high on any government's list of reforms . . . But sometimes I wonder if the students in teaching hospitals crowding around as the condition of the patients is hurriedly diagnosed, feel, as I do, that they are witnessing a tragedy and a national scandal.

So, fortunate though John was to be at the Maudsley rather than at some London alternative – the fact that different doctors were treating him and demanding a new course of shock-treatment undermined my confidence in keeping him there: though having once lost my faith in the Priory as well, I felt like a fish out of water, uselessly flopping this way and that. But five days after he had been admitted, and after another fierce fight with the doctors, I determined, reluctantly, to move him to the Priory again.

This time, before any recommendations were put forward, I made it clear that shock treatment was out of the question – and if the Priory doctors had ever intended it, they did not tell me as much. Instead, John was heavily drugged – and in a few days, as almost always happened after a crisis, he became visibly better.

He was released on the 27th May, after three weeks in the Priory. His next commitment was a visit to Finland in June, at the Jyväskylä Arts Festival; he was going to give a course of Master Classes, in addition to which he and I were to open the Festival with a two-piano recital. Incredibly to me, considering his recent ordeal, he refused to allow me to cancel.

From the moment of our arrival, we both agreed that Finland was beautiful; and, unlike some people, I enjoyed the unending soft summer light, which was as bright at midnight as at noon. John was playing quite well, and he had some very talented students who appeared to enjoy their studies with him. But his depression, predictably, returned: his mouth was so dry and his lips were so chapped from the new medication he was taking, that he developed an insatiable urge for ice cream. At the same time, he was never without a cigarette – after every one of his classes, the stage would be littered with stubs.

Only once did he briefly perk up, and that was with the Soviet pianist Emil Gilels, who had been chairman of the jury when John had won First Prize in Moscow, and who was to give the Festival's final recital. Stocky and unusually urbane for a Russian, he spoke immaculate English: and one night John and I took a walk with him after a party, through the streets of Jyväskylä. He was quizzing John about the respective merits of various agents in Britain, and I was happy to see that John, for a change, was informative and even quite animated ... But back at the apartment we were staying in, he reverted to his blanketing silence.

Chester Terrace was still unsold. Before leaving for Finland, I had had one offer from an Arab of £90,000 in cash; but after a moment's temptation, I had decided to turn it down. Now, back again in London, I faced the fact that our financial situation had become even worse. Indeed, by now things were so bad that – even if Chester Terrace were to go very soon and for a realistic price – our only hope for financial survival lay in selling Plot 32 as well.

Up to this point, I had hoped to see the house finished completely – at least its value would have been increased, even if we could not have kept it to live in. But after two years of construction work, no more cash was available to us ...

"Property abroad" the *Times* advertisement read, "Magnificent house for sale in Marbella vicinity. High location, eight kilometres from the sea. Panoramic views of mountains and sea. Five bedrooms, four bathrooms, large drawing room with terrace facing south, dining room, kitchen, laundry area, self-contained staff accommodation, garage, patio, and several extra terraces. Just under two acres of land. Payable in sterling or dollars. £50,000."

But no description could do the place justice – nothing could convey the warmth of the stones to the touch, the chorus of crickets under the sun, the vistas of blue sky and sea, the heart-cleansing beauty, that lay behind those cold words. Every time I looked at that advertisement, it was all I could do not to cry.

Selling both the houses would ease, but not solve, our problems – and I was beside myself wondering what was in store for us. It seemed only so recently – it *was* only recently – that we had thought ourselves on top of the world ... How very fast we had fallen!

There was one faint glimmer of hope in the blackness ahead. In the three years since John had first been asked if he would consider joining the faculty of Indiana University, he had received several more letters and telegrams repeating Dean Wilfred Bain's offer; meanwhile, I had been doing some research of my own. It appeared that Ruggiero Ricci had not exaggerated the Music School's high reputation; a recent questionnaire sent out to the Deans of over a thousand accredited and university-affiliated schools had resulted in its being voted the very best in the States, ahead of the Universities of Rochester and Michigan as well as New York's famous Juilliard School. The faculty could also boast some impressive names in its recent history, besides Ricci's – names such as Jorge Bolet, Eileen Farrel, Abbey Simon, Janos Starker, and Menahen Pressler.

It seemed to me that once our overdrafts and mortgages had been cleared, a simpler way of life might do John good – and a teaching post would give him the chance of taking a solvent rest from the platform if he wanted to do so, as well as providing him with a congenial musical environment. I was enthusiastically encouraged in this train of thought by Simon Eccles and his wife Sheelin; together they had been a constant support to us since the breakdown, and I respected their advice.

John had an American tour coming up in October; I resolved that I would go with him, and that we would visit Bloomington together.

Before the October commitments, John had a single engagement in Maryland in July followed by a tour of Australia. And that presented us with a problem – because I would not be able to accompany him. For one thing, it would have been unbusinesslike to travel to the other side of the world with both of our houses still on the market; and of course, the children would be on holiday at that time, and naturally I wanted to be with them.

But after the San Antonio experience, I was not about to let John tour on his own – particularly as he was still profoundly depressed. His pills had to be hidden away from him and very carefully monitored, and I felt the need to check up on him regularly when he was alone for hours in his room. Not that he was disturbed or suffering from mental delusions – but as he himself told me later, suicide was preying on his mind all the time.

So I put another advertisement into *The Times*, on this oc-

228

casion for someone who would act in "a secretarial and general chaperone capacity"; and from the many people who answered, I engaged, towards the end of July, a Mrs. Valerie Lines. She is a divorcée with a grown family, about fifteen years older then us; smallish, blonde and energetic, she struck me – and rightly so, as it proved – as being reliable and conscientious. She, in her turn, was eager to see the States and Australia, not having travelled much in her life – and she appeared to be totally undaunted at taking on responsibility for John.

So almost as soon as she had joined us, she and John flew off for his US recital, which was given at the International Piano Festival at University of Maryland College Park. On their return a few days later, I asked Mrs. Lines how John had played.

"Oh, very well" she said cheerfully. "It was a *very* good concert!"

I was delighted at the news – and not until two or three weeks later did I find that she had been prompted by loyalty rather than conviction. The concert had been one of John's worst, which was doubly depressing considering that many other pianists and professional musicians had been in the Festival's audience . . . If I had known the truth, I think I would not have let him go on to Australia.

John's doctor was for once less credulous than I and he insisted that Mrs. Lines must stay close to John wherever he went. The Australian Broadcasting Commission had arranged first class travel for him, as always, but they were not responsible for Mrs. Lines's fares – and so we found ourselves landed with yet another horrendous expense.

While John was away on this tour, I mixed business with a holiday in the sun for the children by renting a very small house on El Madronal called Casa Rosa. I wanted to see how Plot 32 was progressing, to be on the spot for a while and to ascertain just what we were selling. And in fact, from the Casa Rosa, we could see the house clearly – not that I could stand to look at it very often . . .

While we were in Spain, I received a couple of offers for the place: the first was from a Dutch husband and wife, and the second one was from a friend of ours, Mrs. Jean Guepin, together with – to my astonishment – Paco Parladé himself.

229

But in both cases, they wanted to pay me less than the asking price, and so I decided to sit tight a while longer.

Meanwhile, I was getting an occasional letter from Mrs. Lines in Australia. She told me that John's behaviour was showing an improvement, and that he was playing impressively well; and later, to my heartfelt relief, I discovered that this time no wishful thinking had been involved, and that John's tour had indeed been a success.

The moment John walked out of the customs exit on his arrival back in Heathrow, I could tell by his walk and expression that he was indeed very much better. Over the following weeks, his improved condition sustained itself; and so it was with an element of optimism that, in mid-October I set off with him for the States.

Alas, the performance he gave of Ravel's G Major Concerto with the Atlanta Symphony was not as good as I had expected. But his appearances with the Minnesota Orchestra in St. Paul and Minneapolis found him in much better form.

It was on this trip to America that we both went to Bloomington for the first time. I had imagined Indiana to be flat and carpeted with cornfields – instead, we found ourselves in undulating green countryside: many of the hills looked so densely wooded that it was not hard to imagine that a lost Indian tribe might still hide there. There was a huge lake not far away from the town as well, that was no less attractive for being man-made.

The University itself – one of the oldest outside the east – is ranked the tenth largest in America, and its students come from every state in the nation and almost forty countries abroad; it has more than 100 departments and a faculty in excess of 3,000. But it is for the Music School that it is perhaps best-known today.

Wilfred Bain, the Dean who had originally approached John, and who had done more than anyone else to build up the School's reputation, had unfortunately by this time retired; but we were greeted warmly by his successor Charles Webb, who must surely be everyone's idea of the small-nosed, clean-living American. The list of musical activities he described to us – the concerts, recitals and operas – was very impressive indeed; and though the School was famous above all for voice, it was still, in every respect, the most lavishly equipped we had seen in our lives.

John was told that if he decided to teach there, he would have to give a minimum number of lessons each semester – the students needed so-called credit hours in order to get their degrees. But he would also be allowed to go off on tours – and if he was away for much more than a fortnight at a time, an alternative teacher would deputise for him.

Back in our hotel after meeting the Dean, I said "It seems an ideal arrangement to me."

"Yes" John replied vaguely, "I would rather like to teach here, I think."

And so, though we made no instant decision, the wheels of our future had at last found a track.

It was strange moving back into Chester Terrace again; although we had not yet sold it, emotionally it was no longer ours. Deeply though I had loved it, I found I was unconsciously distancing myself; sometimes I felt like a stranger in the house I had run for so long.

The estate market was showing no improvement, and no change for the better was forecast. Our finances remained as desperate as ever; and practical as well as emotional considerations dictated that action could not be postponed any longer. And so, in November 1975, I accepted an offer for No. 13 of £97,500.

Less than four years later the house was valued at well over £300,000. Still, what has been done has been done: I was left with no choice in the matter.

At about the same time, in November, I decided to accept the offer made by Mrs. Guepin and Paco Parladé for the unfinished house on El Madronal.

When John's doctor heard that we were selling the English and Spanish houses and that we were considering moving to Indiana, he advised caution at once – what would happen, he asked, if John were to have a relapse? There were doctors in Bloomington, I told him – thinking to myself as I did so that I would not trust them less than the British...

Even more upset by our plans was Wilfred Stiff of Ibbs and Tillett. He did not conceal that for the agency, John remained a most lucrative artist. "Bloomington's a crazy idea!" he insisted. "It'll kill your career over here, John – go anywhere in Europe you like, but not half way round the world to America!"

But I still thought that in the long run, the life and the alternatives offered by Bloomington would be the best thing for John. So, at the end of 1975, he gave his formal acceptance to the offer that had first been made three years before: and it was arranged that he would take up his post at the Music School in August the following year.

29

I was glad to see 1975 approaching its end: it had been a horrible year.

In December, all our furniture and most of our belongings were put into store. After the movers had left No. 13 I stood alone in the living room, thinking of everything that had happened there – the long hours spent practising, alone and together, the dinners, the crowded parties after John's concerts... Now it was silent and empty, with light squares marking the walls like ghosts of the pictures that had hung there... I too, belonged to its past, with no more substance for it than a shadow. I succumbed to an involuntary shudder, and, for the last time in my life, I walked out of the house.

We had made no plans at this point about where we would live until the move to America next August; but to start off with, we stayed, with the children, at the Savoy Hotel – which might have seemed very extravagant to anyone who did not know that it gives a discount to well-known musicians. We were there for most of the month.

As if to wipe the slate as clean as we could, our first important act of 1976 was to go to Spain; and, on 5th January, we completed the formalities for the sale of Plot 32. After commission and other deductions, we returned to England with a certified cheque for 3,100,000 pesetas – which, with the dollar premium taken into account, came to roughly £43,000. That entire amount was swallowed by the overdraft we had run up at the Midland Bank.

And so we had lost almost everything – one of the loveliest houses in London, the home of our dreams in the sun, and a small fortune into the bargain.

One dark rainy morning towards the end of December, my

cousin Helen Bullock phoned us to say that she had found a house that we might like to rent, close to her own home in Kent.

We drove down to look at it once. It was called Four Wents, and was not far from Tonbridge; it was old, with low beams of black oak, on which I kept hitting my head until at last I got used to them. Its owner had been sent to New York by his firm, and was likely to stay there for some time; we agreed to take the house right away.

We moved into Four Wents in the cold dead of winter. Though it was furnished, it was not well equipped – so I got many of our things out of store again, including my cutlery and my spacious refrigerator.

For the first two or three months we spent in the house, the weather was dreadful – bitterly, icily cold; but from the start we enjoyed living there. All Helen's friends were congenial; Annabel, whose school, Benenden, was not far away, found that many of her classmates lived within easy access – while Richard had no difficulty at all in finding new friends of his own age.

For me, the biggest bonus of all was having Helen and her family so near. She had often come to see us at No. 13, and she had become dear to me over the years. Very much the English country lady, with the greenest fingers I have ever encountered, she is an excellent skier and tennis player who also has a deep love of music. As if that were not enough in one family, her husband, Francis, is no less remarkable than Helen. Saint Francis, we used to call him; he is the only person I know who seems to have no faults at all!

The only thing, apart from the weather, that darkened family life at Four Wents was John's tenacious depression. At the end of February, he even returned to the Priory for a week – not because of any particular incident, but because his doctors wanted to keep him under close observation and to concoct yet another variation in his "cocktail".

Helen, seeing my frustration and disappointment, talked to me frankly one day. "Don't desert John" she told me – "stay with him whatever you do. It can be horribly difficult for you, I do realise that – but he desperately needs you, you know. Without you, he'd be utterly lost."

It was a rare experience for me to receive such personally positive encouragement. It made it that little bit easier to go on

234

caring for John.

In spite of his miserable mood, John was playing quite regularly that winter and spring: in February and March, I remember, he gave some concerts in Germany and Austria, including the Busoni Concerto with the ORF Symphony Orchestra.

In March, I again went with him to America; and after a concert in Seattle, we flew to Indiana to look for a house.

Bloomington itself is typical small town America – agreeable enough in an anonymous way, with brightly-lit supermarket complexes floating on a sea of car-littered asphalt, alternating with residential areas made up of bungalows, unhedged lawns, and plenty of trees. The green and spacious campus itself, however, impressed us as much as it had on our first visit; its striking variety of buildings includes a superbly-equipped Musical Arts Centre with a 1500-seat auditorium, while the students' facilities, from canteens to sports places to bookshops, were very impressive indeed. The University – if not the students themselves – was obviously financially backed to the hilt.

We were helped in our house-hunting by an adorable lady with a strong southern accent called Hazel, who turned out to be the wife of the violinist Urico Rossi. After looking over several houses, none of which inspired us much, we were shown a modern ten-roomed rancher which perches on the crest of a hill a few miles away from the campus. Huge plate glass windows and a balcony overlook a swimming pool built on to the slope, and from all of them there are beautiful views across a deep, tree-shaded valley. Though the place needed repairs and improvements we both fell in love with it on sight. We slapped down a deposit immediately, and set about arranging a mortgage.

Very soon after that American visit in March, John's mood – wonder of wonders! – began to pick up remarkably: indeed, he was soon more positive and cheerful than at any time since 1973, but without the pontifical aggression that had been so difficult to deal with then. By now, though, my days of blithe optimism were over, and I kept watching for signs of regression.

Yet the weeks passed, and those signs did not reappear. There was no apparent reason for this sustained recovery,

235

there had been no dramatic changes in his course of pills: the doctors could explain it no better than I.

Meanwhile, John was playing ever more frequently, keeping all his engagements – early that summer, he gave concerts in Italy and Austria, and in June I accompanied him on his first-ever tour of Latin-America.

For both of us, the long trip was a fascinating experience. Rio, so spectacularly sited, with its mountains and its vast, famous beaches from which, disappointingly, it is dangerous to swim ... Brasilia, an artificial and oddly empty city, rising from fiery red earth like a sci-fi vision of the future or some abandoned relic of a mythical past ... Bogota, a lovely old city perched dizzyingly at the top of the world ... Santiago, over-shadowed by the mighty Andes, and plagued almost constant-ly by earth-tremors ... The tour was far from a smooth one; flights were mysteriously cancelled, I was forced to learn more about the subtleties of bribery than I had ever known in my life, and both of us came down a couple of times with virulent attacks of food poisoning. In Buenos Aires – which, superfi-cially, is the most European-influenced city on the entire American continent – the streets were crowded with tanks all the time we were there; and John's scheduled concerto per-formance was cancelled because the orchestra went out on strike. But he played very well throughout the length of the tour, and his mood of active enjoyment showed no signs what-ever of strain.

Still, I could hardly believe in the change in him: I was even frightened to credit it in case it turned sour on me. But the evi-dence was right there in front of me, every day and every night of the tour.

It was just like the old times again, the halcyon days of the sixties.

At the end of this trip John told me that he wanted the chil-dren – who by now were sixteen and eleven – to continue their education in Britain. I was absolutely appalled – if I had re-alised before this that he had no intention of bringing them to America with us, I would have discouraged him from moving to Bloomington after all. But it was too late to change our plans now.

However much John may vacillate in general, it has always

236

been his habit, in matters of the utmost importance to him, to present me with a fait accompli. Now was one such occasion: he would not countenance my tearful protests – the children could join us for the holidays, he said. I pointed out that that would prove very expensive. He had plenty of concerts, he parried, not to mention an excellent job . . . How *could* he assert that, I wondered aloud, after everything we had been through, after only recently losing so much we had owned? I began to fear that in his assertiveness, I was hearing ominous echoes of the months before that first major breakdown . . .

I did persuade him to look at a handful of American schools with me, including the famous Deerfields in Massachusetts. But "No," he was not impressed, he said: the children were staying in England.

Many people find it difficult to credit that anyone so apparently amenable as John could ever make an important decision and, having made it, continue to stand by it – particularly after 1973. I can only repeat they do not know the man as well as they think. When it actually comes to the crunch, John has always proved stronger than I.

So I did not take the children out of their schools: but I was very unhappy about it.

In their holidays over the previous two and a half years, both Annabel and Richard had been consistently supportive and gentle to John – amazingly, in a completely natural manner, with no outward signs of stress or bewilderment. All the same, it had been a mercy and a blessing for both of them, as well as for us, that they had been away at school for so much of the time.

But now, this last summer holiday in England, there was no more need for sympathy or tactful behaviour: they could treat John like a father again. An eccentric, absent-minded one, true, who came in for more than his fair share of teasing – but, nonetheless, a real father.

At the beginning of August, Annabel went with him to Yugoslavia, where he played at the Dubrovnik Festival, and together, they enjoyed themselves hugely. She had grown tall and dark, very pretty: and already it was evident to everyone that she had a special knack in managing John.

Soon after their return to an England sweltering in one of the hottest summers it has ever known, John and I gave a duo piano recital at the Aldeburgh Festival. It was the first I had given with him for some time, and I was very uneasy about it; I had hardly touched the keyboard over the last couple of years, not through any deliberate decision, but because the pressures of coping had left me too drained. But at least, with his sustained improvement, I had been able to return to my practising, and we carried off the recital successfully.

As well as marking a return to the platform for me, this was John's last concert appearance in Britain before his move to the States. And so, on 15th August, he flew to Indiana and Bloomington to join the Music School's faculty.

I did not travel with him. There were the children to see back into school, besides which, the house we had bought on the hill was not yet ready for us to move into – and as John was due to leave for South Africa in hardly more than a fortnight I did not relish the prospect of being left alone in a Bloomington hotel throughout the length of his tour.

It was the most welcome luxury imaginable to know that I could safely let John settle in at the University and then make a major tour, all by himself. Even so, I remained chary of taking too much for granted, and I still kept on pinching myself to make sure his recovery was not just a dream.

But it was *not* a dream – the confident phone calls from his Bloomington hotel room left me in no doubt of that. To both of us, the omens all seemed to be promising for our future life in the States.

Part Four

The Road to Recovery

30

On his way from the States to South Africa, a happy and confident John stopped over in London for most of one day, which we spent together in the Post House Hotel.

One of the great joys about John's improved state was that we could discuss future plans with each other. Now, amongst other things, we talked about a subject that had been raised several times in the more recent past but which we had never completely resolved – the fate of the furniture we owned. Sending it from London to Bloomington would be very expensive indeed; but on the other hand, storing it would be equally costly over a number of years. The alternative to shipment or storing was, of course, to put it on sale: but neither of us wanted to do that. Much of the furniture we owned would have been irreplaceable in the States – and even equivalent replacements for the rest would have cost us a fortune over there.

In the end, we agreed that the proceeds of the South African tour should be used to pay for shipping our things to Indiana. "We can afford to do that anyway" John told me cheerfully, "I'll be earning plenty more money – over the next five or six months I'll be playing almost as often as I have in my life before".

The realisation that he was not joking produced very mixed feelings in me. The whole idea of moving to Bloomington had been to ease the pressures on him; and besides, though the University officially offered the freedom to go off on tour, it would not take kindly, presumably, to John spending almost all his time away on the road. "John, I don't know..." I said. "perhaps we should ask Ibbs and Tillett to slow down on the bookings a bit..."

"Don't worry, this is how I want it" he told me. "I feel ready for anything, B!"

John's optimism proved to be justified. The month-long tour included dates in Johannesburg, Durban, Cape Town and Port Elizabeth, as well as Nairobi in Kenya: and John played everywhere at the peak of his form. Critics all over the country piled superlatives onto superlatives. John Davies of the *Johannesburg Star* was delighted with John's "stupendous controlled power" in "a magnificent and authoritative reading" of the Grieg Concerto. In Port Elizabeth, Phoebe Lange wrote about "the sheer wonder" of his performance. His interpretation of Chopin's Twelve Etudes, Op. 25, she said, was to "enter a world of new enchantment", while in Mozart's Sonata in A Minor, K.310, "despair was plumbed to the depths." Schubert's Four Impromptus, Opus 90 were "lyrical, tender, and poignant" – "a revelation": while Scriabin's Sonata No. 5 was "spellbinding." She concluded "Who could have asked for, or received, more?".

Meanwhile in a mood of mounting excitement and optimism, I was arranging for our belongings to be packed up and sent to the States. This proved to be no easy task – we were shipping not only linen, china, and pictures, but beds, sofas, dining room furniture, a sideboard – plus the Steinway Grand that John owned! But by the time he came back to London on 4th October, the arrangements had all been completed, and I was ready to fly to Indiana with him.

Before we left, Wilfred Stiff lectured us again on the folly of moving to Bloomington. "It will ruin John's career!" he repeated, with a stern and stentorian conviction: but considering John's up-coming schedule, I found it hard to believe him.

The break from London and Britain did prove quite difficult for me, and I hated parting from so many friends: while worst of all was leaving the children. But because John was so much himself again, I faced the prospect of our future in America with confidence and even with pleasure.

John spent most of October teaching in Bloomington; and by this time he was so healthy that he was taking no drugs at all.

His students, he told me, had not been assigned to him in advance, and neither had he chosen any of them; rather, it was they who had been allowed to select the teachers they wanted. The outstanding French pianist, Michel Block (a witty and wonderful man who, to our delight, was to join the faculty a year later) once told me that during his first days at the Music School, he had been reminded of the red-light district in Amsterdam, with the staff on display in their studios like whores while the students strolled past looking them over before deciding who would best satisfy their particular needs... Fortunately, John had attracted an interesting group, some of them very promising indeed: he gave them lessons in his studio in the Music School, and, after we had moved into our new home, the more talented amongst them were sometimes invited to work with him there.

As one would expect, John is not a pernickety teacher, worrying at fine points of detail – it is the overall approach to a composition that, as always, interests him most. He interrupts student performances less than do most of his colleagues, but his few comments are deeply-felt and clearly thought out – and those who are gifted and technically competent are able to prosper under his guidance.

John, however, found it difficult to summon much interest in all the forms and various reports that the teachers are required to fill out. Faculty meetings usually bored him as well; he would sit swathed in clouds of cigarette smoke, smiling benignly while his mind wandered down channels that were of more interest to him. Many performing artists, of course, share this indifference to administrative detail – but it meant that in matters of day-to-day business, I always had to push him to get the work done.

The improvements to our beautiful new home on the hill were still very far from completed, and so we were living out of local hotels. Not that we were spending much time in Bloomington, at least not after October; during John's first months in the job, we were away for the most part on tour. John was continuing to play quite superbly – and even before October was out, he had given a much-acclaimed "Emperor" in Harrisburg, and another concert at Birmingham, Alabama, after which he had been re-engaged on the spot.

November saw us back in London, where we took a service flat at the Grosvenor House Hotel – the first of several we were to rent there during our return trips in the following months. After playing three major concerts in Britain in the space of less than one week, John embarked on a Scandinavian tour. As was

243

usual by this time, I let him travel alone, with no qualms on my part – besides which, I knew that he would get immaculate care and attention from one of the most honest, reliable and generous agents we have ever known – Henrik Lodding. From Scandinavia, John went on to Hungary, in early December, where he gave several more well-received concerts – and then he joined the children and me in Geneva, where we had been visiting my cousin Geoffrey and his wife Gill (who had been so thoughtfully frank with me in the early days of John's illness).

From Geneva, we went to Verbïer, the skiing resort – in this, the pre-holiday period, it was both quieter and cheaper than in the approaching high season. As I had feared when I had seen his itinerary at the Post House before the South African tour, John was obviously tired after playing and travelling so much. I was worried, and wished we could have stayed in Verbier longer – but after only a matter of days, we had to leave for the Soviet Union. We took an Aeroflot flight out of Zurich, and arrived in Moscow in time to spend Christmas there.

The Russians do not, of course, celebrate Christmas, so though we gave a family party of our own for the children, the festive atmosphere was very much missing. All the same, we were excited just to be in the Soviet capital, where a Winter Festival was being held; it included not only instrumental music, but ballet, opera, theatre, and painting as well. What made the occasion special for us was that John was the first Western pianist ever invited to take part in it.

It was bitterly cold, I remember, and the snow fell with a monotonous and silent persistence. I toured the city and the Kremlin with the children: but wrapped and fur-hatted though we were, we were all frozen through to the marrow.

Soon, I was suffering from a very bad cold. I phoned the British Embassy doctor, who prescribed a drug without visiting me. That same night, I ordered fish in the hotel restaurant, which may not have been totally fresh – or perhaps I was not after all the victim of an ordinary cold, but of a bug then plaguing the capital. In any case, I had not been asleep very long before I woke up feeling violently sick. I got up to go to the bathroom – but suddenly my surroundings were spinning, and I blacked out as I fell to the floor.

I regained consciousness to see John's image swimming above me – "Brenda, Brenda" I heard him saying, as if from a

244

distance. "What is it? Are you all right?" With his help, I managed to sit up – and felt the blood wet on my lips. I did not realise it yet, but in the fall I had broken my nose.

John, seeing that I was still groggy, acted for once with despatch and phoned down to the hotel's reception desk. In no time, three women came up to the room; after hurriedly looking me over, they telephoned for an ambulance.

When it arrived, John announced his intention of accompanying me to the hospital – but he was so very upset that he was ordered to stay where he was. So, dressed only in a mink coat and pyjamas, I was driven away on my own through Moscow's dark snow-lined streets.

What followed was a protracted and wide-awake nightmare. Instead of medical attention, I was subjected to a barrage of questions, fired at me unrelentingly and in incomprehensible Russian by one man and three very butch women. Finally someone was found who spoke fractured English; and through him, the interrogation went on. "Are you on drugs?" "Have you been drinking?" they wanted to know. "Are you a tourist?" they asked – they had to get my category right, they explained. I told them I was here with my husband, who was a pianist of international fame. "Then you are in the Soviet Union on business?" No, I explained, not exactly. I was just travelling with him. Passionate discussion followed: "Ah" the English speaker said finally, "you are in the parasite category."

I was X-rayed and tested for pregnancy: I was shunted from one room to another. Again and again I repeated that I had taken some pills for a cold, which possibly had not agreed with me – or maybe I was the victim of food poisoning as the result of the fish I had eaten. "No, no, that is impossible!" a nurse retorted outraged. "You cannot get food poisoning in Moscow!". Eventually after being pushed around for almost three hours, I became as incalcitrant and stubborn as my questioners.

At about 6 a.m., I was told that my nose would heal on its own, and I was shut in a room by myself. I lay on the bed in utter exhaustion.

An hour later, I was brought a thick slice of bread and some jam – and then a woman I had not seen before came self-importantly into the room. "Are you on drugs, or had you been drinking?" she asked. "Are you a tourist or are you on business?"

"I will not answer any more questions!" I yelled. "I refuse, you hear me? I refuse!"

She stalked out, slamming the door – and when, shortly afterwards, I tried to open it, I discovered that it was locked. For the first time, I became really frightened – no one will know where I am, I thought, I will never see my family or the Western world ever again! I began to beat on the door: "Let me out!" I implored. "Let me out!"

For another hour, nobody came.

But at last, after I had given up shouting, defeated, and returned to lie down on the bed, I heard the key turn in the lock – and Annabel and Richard rushed towards me, followed by our interpreter, Eugenia, and an extremely bewildered-looking John. "What do you think you've been doing?" Eugenia demanded, as if the episode had all been my fault. I shook my head, too relieved to resent her harsh tone; never, in the whole of my life, had I been quite so happy as now to set eyes on John's bearded bulk.

Evidently Gosconcert had insisted to the hospital that I was indeed the wife of somebody famous, and that it was to release me at once. My broken nose was covered with a plaster, and I was shown on my way with ill grace.

John, who had had his usual rapturous reception in Moscow, was due to leave imminently for Riga – but because of my nose and my hospital experience, I was forbidden to go with him. So while I remained convalescent in Moscow with Annabel, Richard went with John on the day and a half's train ride to Riga; they travelled first class, in luxury, and it should have been a enjoyable experience except that Richard, too, caught the virulent cold – or the bug, or whatever it was.

He was much better, however, by the time the four of us went on to Leningrad, just before New Year's Eve. This time there were officially recognised celebrations, one of which we joined in the Europaisky Hotel. While they waited the usual hours between courses, the Russians at the tables around us would burst enthusiastically and sometimes tearfully into popular folk songs, the rhythm almost always picking up speed as the music built to its climax. The women's brave and spirited fashions – downright tarty by most Western standards – reduced a group of French tourists to noisy, near-hysterical

laughter – but they expressed appreciative Gallic astonishment at the excellence of the food we were served, and we all
joined in the boisterous and good-natured reception when, at
midnight, hundreds of balloons floated down from the ceiling,
and exploded around us like firecrackers. John, sweating from
all the food and the heat, was shiny-eyed with enjoyment.

All in all, my hospital ordeal and Richard's brief infection
apart, it proved a most happy trip: for the children, it was a
fascinating experience, and John remained in good health as
well as playing beautifully throughout.

After the Soviet Union, and having seen the children back
into school, John and I flew on to Bloomington: and this time
we took a room in the Memorial Union, which is part of the
University itself.

Meanwhile, the Russians had proved right in predicting that
my breakage would soon heal itself. Every now and then, even
today, I check in the mirror half expecting to discover an ugly
and untoward bump: but my nose is as symmetrical as ever.

Winters in Indiana are generally bad, with below-zero temperatures and guaranteed snow: but the weather early in 1977
was even more savage than Moscow's had been – some of the
worst on record for the region, in fact. Blizzard pressed hard
after blizzard, and work on the new house was forced to a stop –
while the entire basement area was flooded, totally ruining a
carpet. It soon became depressingly obvious that we would not
be able to move in before March, at the earliest.

By now, I was getting impatient with our rootless existence –
but John seemed contented enough with his teaching. Even so,
the snowstorms permitting, he left Bloomington several times
during January to play in other parts of the States.

In February – unwilling to stay by myself in our rented Bloomington room – I went to Switzerland with John for a concert
in which he was playing in Zurich. Then we flew on to Britain,
where he was to give five duo recitals with Ruggiero Ricci, the
violinist he had first teamed with at Shawnigan Lake in the
summer of 1973. Ricci, to our disappointment, had resigned
from the Music School at Indiana University before John had
joined the faculty there – but their musical rapport was as
strong as it had been, and John was looking forward to their
short tour together. The programme they were to play was a

247

full-blooded and difficult one; it included works by Mozart, Busoni, and Paganini, as well as the Debussy Sonata and Liszt's Grand Duo Concertante.

The first of these recitals took place in Cardiff – it was a popular and critical success, as were the three concerts that followed. The fifth and final one took place in London on 20th February, at the Queen Elizabeth Hall: the reviews for both artists were excellent, with Peter Stadlen of the *Telegraph* claiming to have been "riveted by Ogdon's marvellously spontaneous natural grown pianism, a superb mixture of musicality and outsized virtuosity."

It was all so reassuring for both of us – far more than reassuring, in fact. Now, for the first time, I was allowing myself to believe that the bad days really were over.

Together, we flew back to the States and to Bloomington: the new house, to our excitement, was ready for us to move into, and the delivery of our belongings was imminent. I was present, naturally, when they arrived at the house in a vast 40 ft. container of steel, causing a local sensation.

The unpacking and placing of everything was completed in only one day. It was a delight for both of us to see our familiar possessions again: a beautiful and valuable Japanese screen which we had bought together in Kyoto, a Sheraton sideboard and table, and of course, John's Steinway Grand – all of them brought back to new life in such dramatically different surroundings.

After two weeks back in Bloomington, and even less in our home, John had to return to Europe for several more concerts – but this time, I stayed behind. I busied myself with the task of seeing that the house would be immaculate and gleaming, and the garden in much better shape, by the time John returned in a fortnight.

And so it was the most unexpected and painful of blows when I received a telegram from Ibbs and Tillett in London, telling me that John was back in the Priory.

31

John had given a concert in Nottingham, after which he had been supposed to fly on to Holland. He had gone to Heathrow as scheduled, and checked his luggage on to the flight – but once he reached the Departure Lounge, he lost all sense of orientation, and became confused about where he was going. And so he remained there for several hours, until an airport official recognised him and contacted Ibbs and Tillett to tell them that John appeared to be lost.

Wilfred Stiff had gone out to Heathrow at once, and alarmed by John's utter confusion, had arranged for his immediate admission into the Priory. But his stay in the hospital was a short one: he was released on 12th March, after being there only a week. He was now on yet another new cocktail; and so the list of drugs he had taken at one time or another – including Perpenazine, Parstellin, Valium, Phenothiazenes, Chlorpromazine, Stellazine and Norpramin – continued to grow ever longer.

John's next public engagement was scheduled to take place only five days after his release from the hospital; he was to play Richard Yardumian's Concerto followed by the Fantasia on Hungarian Folktunes by Liszt, in San Diego, on the West Coast of America. I was unhappy about his keeping the date – but when I spoke to him in London over the phone, he sounded totally normal. He had been travelling too much for the past two months, he said, which was why he had lost his orientation; he did not believe that the set-back was serious, and he did not think he should have been sent to the Priory. Certainly, he told me, he was feeling on fine form again, and was looking forward to making the California trip.

Only slightly reassured, I promised I would go to San Diego to join him.

But to my indescribable relief, he seemed as much his old self in the flesh as he had done over the telephone. There was also no discernible fall-off in his standard of playing, and he was hailed in the Press as a pianist of outstanding calibre.

I would have liked to stay on an extra few days in San Diego's warm weather and lovely surroundings, above all to give John a chance to relax. But, at last, the Dean had expressed his impatience to me over John's long absences from the Music School, and had been insistent that he return to his teaching post as soon as he possibly could.

So the morning after the concert, we were on our way back to Bloomington.

Fortunately for my peace of mind, John's upcoming concert schedule was lighter than it had been in months. He went back quite happily to teaching, and he professed himself completely contented to be living in the new house. Indeed, he claimed that he liked it as much as any of the houses we had owned; and though it was less elegant than No.13 and not as spectacular as Plot 32, I could understand what he meant. The place was so spacious and light, so convenient in the practical, American sense – and there was always that beautiful view of the wooded hills falling away below the swimming pool terrace.

The children both came to visit us during their Easter vacation – and they took to the climate and the house without any hesitation at all. Crossing the Atlantic on their own had not worried them in the least and they both expressed themselves enthusiastically in favour of a life divided between two continents.

In April, we were off on our travels again – this time on our first visit to Mexico, where John played the Busoni Concerto with the Orquestra Filarmonica de la Unam. The occasion was the start of a love affair.

For all its sprawling size, its poverty and its impossible traffic, we both fell for Mexico City and its pine-covered mountainous surroundings. The new and the grand, the old and ornate, the poor and rundown bump into and run right across each other. The huge and paved cathedral square is unforgettably impressive: and the churches – some so old they seem about to topple over – are gold and white inside, with dark, carved wood, combining, like so much else in Mexico, the stark magnificence of Spain with an inventive Indian exuberance... As with all countries, there were disturbing aspects – the modern Mussolini-style villas guarded by fierce dogs and lava-stone walls as much as the garbage dumps on which people eke out a living. But flowers are everywhere – as are musicians; fiddlers, trumpeters, guitarists in huge hats and colourful costumes, playing on street corners, restaurants and night-clubs, for Mexicans as much as for tourists...

But if we were delighted with Mexico, the compliment was whole-heartedly returned. Audiences and critics alike were intrigued not only by the masterful performance of the mammoth and rarely-heard Busoni, but by the bearded and over-weight Englishman himself. We were asured that John would be invited back soon, without fail.

John's playing continued to maintain the truly phenomenal standard he had been setting for over a year now. Later in April, he gave a beautiful Faculty Recital: and he followed it very soon with a compelling performance of Tchaikovsky's 1st Concerto in Vancouver. Then he travelled to Indianapolis for a Romantic Festival being held there – and no one who heard his recital will, I am certain, ever forget it. Amongst the pieces he played were Chopin's Nocturne in E Minor Op. Posthumous, Busoni's Sonatina No. 6, Liszt's Totentanz for Solo Piano – and most hair-raising and dazzling of all, Alkan's Concerto for Solo Piano.

And there was one other recital the following month that showed him at his magnificent best, both as a musician and a technician. Composed entirely of Scriabin's works, it was given at the Spoleto Festival held at Charleston in South Carolina: and Robert T. Jones of the *New York Daily News* could hardly believe what he heard. "He really is an immense pianist, a genuine Titan of the keyboard" he wrote – adding quite simply "A genius."

In June, John's first year of teaching at Indiana University came to its end. In spite of spending so many weeks away on his various tours, he felt that his time there had been a success; and our decision to uproot ourselves and move to the States appeared, in our eyes, fully justified.

Encouraged by John's recent history of artistic and financial achievement, we allowed ourselves a summer extravagance, and rented a villa on the remote North East coast of Corfu. We

251

went there via England, where John gave a concert for the Appeal Fund of Benenden, Annabel's school: and then on the 20th July, the four of us, plus a school friend of Annabel's, flew off to spend four weeks in the sun.

The Villa Virginia, which had a view over the sea to the hills of Albania, turned out to be close to a house that had been rented by David Cornwell – the real name of the author John Le Carré. Tall, with a fair and very English attractiveness, he is a gregarious and extrovert man – at least, he is when he is not writing: and we were soon exchanging regular visits with him, his delightful wife Jane Eustace, and their youngest son.

He was referred to by everyone as "David" but I could not help but think of him as being John Le Carré. One day I told him as much.

"Oh God," he answered emphatically. "I don't!"

One similarity he shared with John – a prodigal, unstinting generosity: indeed, if possible, it was John who was outdone! In any case, we spent many days together on luxurious hired boats, sunning ourselves and drinking champagne.

Before being in our villa for long, we learned that an old friend of ours, Humphrey Burton – the head of BBC Television's Music and Arts Department – had also taken a house on the coast: and soon his family joined ours and the Cornwells in exchanging convivial visits ... What with the weather, the scenery, and the company, the holiday should have been perfect, and in most ways it was: but only a day or two after our arrival, I had swung off the edge of a platform on which I had been attempting Greek dancing, and broken a bone in my foot. The medical attention I had received had been no better than that in Moscow seven months earlier, though administered with far greater grace; my foot – quite unnecessarily, as I was to discover – had been swaddled in plaster, which slowed me down and put all sport out of the question.

John kept busy for much of the time composing a sonata for solo flute. Perhaps that was why, even more than was usually the case, he seemed not completely to take in half the things that were said to him. "Yes" he would say, smiling pleasantly, and "M-m-m" and occasionally a "Really"; but his conversation both in private and public did not range much wider than that. Most of the time he sat frowning slightly, occasionally, quietly, grunting, as if in response to his own private thoughts.

But to be fair, even a more naturally articulate man than my husband would have found it difficult to compete with David and Humphrey when they got going together – for fascinating days, both of them hardly stopped talking... And John was showing no signs of agitation or of depression, and no desire to withdraw from society. And so I continued to treat him as one might a much-loved but overgrown child, part encouraging and partly reproving; and, as throughout so much of our life together, it proved an approach with which he was happy.

In fact, his good mood was such that he told me he wanted to extend our holiday by a couple of weeks. That would be impossible, I pointed out, as we had booked our house for a limited period, and someone else was due to take it over as soon as we left. And so John made one of his rare but definite decisions – without consulting me or anyone else, he reserved a large yacht for the relevant fortnight.

I was horrified when I found out – there was no way that we could afford it. But fortunately, and in spite of John's vociferous protests, this was one fait accompli I could unaccomplish again, and we flew home to Bloomington on schedule.

Annabel and Richard still had a month's holiday left, and they came with us to the States. Bloomington was predictably stifling, and subject to thundery storms; but the children were able to play in the pool or their games room, and to explore the lush countryside, and once again, they enjoyed the few weeks they spent with us. Their trip, on top of Corfu, was very expensive, of course: but for John and me, it was worth every cent.

It was a cruel wrench when they left us to fly back to England and school; but soon we were comfortably back in the familiar academic routines. Barring the one brief, unimportant relapse, our first year based in America had gone as well as we could have hoped: I prayed that the second one would be as good.

32

In September, after a few weeks' unbroken teaching, John left Bloomington to go to Fort Worth, Texas, where he was to be a jury member in the Van Cliburn Piano Competition. Under the chairmanship of John Giordano – a conductor and composer, and leader of the Fort Worth Symphony – the 14-member international panel included such distinguished musicians as Rudolph Firkusny, Leon Fleischer, Nikita Magaloff, and Leonard Pennario; there were no less than 88 competitors from a total of 26 countries.

Inevitably, with such a turn out, we spent a pressured couple of weeks there: but very hard though the work was, the legendary and lavish hospitality of Texas was constantly to the fore. John threw himself into the party-going with all his pre-breakdown enthusiasm, as well as listening to every competitor. Van himself took no part in the judging, but he was of course deeply involved in the proceedings: he is the most unpretentious person imaginable, and it was a pleasure to see him again.

As the first round gave way to the second, as the number of competitors dwindled and the outstanding talents began to emerge, I was reminded of Brussels and Liverpool so many years in the past... Of course, here in Fort Worth it was hot and continually sunny, and there was no comparison in the facilities provided – but the tension and excitement were identical, and my heart went out to all the young players, so anxious, so eager, so dedicated. Memory lapses are upsetting at any time, but in a competition, with so much at stake, they are enough to make one's heart stop – though however much mine palpitated at times, it was certainly much more enjoyable to take part, not as a sweating contestant, but as a privileged spectator!

In the end, Jeffrey Swann, a local Texan, came third: Alexander Toradze of the Soviet Union was second; and the winner, whom John described as "a classicist whose finely arched style of playing is heard all too rarely these days," was the South African Steven de Groote.

And so, this time with John's participation, another major career had been launched: and in his moment of triumph, de Groote must have felt, as John had in Moscow, that the music world lay at his feet. We wished him well on his road, and hoped it would prove to be a straight one.

At the end of September, the performing pressures on John made themselves felt once again. He went first to London, Ontario, where his interpretation of the Liszt No. 1. concerto and the Franck Symphonic Variations with the LSO earned him a standing ovation. Soon after, at the start of October, we flew off to Italy and Venice, where he played a recital in the beautiful Fenice Theatre.

The rest of October was a scramble of travelling and playing. First we flew to Iran, for the British Cultural Festival there – and between the tenth and the nineteenth of the month, John made three solo appearances and gave two performances of the Brahms D Minor Concerto with the Teheran Symphony under Norman Del Mar . . . But in spite of the arduous schedule, we found time, on John's insistence, to make the long trip out to the awesome remains of Persepolis, as well as to gain an impression of the capital as it was before the Shah's downfall. The contrasts between rich and poor were even more marked than in Latin America: palatial mansions kept company with slums, scented gardens vied with rank open drains, and the elegant and bejewelled women who came to John's concerts were several centuries removed from the cloaked creatures with half-covered faces whom we saw sidling shadow-like through the streets . . .

From Teheran, we flew to Vienna, and from there we were driven in a hired car to Czechoslovakia, where, in a succession of grey deprived cities, he played wonderfully, as usual.

Fog delayed our flight out of Prague for over twenty-four hours. Though John had no concerts in Britain, we had hoped to have a meeting with Wilfred Stiff during a single day's stopover in London en route to Halifax, Nova Scotia; but the hold up aborted our plans. So we sent a telegram to Wilfred, explaining that we would barely have time to change planes at Heathrow, let alone manage a conference.

Wilfred, we have been told, was much put out. Perhaps, to him, it was one more proof that our move to America was making the representation of John too difficult for the agency to deal with: or perhaps he suspected – wrongly – that John was not well again and so could not travel, and that I was trying to conceal the fact from him. Anyway, it was unfortunate that a deterioration apparently took place in a vital professional relationship.

In Nova Scotia – that chilly but beautiful land – John played the Beethoven Fourth Piano Concerto several times with the Atlantic Symphony Orchestra under the baton of Victor Yampolsky. And then, in the bleakness of a wet mid-November, we flew back to Bloomington again – and to the unfamiliar prospect of two months with almost no concerts.

From the University's point of view, as we were aware, the break in concerts was long over-due – and so in that sense it was welcome. But for other reasons it worried us.

It worried us because it had not been planned. Every year since winning First Prize in Moscow, John had given five or six concerts at least in December and considerably more during January – so why were there almost none now? Had Wilfred Stiff been right after all – had the move to Indiana undermined John's career? Was he in truth too far away from the European market – and if so, would Harold Shaw, our American agent, be able to restore the balance with a comparable number of US based concerts?

Or was the trouble not so much our physical location, but the result of John's brief relapse at the beginning of March? Was the concert-organising world losing confidence in John?

If the latter alternative was the right one, then it was very unfair – at least, at this particular point. True, in the two crisis years of his illness, he had had to cancel fairly often, and had at times performed well below standard: but two more years of consistent success had passed by since then. And though, in 1976 and 1977, John had been in the Priory twice, it had been for only two weeks altogether – and neither visit, to my mind, had appeared to be really essential. In any case, his standard of

256

performance had not been affected, and there had been no convalescent periods necessary after he had been released.

Oh well, we told ourselves – a soloist's career is not, and never has been, predictable. Anyway, John would be busier from February on, while May and June would be hectic: in the meantime, how pleasant to be at home with the children throughout the Christmas holiday period . . .

But the mortgage had to be paid, and, like incorrigible children, we were yet again living at the limits of our income. So, still, the question mark hovered.

Late in January, after Annabel and Richard had left us for Britain, I found myself thinking increasingly that John was not as well as he had been. And yet, I could not be sure – all his life he had been difficult to "read", and uncommunicative on personal levels – he had always been subject to silences, and sudden questions that sound like non-sequiturs are an integral part of his behaviour. Certainly he did seem more irritable – though perhaps it was nothing worth worrying about. Possibly I had become so geared to spot symptoms that I was beginning to invent them.

In any case, his tetchy mood had little adverse effect on his teaching – and any complaints on his students' part were aimed above all at the amount of time he spent away from them touring.

These criticisms did not by-pass the Dean, who, despite John's residence at the Music School throughout January, requested him to cut down on his concerts for the following three months as well. And so John found himself trapped in a strange vicious circle – on the one hand worrying about too few dates being offered him, and, on the other, feeling unable to accept them if they were, after all, to come his way.

Nonetheless, he did give several more astounding performances between the beginning of February and the last week of April, including a CBC Broadcast recital from Ottawa, after which he was hailed by one of the critics as no less than "the reincarnation of Liszt".

At home, as the heavy snows thawed and winter faded slowly away, there could no longer be any doubt that John's irritation was getting more pronounced – indeed, his temper

257

was sometimes explosive.

And then, a matter of days before we were due to leave on a major international tour, he received a demand in the post for some very steep English VAT charges – much higher than we had anticipated. In a sudden and violent rage, he struck out at a crystal chandelier that hung in the hall. Luckily, he did not cut himself, but the chandelier itself was badly damaged, with many pendants smashed on the floor.

This was still a long way, in crisis terms, from December, 1973; even so, the parallels with previous crises were too obvious to be overlooked. The time had come to consult an American doctor.

The local paractitioner we saw said that for the type of medication John needed, he would have to consult a psychiatrist. And so, on his recommendation, we made an appointment with Michael Johnson.

A youngish and personable man, he seemed rather distant at first; but that impression was quickly erased by his professional efficiency. Instinctively, I trusted him – at least, as much as I was willing to trust any doctor by this time; and I explained that John was due to leave imminently on a tour of Mexico and Europe. Michael was honest in his response – and though not forbidding John to fulfil his commitments, he did not raise any false hopes about an immediate improvement in his unsettled condition. And in fact, as we were soon to discover, one of the two drugs prescribed, known as Haldol, was to prove far from suitable for John.

The first stop of the tour was in Mexico where, true to the promises he had been given, he had been fast re-engaged. But – though his mood did in fact lighten – we had no sooner arrived there than he began to complain about a very dry mouth and, far more seriously, a lack of physical control. Both of us, naturally, were scared – he was going to play the Liszt A major Concerto at the Festival International Cervantino in the lovely old town of Guanajuato, and we did not want to jeopardise his fledgling Mexican career by an indifferent performance. We were of course both of us amateurs when it came to new drugs and their possible affects, and so the decision about how best to cope was an extremely nerve-wracking; but in the end, we took a risk and cut down on the dosage of Haldol. To our mutual delight, the gamble turned out to be a success; John played brilliantly, and without any physical troubles.

After Mexico, he gave concerts in Alabama and Kentucky before we flew on to Holland, where he was to perform the Schurmann Concerto in Hilversum. Gerard and Carolyn had turned up to hear him, and they were worried – and rightly so – by the way John played in rehearsal: again, the Haldol – not helped in any way by jet-lag, to which John was more susceptible than he had been in the past – had affected the co-ordination of his hands. Another hasty reduction of the dosage solved that problem in time: and John's public performance was not only memorable, it helped to re-consolidate Gerard's reputation in his own country.

Next, we travelled to England, where John played several times. Meanwhile I went on juggling his pills – trying to keep a positive balance between his mood and his ability to play. Somehow, by luck and instinct rather than skill, I managed to hit combinations appropriate to each occasion, and John's British performances kept up his very high standard. But of all the concerts he gave there, the one that mattered the most professionally was to be given on 4th June at the Queen Elizabeth Hall in London.

It was of vital importance to John that this recital should be a success. We were beginning, belatedly, to realise that London is not at all interested in what happens, musically, outside it, and that consequently the people of influence there were quite unaware of how magnificently John had been playing ever since the summer of 1976. Indeed, some of these people were still being openly sceptical about John's professional form, preferring to remember the Wigmore fiasco of 1975 rather than the fine concert he had given with Ricci only the previous year.

As the minutes ticked by before John made his entrance, I looked away from the great black piano waiting silently in the middle of the stage, and glanced round the body of the hall. I saw many old friends and acquaintances, all of them hoping, I supposed, for the best: I recognised some of the critics as well. But the vast majority of the audience consisted of strangers to me, and I wondered if any one had turned up in the hope of witnessing the performance go wrong. Not for a very long time had I been quite so nervous for John . . .

Portly, with an authority that was by now almost Brahm-

259

sian, he hurried on to the platform. He received a warm round of applause: it had not yet died away, indeed, he had hardly sat down, before he had started to play. A few bars into his first piece, I knew that, as ever these days, all was going to be well.

When the recital came to an end, John was given a rousing reception; and next morning, as I had hoped and expected, the critics were loud in their praise. Bryce Morrison, in the *Daily Telegraph,* described him as "among the most gifted and original of all young pianists": he wrote that "heaven-sent touches" had been scattered liberally through performances that were "thrillingly spontaneous and communicative". Scriabin's Fifth Sonata "was conceived in an astonishing spectrum of colours and dynamics"; in Schubert's Op. 90 Impromptus "tempi (slow as well as fast) forbidden to lesser mortals made a deeply poignant experience of numbers one and three, whilst two and four glittered and cascaded in astonishing fashion": in Beethoven's 101 Sonata some "skimped detail seemed a small price to pay for such tonal delicacy and imaginative freedom"; while Liszt's B minor Ballade and Dante Sonata were given performances of "blazing panache and poetic engagement."

For a while, I was transported back to the days of John's triumphant London debut – the difference being, of course, that this was something in the nature of a come-back. Alas, time was to provide another difference as well; because whereas the 1959 Wigmore recital had led in no time at all to regular appearances in the capital, on this occasion almost three years were to pass before he was invited to play in London again. Neither his residence in Bloomington nor exaggerated rumours of his mental condition have seemed to us to be an adequate reason.

Anyway, Wilfred was obviously right in predicting a slump in John's British career...

From England we went back to Mexico, where John appeared in the capital with the Orchestra of the University conducted by the excellent Jorge Velasco. He played both Brahms concerti in one concert – a feat of physical endurance as well as of artistic stamina, but a feat triumphantly executed.

Quite recently, Artur Rubinstein, recalling his youth when two major concerti were not unusual in a single concert, spoke with an edge of disparagement about today's younger artists who consistently play only one. I believe, though, that the Maestro has not taken into account how much the power of conductors has grown; and very few indeed of these gentlemen are willing to let a soloist dominate a concert. I assure Mr. Rubinstein that if the opportunity were to present itself, a great many contemporary pianists would jump at the chance of playing two – or better still, three! – concerti in the course of an evening...

From Mexico, well-pleased but tired, we returned to our ranch house in Bloomington;and rather than take an expensive summer holiday away somewhere, we planned to spend two quiet months at home. After so many weeks of attempting to balance John's intake of pills, it was for me a welcome relief to hand the responsibility back to his doctor.

We reclined by our swimming pool under the warm summer sun, and waited for Michael Johnson to mix another new cocktail.

33

Michael Johnson is honest, making no trumped-up claims for himself: indeed, he told me bluntly that he puts our knowledge of mental illness today on a par with surgical skills at the time of the American Civil War in the 1860s. But he does believe that at last great strides are being made both in diagnosis and treatment – more and more people are realising, he said, that problems of the mind can be a purely chemical malfunction; and, within only a year or two, he thinks it perfectly possible that doctors will be prescribing effective medication based on simple urine, blood and cerebrospinal analysis.

As if to underline the physical source of John's illness, he treated the problem with no more mumbo-jumbo than if he had been dealing with a mild case of flu, or a cold. I remember saying to him one day that shame was still attached to mental illness these days: "Oh no" he replied, with a shrug, "no, it's quite popular, almost fashionable, now." He was deliberately making light of things, of course; but, in general for me, his whole approach came like a breath of fresh air.

Not that everything he said to me was reassuring or easy to take – very far from it, in fact. For example, he told me what no one had admitted to me directly before – that schizophrenia is a potentially degenerative illness . . . But he also laid more emphasis than I had been used to on manic depression in relation to John: it was a condition that had played little part in earlier clinical reports, but which a doctor had mentioned as relevant as far back as one of John's original spells in the Priory. Michael told me that this illness, with its severe highs and lows, usually peaks by the mid-forties – and that it is being ever more effectively controlled.

How much more useful were Michael's frank discussions than the hinted-at mysteries to which I had been subjected so often. Of course, I realise it must be difficult for doctors to gauge when to reveal and when to conceal; but too many of John's British doctors, to my mind, assumed an identical all-knowing mask, behind which we lesser mortals were not permitted to see. Straightforwardness – including, I believe, an open admission of medical and professional fallibility – is usually more helpful to everyone.

During the humid summer months in Indiana – during which John taught some special students – Michael altered and readjusted the dosage, always seeking the one magic formula.

Alas, John's state got slowly, but visibly, worse. His silences grew longer and longer: it was a fight to make him get up in the mornings, and he seemed to have no energy at all; while the dreaded name of the charity organiser was once more starting to dominate what little conversation he had.

Why, I cried to myself – why should fate be so cruel all over again? Why, when John had been more than holding his own for so long, should he now have another relapse? Such suffering was so useless, so unfair – why us, why me, and why John? *Why?*

The children spent their holidays with us in Bloomington, apparently happily enough: and as usual in the less easy times, they were marvellous with John. And so the summer passed by, with periods of blistering sun broken by sudden barrages of thunder and heavy outbreaks of rain: while John's mood got steadily darker.

At the end of August, when the semester – and John's third year on the faculty – began, he was still capable of resuming his teaching duties and of fulfilling his performing engagements. But once again, these latter commitments caused the Dean to voice an objection in the first week of September. John had been invited to sit on the jury of a Washington piano competition that same month, and he was also due to record some Liszt pieces in London as well as making a heavy international tour in October: and at least one of those commitments, the Dean told John, would have to be cancelled. It was the beginning of the school year, and it was John's duty to assess, and establish contact with, his students.

As a result of this blast from the Dean, we decided to ask

263

John Boyden of Enigma Records, to postpone the projected recording of Liszt's Transcendental Etudes by three months – after all, cancellation rather than postponement would have been the only possible course where both the competition and the tour were concerned. Very much to our surprise, however, Mr. Boyden called off the recording completely – and Enigma has not approached John since.

In any case, John kept his commitment to sit on the jury of the Rockefeller International Competition for Excellence in the Performance of American Music: and he arrived in Washington in mid-September for the semi-finals and finals.

He remained in the capital for almost two weeks. The largely modern repertoire that was being played held a particular fascination for him: for the finals alone it included Sonatas by Barber, Copland, Ives and MacDowell, plus works by Sessions, Babbit, and Cage. Over the phone, he told me that he was enjoying himself – but the tone of his voice sounded altogether less positive than his words.

I had not gone to Washington with him because, soon after he had arrived there, I flew to England with both the children. John had determined, some years ago, that Richard should be educated at Eton, and even now, after all our financial disturbances, he was eager that we should send him there if we could. And so now Richard was going to start his first term, and the housemaster had suggested to me that I should see him settled in myself.

John was due to join me in London in early October; we would then fly together to Italy for the start of his European tour.

However fascinating John may have found the Competition in Washington, there were no signs of a lift in his pall of depression when he went home to Bloomington. He was looked after with dedicated devotion by one of his students, Edna Chun, for the following ten days or so: and then she personally put him on a flight to Chicago, where he would catch another plane on to London.

But John did not arrive in Heathrow when he should have done. Alarmed, I phoned Bloomington to find out what had gone wrong – and a general panic ensued.

The American police were requested to search for him – but

for a whole day I heard nothing more. I waited in a nightmare of anxiety in Lady Arthur's house in Kensington, where I was staying – and at long last I got a call from the States to tell me that John had been found, and was safe. At Chicago's O'Hare airport, I learned, he had lost all sense of orientation, just as he had at Heathrow early in the previous year: and for twenty-four hours he had been sitting in the international departure lounge before being tracked down by the admirable Edna, who had flown from Bloomington specially to look for him. She put him on the next plane to London.

As I waited for his flight to arrive, I remembered many other times when John had been agitated in airports; and I wondered why I had not fully appreciated quite how upsetting they were for him. To this day, even now that he is better, they remain places where, for safety's sake, he ought to be watched: though I am not sure why this should be. True, he is a little nervous of flying, in spite of the countless thousands of miles he has covered – and there are the crowds and hustle and bustle, plus the constant and echoing announcements for destinations world-wide, all of which are well-known to John... Yet nothing can fully explain why on rare occasions, he can forget where he is meant to be going, or why he then just waits until he is found.

But this occasion was more serious than any earlier one, and my heart sank as he came out of customs. He looked untidy, unshaven, glassy-eyed: far worse than at any time since we had made our move to the States. I also discovered that four hundred dollars he had had with him had either been lost or been stolen – John himself had no idea which. I reported the loss right away and the aircraft was thoroughly searched: but the money was never recovered.

I had to cancel the concerts in Italy. This time, John went to the Maudsley: but again he was kept there for only a week. When they released him, however, his recovery was not nearly so marked as it had been the previous year: and I prayed without very much optimism that I would somehow again find the strength to cope with a major relapse if it came.

The Maudsley doctors, though, were quite reassuring; and they said that John could pick up his tour in Hungary, provided that I went along too. And so we flew off for his first concert there on 10th October – and for the start of several weeks of sheer misery.

Having got used to John playing so well, for so long, it was a bitter experience to hear him in less than his usual form: while in purely personal matters, his condition was very distressing. He showed no interest in anything, and his self-care was appalling in every respect; I even had to help him to dress and to undress.

On returning to Britain after his Hungarian concerts, he played, still rather erratically, in Wales, Shropshire and Leicester: then we flew to Monte Carlo for a single concerto performance before crossing the Atlantic again for an engagement in Vancouver, where he played with the Symphony Orchestra. All in all, it had proved to be a tour that had done little for his reputation.

Back in Bloomington, at the start of November, periods of brooding introversion alternated with his reawakened obsession with the charity organiser – he would startle our American friends and occasional visitors from Britain, Peter Andry included, with his sudden tirades about the way in which he said the man had set out to destroy him, and how he – John – was going to sue... His state was far from as desperate as in 1974 and 1975 – there was no talk of Hitler and plots, and no suicide scares to contend with – but this time round I was not only frustrated and lost, but physically and emotionally incapable of managing him all by myself. And so I arranged, with Michael Johnson, for John to be moved into Bloomington Hospital.

In the past, I had been upset at his having to leave home for a hospital – but on this occasion I confess that I felt overwhelming relief. This was in part because the hospital was by far and away the most pleasant in which he had ever spent time. The security system was effective but also unusually discreet: the elevator to the floor on which John had his room was very carefully controlled, and one had to identify one's self into a mouthpiece before it could move up – or down... On our own, it goes without saying, we could not have afforded so luxurious a place – but fortunately the University paid, being covered for all such contingencies, with Blue Cross/Blue Shield Insurance.

John's agents did not take at all kindly to news of this new confinement – even though, up to this point, he had been in hospital for only three weeks in three years – surely by any standards a pretty good average! What is more, with the sad

266

exception of the last month or so, he had been playing like an angel for virtually all of that time. Even so, Wildred Stiff informed me that in his opinion John should go into the Maudsley for the next year, and Harold Shaw, John's American agent, wrote me suggesting that John should take twelve months away from the platform.

However sincere the reasons for their advice, I do not believe it was medically justified. It was as if John's balanced two – and more – years had been forgotten, or overlooked – as if the excellence of his playing until his last single tour, had made no impression at all.

And indeed, John's state was far from being so serious that he had to be confined all the time in the hospital. He was even let out to give concerts, provided the distances involved were not great. One of these, at the end of November, was a Faculty Recital, given with the violinist James Buswell, entirely of Prokofiev works; and they were all of them superbly performed.

John had not been in hospital long when Michael Johnson made a startling announcement: he told me that after close observation of my husband over the better part of a year, he had come to the conclusion that John, though undoubtedly manic depressive, was not after all schizophrenic. Of course, diagnosis in these matters is usually shaded, it is rarely a question of pure black and white: and complicated labels were still used to describe John's overall condition. But where Michael thought a mistake had been made was in not taking sufficient account of John's individual personality, which has always been eccentric and "different", even when he has been his most sane.

In the simplest of terms, Michael believes that John is, and always has been, an obsessive genius, living a vital inner life in comparison to which the "real" world can be shadowy and remote. This interior and often one-track commitment can produce very positive results – but its negative aspects are demonstrated by John's fanatical pre-occupation with the charity organiser, and the criticism the man had once made to him. So – the same obsessive quality that allowed him to transform talent into musical greatness had also prolonged the expressions of his illness.

Now Michael was proposing, not another change in the cocktail, but a different kind of treatment altogether. It is not a

267

treatment intended for a schizophrenic disorder, Michael explained to me, nor is it a matter of the more usual stabilisers – in fact, the pills would contain a salt carbonate only, the affect of which would be directly on the blood. These pills would be easy to take – and, of overwhelming importance, they would have no effect whatsoever on John's physical ability to play. There were, however, one or two drawbacks: for example, the salt could have a toxic affect, and so regular visits to a doctor would be essential, if only for monitoring purposes. In addition, we had to be prepared for the fact that the most beneficial dosage for John would still entail some trial and error – and once the treatment had started, it would have to continue for life... But on the other hand, it had worked many a miracle for hitherto incurable manic-depressives.

So in December – bolstered only by an anti-depressant called Norpramine – John began to take Lithium. It was to be the treatment that altered our lives.

34

An improvement in John's condition was not immediately evident – it took time for the Lithium to take its effect. Even when he came home in January – though he was certainly better than he had been when he had left it six weeks before – the image of the charity organiser was continuing to plague him.

In the middle of the month, very soon after his release from the hospital, he gave a concert in Edmonton, in Canada: and he did not play well. This disappointment proved to be too much for Harold Shaw, who had booked him the date – particularly as we had not followed his advice that John should take a rest from the platform. So he and John parted professional company.

John soon got a new American representative, Joseph Scuro: nonetheless, there was another flurry of panic along the agency grapevine, and the seriousness of John's relapse was exaggerated out of all proportion... The extent of world-wide concern became all too evident to me when I went with him to Japan for six concerts in February 1979. Even before John had laid a finger on the keys of a piano, his agent there was worrying about his condition, and about whether he would be able to play...

But I should confess that at this point – in spite of Michael's warning that I would need to be patient – I had little more faith than anyone else in John's eventual and total recovery. And, sadly, the Japanese trip did little to reassure either me or the agent. At times, John was playing quite brilliantly – but his tempi were sometimes eccentrically fast, and emotionally he was detached from the music. His private behaviour was more of a worry – he spent whole days shut away in his hotel bedroom, writing incessantly the while.

I was to discover, too late, that he had not only penned a number of letters to the charity organiser, but that he had actually posted them too; in them, he had accused the man, amongst other things, of engineering his breakdown deliberately, with a view to destroying his concert career. Yet in spite of the fact that these letters were patently disturbed, and in spite of knowing about John's mental troubles, the man's response was to threaten, formally, to sue him if he ever put such charges on paper again . . .

While we were still in Japan, John's condition began to change for the better – but it was too late to counteract the damage that, professionally, had already been done. If only we had cancelled the tour – or if only it had taken place a mere three weeks or so later! But neither I, nor anyone except perhaps Michael Johnson, could have believed that recovery was just round the corner.

Certainly I had no inkling of the fact when our plane touched down in England after the long flight from the Orient. I was so tired, and so close to despair, that I abandoned my responsibility for John for a short while: I let him go north for some concerts in the company of his sister Ruth, while I went to stay with the Eccles.

But the break from John did me some good: and in the last week of February, I was once again strong enough to go back to Bloomington with him.

Even on the journey, before we got home, I was struck by the improvement in him. His eyes were clearer and far more alert: he was much more responsive to everyone, and also, for the first time in months, he began initiating conversations with me. What is more, the charity organiser was no longer dominating his thoughts – indeed, when his name happened to be raised, John was able to talk about him, as well as about his own previously obsessive reactions, with a totally calm objectivity. As for his depressions – they vanished: and if he did not appear to be deliriously happy, at least he seemed contented at last.

John's continued recovery over our first two weeks back at the house was so dramatic and convincing that, in spite of so many past disappointments, I found myself daring to hope that in Lithium we had finally found the right answer. And after a whole month had gone by, I had even become so confident of his condition that I allowed him, with Michael Johnson's permission, to go to Scandinavia alone.

Henrik Lodding, our agent – as ever reliable and kind – arranged for a Swedish lady, Miss Guelich, to accompany John on the tour: her responsibilities included making sure that he took his pills on a regular basis, because even at the best of times, John has been, and remains, absent-minded. He played the Third Piano Concertos of Prokofiev and of Rachmaninov; and, on a couple of occasions, he performed the Brahms B Flat Concerto. According to the reports Henrik gave me, he acquitted himself well every time.

He came back still in excellent health, and spent the whole month of April in Bloomington. He was of course as vague as ever about keeping appointments, as bored by the faculty meetings, and he was still wreathed in coils of cigarette smoke – but these foibles were so much a part of him that I would have been concerned if they had been any different. But at the same time, there was a reawakened pleasure and interest in the job of teaching itself: and amongst his more talented pupils, he was taking a special and personal pride in Raymond Clipper Ericson and Michelle Koslovsky, both of whom he thinks have the potential to pursue performing careers.

Late in April, he gave a Faculty Recital made up of his own compositions – the Sonata No. 2, the Sonatina which he had written for me, the Dance Suite, the Variations and Fugue, and his Theme and Variations. Also included were two more recent works – his beautiful Flute sonata, which he had finished in Corfu in the summer of 1977, and his Sonata No. 3, which had been written in the same year. The concert was very successful and provoked some excited discussion: "the music" the local critic reported, "is always unpredictable, always fascinating, and a little disturbing. It is also" he added, with good reason, "unimaginably difficult."

Early in May, John went to Italy for some concerts, once more travelling on his own; and in June, I went with him to Britain, where he gave several recitals over a period of almost three weeks. But again, he proved perfectly capable of looking after himself: and so I flew back to Bloomington ahead of him, as Annabel was there at the time and all by herself in our house.

271

In fact, Annabel had left Benenden the previous year, and had been living with us in the States for some months. She was by now eighteen years old, a strikingly attractive young woman; and having trained as a secretary at a business school, she was doing part-time work in a legal office as well as serving in a restaurant most evenings. In spite of working so hard, she was loving America – and though she had been entered for Edinburgh University for the autumn of 1980, she was looking forward more eagerly to spending the upcoming year at the University of California in Santa Barbara.

It was such a pleasure for us to agree with each other that John had never been better. Indeed, John was ready again, I was sure of it, to reclaim his place on the circuit as one of the world's finest pianists.

Things have not proved as simple as that.

35

The problem we have found ourselves faced with is that for some agents, if not the public, John's recovery has come that little bit late.

The seriousness of his relapse at the end of 1978 has, as I have said, been exaggerated: in fact, he was put into hospital mainly to give me the break that I, and Michael Johnson, felt I needed. But then his removal from Harold Shaw's books, followed by the largely disappointing Japanese tour, further compounded the damage. And so, in the late summer and autumn of 1979, John found himself with fewer international engagements than at any time since winning first prize in Moscow. He played in Mexico, Britain, and the US – nowhere else.

The professional situation already seemed dispiriting enough – but there was to be another set-back that year when Wilfred Stiff wrote saying that he also no longer wished to represent John.

Now, I am happy to say, John is represented by Basil Douglas, a Scottish gentleman of the old school, who had done such an excellent job of arranging the 1977 tour together with his own artist, Ruggiero Ricci.

Even though the confidence of some other agents had been shaken by the departure of Harold Shaw and Wilfred Stiff, I was confident that the new and healthy John – or perhaps I should say the restored, familiar John – would, with little trouble, inspire a world-wide demand for his services.

But, for several months at least, another, and unexpected obstacle stopped the tide running in his favour: and that obstacle was John himself!

Quite simply, after all the years of driving himself and being driven, after all the constant travelling and stress, after the long and arduous struggle against the illness that had threatened him for so long, he felt a need to ease up on giving concerts and on racing all over the world. Now that he was mentally balanced again, he was determined to take time out so as to come to terms with what had happened to him and with what he was hoping for from the future.

He had fully earned a break, no one could argue with that. But this months-long period of personal stock-taking did include a few concert dates – and his attitude to these commitments marked the temporary re-emergence of an old fault. He performed too often with almost no preparation at all, relying more heavily than was prudent on his talent for learning fast – and sometimes he was caught out, musically, to his cost, as happened in South Africa in January 1980. The disappointing concerts that he gave on that tour were not, as sometimes four or five years before, the result of drugs or of illness: he just had not practised his repertoire!... And yet, during this same period, he would occasionally get down to work for a while – and play like the great pianist he is.

In any case, the fall-off in the number of John's engagements, however much in harmony with his wishes, did present us with major problems in practical and financial terms – because by this time, John had parted company with yet another important organisation with which he had been closely involved: he was no longer on the staff of the Music School.

His engagement there had come to an end for a variety of reasons. His heavy touring schedule, particularly in the first two years he had been there, had kept him from his teaching for too long – though any University wanting to employ names of major stature in the performing world must expect them to travel: it cannot have things both ways! I am sure, too, that John's weeks away in the hospital had done nothing to his advantage. But there were also other factors involved. Just as John could not help being an artist of world calibre, so was he incapable of channeling the marked individuality and eccentricity that sometimes go with phenomenal talent into a conservative academic world. Even if his life were to depend on it, he could never become an administratively-dedicated college operator, attuned to the right kind of "game".

I was not prepared to press John back into a full time concert career or a new University post until he felt ready for one or the other – or a combination of both. But in the meantime, we needed money.

And so I took the decision that some people thought I should have taken in 1974 or 1975, when John was at the height of his illness: I set out to earn my own living. But, however paradoxical it may sound, I did so only because John was now better; it would have been impossible otherwise.

What complicated the situation the more was the fact that John was considering staying in America – he likes the way of life there, and he will not easily forget that it was in America that his breakthrough to recovery was made. I, too, had been happy in the States; but my name is not known there to people who count in the music world, and I considered that it would be at home, in Britain, that my best chances would lie both as a performer and as a teacher.

So after a great deal of soul-searching, I returned to England in March 1980 and took a small flat in Chelsea. Soon I got myself a few private pupils – though a teaching job in a college or school has so far proved impossible to come by – and Basil Douglas became my agent as well. I kept in constant touch with John on the telephone, and we managed to see each other surprisingly often – several times, when he was en route to Europe or the British provinces, he stopped over for a week or so in London, and once I went with him to Switzerland.

I cannot pretend that John was pleased we were living temporarily apart; but he appreciated my reasons for coming to London, and he was in no way resentful of me . . . It was a question – it still is a question – of needs must: Richard is going to school, while Annabel is at University: and it takes money to keep them there. If I had stayed on in Bloomington, I would be a financial burden to John at a time when he is hard-pressed: and until he is firmly back on his feet, I will continue to fend for myself.

In the early summer, a couple of months after I had come to London, John announced that his period of professional withdrawal was over – he told me that he was concentrating on polishing his repertoire. And there is no doubt at all that his recent playing has been superb.

He sees composing, as well, playing a major part in his

future: and he began working hard on some new piano pieces during his periods in Bloomington. He also started preparing his own libretto for his first attempt at writing an opera, based on James Elroy Flecker's *The King of Alsander*. Of course, I did not leave him alone in the house (which up to the time of writing we own, although it has been put on the market): for some time he was looked after by a Mormon lady, and Annabel was now old enough to take a willing responsibility for him during her summer break from the University. Indeed, there is a quality of determination and strength in her that reminds me very much of Dorothy Ogdon... But she could only be with John for a couple of months – and so, for the first time in his life, he found himself without a managing Mother figure permanently at his side.

In purely domestic matters, he got himself involved in a number of predictable escapades. True to the style of a lifetime, he forgot to pay the telephone bill, and so, of course, was cut off. And he fell behind with our mortgage instalments, which caused another brief flurry of trouble... But there was only a single occasion when, briefly, I feared for the worst.

He had been on the jury of a piano competition in Montreal during June – and, after the judging was over, he apparently vanished from the face of the earth. Annabel, who was waiting for him to come back to Bloomington, had no idea where he was: I found that he had checked out of his Montreal hotel; and enquiries very soon ascertained that he was not sitting about lost in the airport.

After three or four most anxious days, the phone rang in my flat very late. "Hallo, B" John's voice said. "How are you?"

"John!" I screeched. "Where are you? Where have you been all this time?"

"Me? Oh ... um, I've been staying at the airport hotel." Innocently, he added "Why?"

"*Why*? John, we've had no idea where to find you – we've been going crazy with worry!"

"Oh" he said, sounding surprised. "I'm sorry. I just didn't think to let anyone know, I suppose..."

It turned out that he had not renewed his American visa, as he should have done, before he had left the country for Canada – and its validity had expired while the competition was on. He had been prevented from boarding the plane for his journey

276

back to the States; and so, he explained to me, he had been staying in Montreal while he tried to get a new visa.

The story did not end there, however. Fed up with the complications of getting the visa all by himself, he flew on to Vancouver only a day after his phone call to me. There – successfully – he passed the responsibility of getting him home on to the organiser of the Summer School at Shawnigan Lake, where he was soon due to give master classes.

As I say, at the time I had been very scared; but in fact the whole episode is typical of John and the way he has been all his life.

Late in October, 1980, John flew to England for a concert, arriving a couple of weeks early specially to hear a recital I was giving at Pro Pantera, a small hall in the Brompton Road, and to my astonishment he announced that he would not be returning to the United States – at least, not in the foreseeable future. Whether this is one of his unshakeable decisions or merely a temporary impulse, it is too early to say – for him, I think, just as much as for me.

John's presence in London, however welcome to me, has not undermined my determination to make my own living; indeed, I have no choice in the matter, because to put it bluntly, we are at the moment broke. And so I still cannot devote the greater part of my time to my husband, as I have done in the past.

Michael Johnson did warn me that John might find the transition back to Britain quite difficult, if indeed he was determined to stay – and once again, Michael has been proved correct. Hopelessly impractical in the best of circumstances, John soon found that being much of the time on his own with virtually no money to spend was a most unsettling way of existence. And so, one day towards the end of January, he readmitted himself to the Maudsley – not because he was once again mentally ill (as the hospital, rather perplexedly, has confirmed he is not!) but because he needed to escape from those everyday problems from which I can no longer shelter him.

But his British return has proved to have had the most positive – if unforeseeable – aspects as well. Early in February, John was invited to make his first London recital appearance in almost three years, as a replacement for the late Hans Richter Haaser at the Queen Elizabeth Hall. However – largely due to

277

the advance announcement of this book and thus the first public acknowledgement of John's breakdown – the *Sunday Times* traced him to the Maudsley: and only four days before the recital was due to take place, the paper published a long and revealing interview with John as well as a photograph of him at a piano in the hospital's gymnasium.

Hard on the heels of this coverage there came an unprecedented wave of pre-concert publicity. Almost every national newspaper carried a picture and a story of him, hailing his professional return to the capital after his long battle with mental illness.

After the recital, the critics too were warm in their welcome (his triumph was even announced on the *Guardian*'s front page the next morning); the packed house gave him a rapturous reception, he was featured on BBC 2's 'Newsnight' while still wearing his tails, and the following day he gave several interviews – and heard many of his recordings played – on the radio. And he is surely the first pianist ever to have had his concert, and the standing ovation that greeted it, reported as a matter of national interest on ITN's 'The News at Ten'.

John was beside himself with delight and new confidence: another London recital was very soon arranged, and there was talk of a forty-minute profile of him on Thames Television. So it could well be – as John himself has written in his Foreword – that this book is ending with a new, and wonderfully positive beginning. Whatever predicaments John may land himself in, of one thing I am convinced: he will, always, somehow, overcome them – or, more likely, someone (most probably myself) will be called on to overcome them for him. As has almost always been the case, the very fact of his practical helplessness, combined, of course, with so very rare a talent, ensures that he is a survivor.

Afterword

It has been suggested to me that this story, or at least that part concerning John's breakdown, should not have been written: that it is a too-intimate glimpse into something frightening and painful.

And yet so many books are being written about personal fights – both successful and unsuccessful – against all kinds of illnesses, such as cancer and heart-disease: why should mental illness be considered shameful when they are not? Clara Haskil's triumph over the troubles that plagued her – curvature of the spine and a brain tumour – have been discussed in print often: why then should John's struggle, and his victory, be shrouded? Jacqueline du Pré not only leads as full a life as she can, she openly campaigns for better understanding of the disease from which she is suffering, the dreaded multiple sclerosis: so why should a curtain be drawn over the most misunderstood illness of all – the illness afflicting the mind? It is as if the objectors believe that mental illness is something remote from most of our lives, and about which we do not need to know: as if it is something quite rare.

But it is not rare! And we do need to know!

If John's story is exceptional, it is because he is an exceptional man: his illness (or variants of it) is not exceptional at all. I know that it is often said that unusually talented people are more prone to breakdowns than others – but that is a sweeping, and questionable, generalisation. The truth is that mental troubles can attack anyone. The artist, performer and philosopher are no more vulnerable than the stevedore or the company chairman: the placid are at risk as much as the excitable, the stupid as much as the brilliant; and leaders as much as their followers.

Almost every family in the country has been affected, if only indirectly, by mental illness of some kind or other. Since John's breakdown, and more particularly since his recovery, I have been amazed how many people have confided in me, as if to a comrade in arms, that a spouse, a relative, or a friend – even, on occasion, they themselves – had undergone a comparable ordeal (if not often so extreme a one). But why have they hidden that experience from the world? Why, when most of them admit to having been deplorably ignorant when they were first forced to cope, do they not give advice and warnings to others? What is it that they are ashamed of? . . .

I repeat – we do need to know more about these things, which means that more needs to be told. More general education is vital: not so much where labels and categories of illness are concerned – we can leave the experts to grapple with those – but so that we, the affected, can deal with them, and our reactions to them, more adequately. We have to accept that those who are ill cannot help themselves – believe me, a difficult lesson. We have to realise that they need our support, even though they may seem unaware of receiving it, even though it is so often difficult to give. And we must remove every inference of shame, because there is no reason for shame.

Our particular story does not offer easy solutions. And it is no use claiming that after going through such an ordeal things can again be the same as before the breakdown took place: love may survive and even deepen, but our lives, our perceptions and our hearts will of necessity have been changed for ever.

I know that it is in most of our natures to avoid pain if we possibly can. Almost the hardest battle of all is making oneself face reality: but in the end, the intolerable *has* to be suffered because there is no other alternative . . . But then, once one has accepted that fact – at least, speaking from my experience – it gets a little easier to go on.

But I do not wish to end on too pessimistic a note: if John and I could get through, if he could find a way back to health, then there must be hope for almost everyone else. Certainly the outlook today is far brighter than it was only twenty – or even five – years ago. In spite of all the pitfalls and ignorant behaviour that one is almost certain to meet, in spite of the over-worked doctors and so many understaffed hospitals, medicine *is* making great strides, and in the great majority of cases where mental illness has struck, the future should hold a genuine promise.

The tunnel to recovery, however short or long it may be, is always going to be a dark one: but those who are forced to go through it should remember what Gill taught me – that in their suffering, they are not alone.

So what does the future hold for John and me now?

There will always be the pleasure we share in the children. These days, though, I am missing Annabel very much – because having spent a year at the University of California, she is determined to stay there if she can. She has made several close friends, she contributes regularly to a student newspaper, and she is enjoying her studies: Edinburgh is no longer mentioned, and I shall be very surprised if she returns to Britain to live.

Richard is doing well at school, and has proved a more than adequate cricketer. He is a big boy for his age – 15 – and is beginning to look more like John every year. And what is exciting – and naturally a little alarming for John and me, knowing the concert world as we do – is the flowering of his musical talent: he has already developed into a considerable pianist. But where his future will eventually lie, it is still too early to say.

As for me – I will give music lessons for as long as I must. And I will keep up the practising which once again occupies happy hours of every day – and now that the children are so nearly grown, I will fight to pick up the solo career I had yearned for all through my youth.

And I hope to give more duo recitals with my husband. That, like so much else in my life, depends entirely on him.

John, in addition to playing in public, intends to continue to teach. Perhaps his forte might be as a lecturer – his strength has always been for the one-sided, brilliant address rather than a two way conversation. And I would dearly like to see him give classes on composition – the subject perhaps closest of all to his heart. It would be sad if these qualities were not made the most of.

By all accounts, John has been thrilling his audiences recently with some of the most memorable performances he has ever given and certainly, on the few occasions I have been able to hear him, including a recital in Lancaster and performances of the Liszt E minor and Chopin F minor Concertos at Milton Keynes his playing has been accurate, exciting, and moving – even, dare I say it, demonic... But as always, he is uninterested in impersonal perfection and remains subject to the influence of moods: and so, on a few future occasions, he is bound to be slapdash and possibly wilful... But I can say this much with confidence – in the tradition of the greatest piano playing, every performance John gives is guaranteed to be an adventure – and boredom is out of the question!

Unless the world itself has gone mad, playing of the calibre of John's will not be rationed for long. Now that he is determined to play widely again, for the sake of all music lovers, he must!

John is still socially awkward; and he is as absentminded, untidy, and impractical as at any other time in his life. He smokes as heavily as always, and is now fatter than I have ever known him... And yet, he is so very generous, so unpretentious and genuine – while he remains a man not only of staggering talent, but of the most formidable intellect in his own field. As much as has ever been the case, he inspires a deep affection in the widest spectrum of people; and he continues to bring out the protective instinct in friends who were hardly aware that they had one. John remains a most special human being, cast in unique, unrepeatable mould.

John – impossible, adorable John – has dominated every aspect of my adult life: he is, and always will be, a part of me. Of one thing I have no doubt: our story is far from over.

Index

285

relationship with John, 219–20; sale of Chester Terrace house and Plot 32, 221–2, 227, 229–31, 233; plays with John at Brighton and in Finland, 222, 226; at Four Wents, 234; house-hunting in Bloomington, 235; in Latin America, 236; and the children's education, 236–7; plays with John at Aldeburgh, 237–8

her move to Bloomington, 241–3, 248; illness and accident in Moscow, 244–6; in Mexico, 250–1; holiday in Corfu, 251–3; breaks bone in foot, 252; at Fort Worth, 254–5; in Iran, 255; at Queen Elizabeth Hall, 259–60; and John's relapse, 263, 265–6; with John in Japan, 269–70; returns to England to earn living, 275, 283; takes flat in Chelsea, 275; and the story of John's illness, 281–3

Lucas, Janet (sister of Brenda), 13, 205, 210

Lvov, 126–7

Maazel, Lorin, 84
MacDowell, Edward A., 264
Magaloff, Nikita, 254
Manchester, 119, 125; Royal Northern College of Music, 3–11, 14, 18, 19, 29–30, 32–3, 36, 200, 212–13; New Music group, 14–15, 24, 58, 105; Grammar School, 18, 19; Midland Hotel, 47, 48, 212; Free Trade Hall, 212
Mancinelli, Aldo, 44, 45
Marbella, 145–6, 222; disrupted flight for concert there, 162–3; Amigos de la Musica, 162
Margaret, H.R.H. Princess, 125, 139
Mary Angela, Sister, 13
Maryland, International Piano Festival, 228, 229
Masters, Brian, and John's illness, 177–8, 181–5, 187–90, 198
Matthews, Denis, 37, 49
Maudsley Hospital, Denmark Hill, 220, 221, 267; John as patient at, 210–12, 216–17, 223–6, 265
Maxwell Davies, Peter, 15, 58, 105, 106
McDonald, Gerald, 40
Measham, David, 161
Mehta, Zubin, 42
Melbourne, 100
Menotti, Gian Carlo, 56
Messiaen, Olivier, 110, 165; "Vision de

l'Amen", 138
Mexico and Mexico City, 250–1, 258–61
Michelangeli, Arturo Benedetti, 86; Festival, 116
Milan, La Scala, 86
Milhaud, Darius, 165; "Scaramouche", 163
Milne, Hamish, 65
Milton Keynes, 284
Minneapolis, 230
Minnesota Orchestra, 230
Monte Carlo, 266
Montreal, 276–7
Morrison, Bryce, 260
Moscow, 73, 125–7, 244–6; International Tchaikovsky Competition, 67–76
Mozart, Wolfgang Amadeus, 3, 4, 18, 35, 71, 105, 111, 163, 248; A Minor Sonata K 310, 242; Concerto in F Major for Three Pianos and Orchestra, 121, 122, 175; D Major Sonata K 576, 57; "Don Giovanni Fantasy", 37; Double Concerto in E flat, 152, 177; Piano Concerto in B flat No. 27, 161, 199
Murray, David, 217

National Health Service, 225
New Music group, Manchester, 14–15, 24, 58, 105
New Philharmonia Orchestra, 69, 123, 165
New York, 90–4, 129–31, 154, 199, 212
New York Daily News, 251
New York Herald Tribune, 93
New York Times, 93
New Zealand, 101, 131, 157, 158
Nielsen, Carl August, 165
Northern Symphonia Orchestra, 152
Nova Scotia, 256

Ogdon, Annabel (daughter of John and Brenda), 67, 69, 70, 81, 86, 95, 101, 102, 145, 146, 166, 168, 203, 207, 237, 246, 252, 276; birth, 65, 68; in Australia and New Zealand, 98–9, 101; and John's illness, 193, 237, 263; at Benenden, 234, 252, 272; in Bloomington, 253, 265, 271, 276, at University of California in Santa Barbara, 272, 275, 276, 283
Ogdon, Brenda Lucas, *see* Lucas, Brenda
Ogdon, Dorothy (mother of John), 16–19, 33, 57–8, 65, 69, 141, 276; and John's engagement to Brenda, 50, 55;

289

291